LEARN,
LEAD,
SERVE

LEARN,
LEAD,
SERVE

A CIVIC LIFE

THOMAS EHRLICH

INDIANA UNIVERSITY PRESS

This book is a publication of

Indiana University Press
Office of Scholarly Publishing
Herman B Wells Library 350
1320 East 10th Street
Bloomington, Indiana 47405 USA

iupress.org

First printing 2025

Cataloging information is available from the Library of Congress.
ISBN 978-0-253-07166-8 (hdbk.)
ISBN 978-0-253-07165-1 (pbk.)
ISBN 978-0-253-07167-5 (web PDF)

Cover image: Tom and Ellen Ehrlich outside the Wells Library following the
"Meet Tom & Ellen" receiving line on the day of his inauguration, October 12,
1987. Image number P0112952, courtesy of Indiana University Archives.

To Ellen, the love of my life
And to our family, our greatest joy

CONTENTS

PREFACE

This is my story, starting when my parents gave me a big, red fire engine at age five as a consolation prize for not being taken to the 1939 New York World Fair. In a more important sense, this is the story of what matters to me and why. It is the tale of what and how I have learned from each step in my personal life and professional career and the precepts that have guided me.

At the outset, I stress my blessings. A wonderful family is center stage. My beloved wife, Ellen, has taught me, helped me, and loved me, even when I was far from lovable.

Right before we were married, her father told us that if we each went two-thirds of the way, we might just make it. Ellen has done that throughout our sixty-six years of marriage.

Ellen is the most curious person I have ever known. Her curiosity led us over countless new horizons together. We have three marvelous children, each different from the other two, but all three bonded closely together. They take close care of each other in ways that neither Ellen nor I were adequately able to do with our siblings. Our children gave us nine grandchildren, who really are grand. And now we have a delightful great-grandchild.

I have also been blessed by my mentors. They made each of my careers possible. We moved many times—Ellen says I could not hold a job—and those mentors always guided me. My father was the first and the best, but there were other great ones you will meet as well, starting with my second-grade teacher, Mrs. Scattergood. Neither Dickens nor Trollope could have come up with a better name for her.

Ellen and I each brought scores of friends to each other when we met, and we have made more friends everywhere we have lived over the course of our marriage. Some are mentioned in this memoir, but the absence of others from these pages should not suggest that our devotion to them is any less.

When this memoir is published, I will be more than ninety years old. What I have written reflects what I remember, aided by some sources that helped me. But I know that I have misremembered, probably often, and I apologize for what I have reported incorrectly. I have told some of the stories in this memoir multiple times and have no doubt that I embellished some of them in the recounting. For these and other errors, I apologize in advance to readers.

Along with my family, I owe special thanks to friends and colleagues who helped me as I wrote and others who assisted in preparing the portfolio of photographs that are included. I owe my editor, Gary Dunham, director of Indiana University Press, my gratitude for asking me to write this memoir and in helping me each step of the way in preparing it. Terry Clapacs and Don Fidler deserve special credit for spending many hours with the photos. Terry helped choose the right ones for my time at Indiana University. Don did wonders in making my photos look far better than I thought possible. I gained advice and support from Bradley Cook, Alec Glover, Catherine Milton, Ross Stein, and Sergio Stone, as well as from my dear friends from our days together at the Carnegie Foundation for the Advancement of Teaching, Anne Colby, Mary Huber, Bill Sullivan, and Lee Shulman. My apologies to those I mistakenly omitted.

I have had the good fortune to learn throughout my life and to serve causes I care about as well. The most important of those causes is helping preserve and strengthen the civic fabric of our country. That has been my privilege.

PART I

AWAKENING

1

Beginnings

M y early memories are like shards of a mirror—quick, brilliant flashes but without anchors in time. My father taking me in a car. My mother talking to me. A nanny walking with me down to the beach. My sister, Ellen, holding my hand. But I can't place those snapshots in any order.

A big red fire engine. That is my first clear memory, from the summer of 1939. My father, mother, Ellen, and I lived in Clifton, Massachusetts, where my family rented a large, rambling, wooden-framed house for two months each summer. The house was set on a bluff overlooking the Atlantic Ocean. A dirt path ran along the edge of the bluff. On the other side of the road that led up to the house, about a hundred yards away, a long flight of wooden steps connected the bluff with a beach below. I have a faint memory of going in the water in those early years, but I also recall being a bit scared of the ocean. Perhaps as a result, I never learned to swim well.

My mother and father took Ellen to the 1939 World Fair in New York and left me behind with a housekeeper who lived with us at the time. My parents gave me a large red toy fire engine just before they left. The shape of that fire engine—long and sleek, with ladders hooked along each side and a bright, shiny body, remains vivid in my mind's eye. I was overjoyed, for this seemed far better than going on the trip with them. I recall playing with that fire engine for hours.

My parents were living in the first house they owned, a red-brick dwelling in quiet Shady Hill Square in Cambridge, Massachusetts, when I was born at Mount Auburn Hospital on March 4, 1934. Coincidentally, this was exactly one year after the first inauguration of Franklin Delano Roosevelt, my great political hero. Perhaps this alignment helped me become a political junkie at an early age.

My parents' first plan was to name me Alexander, after my mother's father, but my sister, Ellen, four years older than I was, had a best friend with a brother named Thomas, and that carried the day. I am forever grateful to Ellen for her persuasive powers at that moment. Unfortunately, her friend's brother was known as Tommy, and that nickname, which I never liked, stuck with me until I was a teenager. Then I started to insist on Tom, which has been with me ever since.

A few years after I was born, we moved a couple of blocks away to a large white clapboard house at 81 Irving Street, which backed onto Kirkland Street, one of the busiest in Cambridge. Fortunately, Irving Street was closed at one end and had little traffic.

A boy my age, Christopher Eliot, son of the minister of the Unitarian Church, lived next door on Irving Street and became my best friend. We played endless games together—cops and robbers, particularly, and cap guns were a favorite toy at an early age. In retrospect, I do not think that the arsenal of weapons I had from age five to twelve did me much harm, though I would be troubled now to see a toy gun in the hands of one of my grandchildren. Guns were not real to me then; instead, they were what Dick Tracy used.

Christopher, known always as Kitsi, and I ran strings between our homes and shot rocket ships on rollers to each other, attached to those strings. We made crude walkie-talkies using the same strings. We also gathered bits of colored glass from the street, tied pieces of wire around them to make rings, and sold them to our neighbors. Baseball and the Red Sox were a passion for me and for Kitsi, and I still have a photo of myself in a Red Sox uniform with my glove.

We also played with a small group of friends who went with us to the Shady Hill School, a few miles away. One was Charles (Chicky) Kuhn, son of my parents' good friends, who lived on Brattle Street and later became my roommate at Exeter. Others were Billy Bourne, Bob Casey (later a hockey star), and Bob O'Neill. No girls were in our group—that came later.

Speaking of girls, my sister, Ellen, was just enough older—four years—that we were not particularly close friends growing up. We often squabbled, partly because my sister believed, with some justification, that I was the favored child, at least in my mother's eyes. In retrospect, as will become clear, she was right—my mother never gave Ellen the affection and maternal attention she needed, while I was probably pampered. My father tried to be evenhanded and succeeded, except that he and I joined in sailing and skiing, but Ellen never had much interest in those sports.

I started first grade at the Shady Hill School in 1940, when I was six. I loved school then and loved it most of my life growing up. Learning has almost always been a delight for me, and there is always something new to learn. My good fortune in loving to learn comes primarily from the genes of both my parents. Neither was an academic, but my mother and father loved to read and were always interested in learning. Luckily, I have been able to spend most of my professional life at schools— as a student, professor, and leader, always learning.

Second grade, because of my teacher, Mrs. Scattergood, was a particular delight. To me, she seemed a wonderful person in every way. One day, I came home from school and, in describing the day's events to my parents, I started calling my mother Mrs. Scattergood. To put the matter gently, this did not please my mother. But I remember Mrs. Scattergood—her everyman name was perfect—with great affection, and the slip, no doubt, says something about the lack of time I spent as a child with my mother. Some sixty years later, when I told that tale to one of my Philadelphia aunts, she told it to Mrs. Scattergood, who wrote a lovely note to me.

Given my mother's feelings about Mrs. Scattergood, it may be fortunate that the following year, in 1942, my father left his job at C. F. Hovey's—a department store where he bought women's clothes from various wholesalers—and accepted a job in the new Office of Price Administration in Washington, DC. The OPA set and enforced prices for all products sold throughout the country and handled the complex rationing processes during World War II. My father was friends with two Harvard faculty members who also worked at the OPA. John Kenneth Galbraith became deputy head of the agency, and Merle Fainsod, whom Galbraith asked to join him, directed the section where my father worked. (Fainsod later served as a wonderful teacher of Russian government for both my wife, Ellen, and me at Harvard.) My father was in charge of helping ensure that prices of clothing were not raised beyond minimal levels despite the severe wartime shortages. It was wartime, and everything was rationed. We used ration stamps along with money to buy necessities.

I recall being very upset at our move to Washington. My irritation began in the summer of 1942 when I was sent to a boy's camp called Lanikila on Lake Fairlee in Vermont. My parents felt that the move to Washington, a hot city—no air conditioning then, of course—would be difficult enough without me underfoot, and my sister had already started at Tripp Lake Camp, a camp for Jewish girls our mother had attended. Two of my aunts had gone to Camp Aloha, the sister camp of Lanikila, and they knew the camp directors, Mr. and Mrs. Luther Gulick.

This was the first time I had spent any time away from home, let alone two months. At eight years old, I was the youngest camper at Lanikila and benefited from all the attention counselors gave me to make up for my loneliness. Campers earned points for outdoor activities like camping, canoeing, and swimming. Those who earned enough points were given awards named after Viking gods—Loki, Thor, and Odin are those I recall. I was the only camper in my group to become a Loki that summer, to my great pride—and my parents' bewilderment, since they could not understand why I thought this was a great honor. The next summer, I advanced to Thor, but not without great difficulty because I had to learn to dive, which scared me, as it still does. During the next three summers, I returned to Lanikila, where I delighted in canoeing and crafts but never learned to love swimming.

My parents rented a little house in Washington, just off Connecticut Avenue, where we lived for a year. Two incidents stand out in my memory. My father used to walk with me to a nearby school, where I was in the third grade. I remember being afraid at first, for everyone else in the third grade seemed to have friends except me, who knew no one. So, one day during the first week or so, I just turned around and walked home after my father left me at school and went off to work. My mother was out of the house as well, and I just sat inside all day. When my father came home, he was furious, but his anger was tempered by his understanding that I was lonely at school and more than a little scared.

"What am I going to do with you?" I remember him asking.

"I don't know, Dad," I solemnly responded. "That's your problem, not mine."

He laughed, much to my astonishment, since I had no idea I had said something funny. In a matter of weeks, I had new friends at school, and loneliness was not a problem. We lived near the zoo, and I recall numerous trips there with special delight.

In the fall of 1942, the efforts to mobilize our country to fight World War II were well underway. I was consumed by stories and pictures of America's fighting soldiers and sailors. The walls of my room were plastered with pictures of US Navy ships and Air Force planes. But I wanted to do more. I wanted to contribute directly to the war effort.

I thought I had my chance when the neighborhood Uptown Theater advertised that it would give free admission to the Saturday morning double feature to anyone who brought five pounds or more of scrap iron to donate to make bullets and battleships. I loved the movies and fondly recalled going to the Harvard Square movie house on Saturday mornings before we moved. I was particularly entranced by the Uptown Theater's fare on Saturday mornings, which always featured a war movie, a Western, and multiple cartoons. Those Saturday mornings gave me my first sense, via the regular short films on the war, of what was happening overseas. My friends and I would arrive a bit before the ten o'clock start time and not leave until mid-afternoon.

But where to find the five pounds of metal that I needed as the price of admission? Why, the iron used for pressing clothes in our home seemed perfect. It was made of iron and weighed at least five pounds.

I did not bother to check with my mother but grabbed the iron and lugged it to the movie theater, where I met my friends and gained admission. Did I honestly believe my mother would be pleased with my display of civic virtue? I am not sure, though I know that by the time I returned home that afternoon, I was convinced I had done a fine thing for our country's war effort and seen two great movies.

That night, my mother asked how I got into the movies with no money, and I reported that I had donated our family's iron as a contribution to fighting Germany and Japan. My mother was upset. Needless to say, our family had only one iron, and it was gone, with no possibility of replacing it until the war was over. My mother immediately marched me down to the movie theater, went directly to the manager, and somehow succeeded in retrieving the iron. As punishment, I was deprived of movies for the rest of the fall.

My father stayed at the OPA for only two years. Galbraith was forced to resign in an administrative shake-up, and many of those he brought with him left too. We returned to Massachusetts in 1944, where my father became vice president of a small chain of retail stores called Touraine, which sold mid-priced women's clothing. My grandfather had bought a half share in the company, and my father's oldest brother became its president. My grandparents moved to the Braemore Hotel on Commonwealth Avenue in Boston, where they lived for the rest of their lives, and we moved into their house in Brookline, on Beach Road, a lovely street one block long that fronted a little park with huge beach trees, which I regularly loved to climb. I quickly found the initials of my father, uncles, and aunts carved in the trees, where they had played as kids.

The Beech Road house seemed enormous to me. When I visited it as an adult, though, it appeared to be a substantial home but by no means as large as I remembered. The house had an ample backyard, a music room, a library, a living room, and a dining room, all on the first floor, along with a large entryway and curling staircase to the second floor. It also had two maids' rooms on the third floor, though they remained unoccupied when we lived there. My bedroom faced Beech Road, while my sister's and my parents' bedrooms faced the yard in the back.

In the house behind ours lived a new friend my age, Freddie Sharf, and we played together constantly. We liked to go to the neighborhood Sears Roebuck & Co. and wander up and down the aisles. For a short time, we stole small items because it seemed a daring thing to do. Fortunately, a store security man caught us, hauled us into the manager's office, and called our parents. My very unhappy father took us home and gave us a severe lecture on why we should never steal—both because it was morally wrong and because if we were caught, we could go to prison. The lecture stayed with me. I knew I would never steal again.

During those years, I was sick a number of times. (My mother claimed I had polio on one of those occasions, which is why my left foot is substantially shorter than my right foot. I have always been dubious about that claim.) During one long illness, I fashioned a spear out of a tree branch and then threw the spear into my bedroom wall. My parents were angry and declared my punishment would be to look at the holes in the wall for a long time. (This did not seem like a punishment to me.) I also had ingrown toenails, so the nails on my two big toes had to be removed.

I went to the Lawrence School, a public school a few blocks from our home, for the fifth grade. It was the same school my father had attended forty years earlier, and I had the very same teacher! In later years, my dad and I used to joke that she was no better for me than she had been for him. I learned little that year.

The next year, I was sent to a private school for boys, Browne & Nichols, in Cambridge. All the kids in my class knew long division except me, and I felt lonely and miserable for the first few months, both because I knew no one and because I was behind in the work. But I quickly caught up and soon had many close friends. Since I traveled every weekday to school in Cambridge, I had few neighborhood friends except Freddie Scharf. As a result, I often stayed in Cambridge and played with my school friends and frequently visited them on weekends. They include Bob O'Neill, Bill Borne, Joe Fletcher, Charlie Walcott, and Gordon Lund.

Once, as a special treat, Bob O'Neill's parents took the two of us for four days to New York, where we stayed at the Plaza Hotel. I was overwhelmed by the opulence of the hotel and by New York generally, especially the Empire State Building.

I continued to love school, particularly English and history, and I had a knack for doing well. At the end of the year, one of my close friends, Bob O'Neill, and I were tied for the best grades. I was especially delighted when I entered a contest that *Time Magazine* sponsored about current events and won the prize for my grade, which was any book costing less than $5. I chose *This Is My Best*, an anthology of writing by the most famous American authors, all of whom were asked to select a work of theirs they liked best. Although I suspect I chose the book because it was the only one on an approved list for $4.95, it became—and still is—a favorite collection of prose and poetry. Many years later, Bob was chancellor of the Bloomington campus at Indiana University, then head of the University of Wisconsin system and president of the University of Virginia. After leaving Browne & Nichols, we lost touch but renewed our friendship when I went to Indiana University.

I stayed at Browne & Nichols for the sixth, seventh, eighth, and ninth grades. I continued to enjoy writing but was never a standout in team sports and did not particularly like them. I played football, for example, but never with great confidence.

Browne & Nichols had many fine teachers. My favorite was Mr. Sindall in English. He kindled in me a love of writing to match my delight in reading. My mother later told me that she often worried because I read so many comic books, but after a time, I turned to adventure stories. Mr. Sindall introduced me to *The Once and Future King*, and I never tired of the stories of Arthur and Merlin, as retold by T. H. White. It is still on my short list of all-time favorite novels. Mr. Sindall also encouraged me to write stories, and I kept doing so through high school and college, though later, I stopped until I started telling stories to my children.

When I was twelve, I stopped going to Camp Lanikila for eight weeks in the summers and instead went to Camp Kennebec in North Belgrade, Maine, where my father had been a camper and then counselor. Kennebec was a camp for Jewish boys, founded because most camps, unlike Lanikila, were not open to Jews. (Kennebec was founded by three Jewish businessmen, whom campers called the "Jewish Indians" since the camp used Indian names for many of the places around the camp.) It was owned and led then, and still in my day, by a man named Louis Fleisher.

Camp Kennebec catered to Jewish boys from the East Coast, with a large group from Boston, New York, and Pittsburgh. I loved Kennebec from the start and made close friends there who remained friends for much of my life. Dan Mayers was my closest friend at camp, and we visited each other's homes during the winter months. We are still friends today. Another was Myron Markle from Pittsburgh, an intense fan of modern poetry who introduced me to T. S. Eliot and "The Love Song of J. Alfred Prufrock." Having read large quantities of Tennyson, Coleridge, Wordsworth, and other nineteenth-century poets in school, this was a fascinating shock. I also made lots of other friends who opened my eyes to other worlds I didn't know about. Fred Willman was another close friend and roommate all the way through college, though we lost touch in subsequent years.

Kennebec was divided into two groups—Crimson and Grey—and one set of our activities centered around competitions between the two. I was never particularly good at competitive sports, especially baseball, but I loved canoeing and hiking, and they were a big part of our lives at Kennebec. We took an increasingly demanding canoe trip each summer, climaxing in our last year with a long journey down the Allagash River. In my last year, I was chosen as captain of the Grey softball team, not because I was good at the sport but solely because it was my turn. I was a pitcher because that was the only position I could play with any ease. We won the tournament that year, and I came home with a giant trophy. (Kennebec gave many awards to campers for all sorts of reasons.) When I got off the train, my father looked at the trophy and, laughing, asked where I had bought it.

I also enjoyed a variety of crafts, such as making a canoe paddle, and I acted in several theater productions. One of my favorites was "If Men Played Cards as Women Do" by George S. Kaufman.

After four years as a Kennebec camper, I applied and was chosen as a waiter/counselor, which was a wonderful way to enjoy all the outdoor benefits of Kennebec while doing only a modest amount of work at meal times and supervising hiking and canoeing trips. My friends and I could play the rest of the time and go into town at night to drink beer, a daring new experience for us.

I loved Kennebec for the fun and friends and because my father had been there. He and I returned there in the summer of 1977 to celebrate its seventieth year in operation.

In the weeks before and after Kennebec in the summer, I worked in a number of different jobs. One summer, for example, my parents insisted I learn to type. It was not fun to sit for hours with a class of young women who were learning to be secretaries, but the ability to type has benefited me all my life.

Another summer, I worked in a Boston stock brokerage firm as a runner. This was an "odd lot" firm—it bought and sold small amounts of stock. The offices were in the Boston Stock Exchange building. My job was to pick up little slips of paper that listed buy or sell orders from various brokers and run downstairs to the desk of an elderly employee, who put the slips in order and gave them to another broker on the floor of the Exchange, where the broker executed the order. This mindless job kept me half busy, and I had ample time to read between runs. I also learned that I had no interest in the world of brokerage.

At the end of that summer, watching all the little slips of paper being passed from hand to hand, I wrote a memorandum to the partner who had hired me, suggesting a way to make the operation more efficient. In essence, I proposed that the runner take the slips directly to the broker on the Exchange floor, thus bypassing the elderly employee. The partner read the memorandum and was silent, looking at me for what seemed a long time. Then he said something like, "The man whom you suggest we fire has been working for our firm all his life. He is sixty years old and has a wife and children. How do you suppose he can live and support his family if we fire him?" He left the question hanging until I left, mumbling an apology and with an important life lesson I never forgot.

During my eighth grade, we moved from the Beach Road house—which was becoming too much for my mother to handle—to a rented apartment at 417 Beacon Street in Boston. It came completely furnished by the architect who had designed it—an ultramodern decor, including a huge living room on the second floor with a picture window and Mies van der Rohe chairs.

I especially enjoyed being with my father during those growing years. Dad was the perfect father. He always spent time with me—much more than my mother did—and was interested and involved in what I did and why. From an early age, I joined him on ski trips, sometimes with my sister, sometimes alone, but rarely with my mother. We went to Stowe, Vermont; North Conway and Mount Washington in New Hampshire; a number of other ski resorts in New England; and once to Mont Tremblant in Canada.

My father also loved sailing and taught me to love it as well. In the summer, we sailed on his small sloop, *Folly*, which he bought when I was twelve. He kept the boat in Manchester Harbor, and we regularly went there on weekends. My mother did not enjoy sailing and rarely joined us. My sister was with us sometimes but often stayed home to be with her friends. We also read books together, walked together, talked together, and became as close as father and son could be.

I think my father liked working at Touraine's in Boston, though I doubt he had a real passion for it. On the day after Christmas, there was always a big sale, and my father had to work late Christmas Eve, visiting each of the stores—at one time, there were eight—to be sure everything was in order, and I often accompanied him on these and other rounds of the stores. I also worked in the Touraine warehouse one summer, using a staple gun to put price tags on garments for eight hours a day, and I hated it. I was just a teenager, but that summer convinced me that I wanted no part of retail sales when I was grown.

During this time, my mother was committed to working as a professional. I cannot think of another woman among my parents' friends who worked then. She worked during the day at the Fogg Museum of Art as a curator of works of paper. She had little interest in household chores, so we had a maid/cook who cooked every day and left a big meal for us on Sunday if we did not go to my grandparents for Sunday lunch. We usually had cereal and toast or eggs and toast for breakfast and meat or fish or chicken at night, along with vegetables, potatoes, and dessert. The Sunday dinner was a large roast with all the trimmings. On Sunday night, my mother made scrambled eggs, the only meal I remember her cooking.

Meanwhile, I was having fun at Browne & Nichols and with a group of friends from Cambridge. They included a number of girls who attended Shady Hill School, which was just across some playing fields; the Buckingham School, not far away; and probably others. I recall some of their names—such as Gay Cross, who had a big house off Brattle Street, where we played Spin the Bottle regularly—the winner had to kiss a girl of his choice. I can vividly recall when Joe Fletcher, son of the dean of the Harvard Divinity School, took us into his father's study, where he showed us the first Kinsey report on sexuality in males. We were stunned to learn how much sex was part of the lives of most men and how many different forms their sex seemed to take. About this time, I recall sneaking into a burlesque show in South Boston and seeing almost-naked ladies for the first time.

My friends all went to dancing school, and I went as well. We also attended a series of dances for seventh-, eighth-, and ninth-grade boys and girls. I learned the foxtrot, the waltz, and a number of South American dances and enjoyed the experience. The lessons certainly helped later when dancing became a key part of social life at Exeter and Harvard.

During the ninth grade at Browne & Nichols, my life changed dramatically for the worse because a number of my close friends, including Bob O'Neill, left for Milton Academy, another private day school.

One day that year, I came home and abruptly told my parents that I wanted to go to Exeter Academy. I am not sure how I got the idea in my head that Exeter was the place for me. I knew Exeter was reputed to be the best prep school in the country. My parents were stunned. They had heard of Exeter; my cousin, Charles Wyzanski, a federal judge, had gone there. It just never occurred to them that I might go away to school.

I wouldn't let the matter go. I had a very, very close relationship with my father's mother, my grandmother, who lived in Boston. She never went to college but was among the most educated people I ever knew. We had lunch often on Saturdays, she would give me a book she had read, usually biographies and history, and the next time we had lunch we would discuss the book. One day, over lunch, I confided to her, "My friends are going away to boarding school, to Exeter Academy, but that's not possible for our family financially."

Looking at me, she said quietly, "Well, we'll see."

One of the great blessings of my life is that my grandmother financed my education as a sophomore, junior, and senior at Exeter Academy. She was a shining example of the power of family to help each other and make a difference.

2

Generations

My father's parents, Adolph and Marion, were a dominant presence in our lives when I was growing up. Before we moved to Washington, DC, in 1942, we went for Sunday lunch almost every week to their Beach Road house, where they had a cook, maid, and chauffeur. We enjoyed a long, elaborate meal of soup, roast beef with potatoes and beans, salad, and pie or ice cream. In the summers, the routine was the same, except that it was at their summer home, even larger, on a beautiful bay in Beverly, Massachusetts, several miles to the north of where we were living in Clifton. My grandfather bought the Beverly home with a large share of his stocks just before the stock market crash in 1929. They stayed there for three months every summer until my grandfather died.

The Beverly home was the command post for the Ehrlich clan of my grandparents and their five children, spouses, and grandchildren. Every September 1, the entire family gathered at the Beverly home to celebrate my grandfather's birthday. A family photograph was part of the birthday ritual, and we still have some of those pictures. I only later learned how deeply my mother resented the pressures and obligations that she felt were imposed by my father's family.

My grandparents were members of the largest Reform temple in Boston, Temple Israel, led by a then-famous rabbi named Joshua Loth Liebman, who had written a bestseller about spiritual values. Later, my friends joked that Temple Israel was so liberal that it was closed on Saturday and open on Sunday. My parents were members as well, but they limited attendance to High Holy Days. My father was a board member of the American Jewish Committee in Boston in the era before that organization shifted significantly to the right politically.

As a family, we certainly never made a secret of being Jewish, though we never publicized it either. I do not remember any effort by my parents to instill Jewish traditions into our lives when my sister and I were growing up, though they contributed to Jewish charities such as the Jewish Federation. Particularly in the days before World War II, assimilation was seen by them and their friends as much more important than asserting Jewish identity, and that feeling carried over into the 1950s.

I also do not remember any antisemitic incidents in my life growing up, with one exception. I recall meeting a group of boys on a street in Cambridge when I was six or seven, having my pants pulled down, and being called "kike," which meant nothing to me until my dad explained that it is a derogatory word for Jews.

My grandmother Marion was warm and loving, and we were close, especially after Adolph died. Her parents were from a prosperous family, and she went on a grand tour to Europe in June 1897. She must have been about eighteen. I still have her diary from that trip.

After she was widowed, my grandmother took me to the Boston Symphony and other cultural events. One of the many books she gave me, which we would later discuss, was a biography of Louis Brandeis by Thomas Adolphus Mason. I can still remember talking about that blue, cloth-bound volume with her. I think one of the reasons she chose the book was because Brandeis was not only Jewish like us, but also more important, he was a great hero in terms of free expression, protecting minorities, and particularly protecting against economic oppression. It isn't a great biography, but it absolutely captivated me that this man could be so wise and do so much to utilize the law to make the country and the world better places. It was a shaping force in my decision to become a lawyer. While I knew I would be no Brandeis, I wanted to use my intellect for the public good, as he had done.

In marked contrast to my grandmother, my grandfather Adolph always seemed a stern presence to me. He started in the textile business; was a partner in a clothing company; and then, in 1925, became a director of Jordan Marsh, a prominent department store in Boston. He held that position until he died in 1952 at age eighty-four.

He was definitely the patriarch of the family—austere, aloof, and a bit forbidding. Once when I was visiting the Beverly summer home, my cousin Louis climbed up a tree near the house and fell, breaking his arm. I was about ten or twelve at the time and recall talking with my grandfather that day. For something to say, I told him I was sorry about Louis's accident. My grandfather, as it turned out, had not heard about the accident and roared at me that he did not know what I was talking about—and why had he not been told? I was totally terrified.

As I have written, Adolph bought the controlling interest in a small chain of retail stores named Touraine. He appointed Richard as president and my father as one of the vice presidents. My mother resented this and often said to me that Adolph favored Richard over my father and that this was unfair.

Turning to my father's siblings, he was one of five children, three men and two women. All five were extremely close to each other. Richard was the eldest, then my father, then Frances, Polly, and Henry.

Richard always seemed to me a complete contrast to my dad, reserved and distant, while my dad was warm and caring. Later, I learned that Richard and my father really were extremely close siblings and frequently shared and discussed each other's troubles.

Richard married a lovely woman, Virginia, after he divorced his first wife. Virginia was the sister of the wife of the movie mogul Samuel Goldwyn. Before the marriage, I think Virginia was an actress. Because she was a Catholic, she had to marry Richard outside the Church. Virginia was absolutely beautiful and a lovely person. She and Richard and their two sons, David and Daniel, stayed in the Beverly summer home all summer, and Virginia ran the household. This unfairly contributed to my mother's irritation that they were favored over my parents. In my own view, Virginia was needed to run the household, as my grandmother could not have done so alone.

My father's sister Frances, a wonderful woman, was also briefly married and divorced before she married my uncle, Elias Wolf. They lived in Philadelphia and had two children, Betsy and Louis. Elias came from a wealthy family that made metal-edged boxes, and he was able to retire at age fifty—he told me he never worked hard before then. He became "Mr. Philadelphia" because he devoted his life to philanthropy in the city.

Polly, the younger sister, was married late in life to Robert Shackelton and worked at the American Institute of Architects until she became deeply involved as a Democratic leader in the District of Columbia, and politics became her full-time occupation. She was an elected member of the DC Council for many years and cochair of the DC delegation to many Democratic conventions. She also almost became mayor of DC when Lyndon Johnson was president, but her appointment was stopped at the last minute by political pressures. Aunt Polly was friends with most of the DC movers and shakers, especially in the JFK and LBJ years. Lady Bird Johnson was one of her good friends.

The youngest of my father's brothers, Henry, was a journalist for *The Boston Herald* before WWII, and then became a successful war correspondent, rising to the rank of lieutenant colonel. He helped uncover a huge cache of stolen art in Italy near the end of the war. Henry joined *Look* magazine when he returned after the war and lived in New York City, where he remained a bachelor and loved high society until his death. He later wrote for *McCall's* and other magazines. He was my favorite uncle, and my wife Ellen and I enjoyed many great times with him, including a trip to China when I was provost of the University of Pennsylvania. Ellen and I also became close to both Frances and Polly and saw them often in later years.

My father, William, known to everyone as Bill, went to public schools in Brookline, Massachusetts, when his family lived at 42 Beech Road. After high school, he went to Harvard College where he was a member of the Harvard Crimson. He told me later that he thought he would have been chosen as the business manager of the Crimson if he had not been a Jew.

My father was always active in a range of civic activities in Cambridge, Boston, and Brookline, including at a center for international students at Harvard. He was also involved in Harvard alumni activities—he chaired at least one reunion of his class. I suspect these activities, other volunteer service, and his garden meant more to him than his lifelong occupation as a retail merchant. He loved gardening—roses, particularly—and spent hours puttering around his beloved flowers.

I had the sense that my father viewed his work life as necessary to feed and clothe his family, but that his heart was not in the business. I saw how hard he worked at Touraine and finally at two pipe and tobacco stores that he and Richard bought. He often worked all day, every day, six days a week, and sometimes on Sundays. The markups were small for retail stores like Touraine then, and the work was demanding because it involved an avalanche of details.

My father worked to earn a living, but his real enjoyment was in his family, his community, and his personal efforts in aiding those in need. My father was my first mentor, a role model in helping me and many others do our best, right up to his death at age eighty-seven. Only now, as I reflect on his life, do I understand the full force of his moral character as my teacher. We were the closest of friends. We looked much alike, as he looked like his father and as my youngest son looks like me. A quartet of photographs used to hang on a wall in my home with the caption, "Four generations of Ehrlich men at age fifteen"—my grandfather Adolph, my father Bill, myself, and my son Paul. We look like quadruplets, though the four generations spanned almost one hundred years.

Like most great teachers, my father taught by the example of his life. From my childhood on, he was always in my corner, listening, learning, advising, supporting. But the example of the way he lived his life—most particularly in his relations with other people—was even more important for me than his support. Over and over, after his death, I heard individuals who had known him tell how much he had influenced their lives by listening carefully and then helping them think through their difficulties so that they could arrive at their own decisions. His employees cared for him and called him "Mr. William."

My mother, Evelyn Seltzer Ehrlich, was a markedly different person. She grew up in Philadelphia with her parents, Minnie and Alexander Seltzer. My mother's father tried a number of businesses, including a plastic manufacturing company, which failed. But over time, Alexander became sufficiently successful to have a small, but pleasant home in Germantown. Because my father's family was in Boston, I became much closer to them, but I also visited my mother's parents, my grandparents, once or twice a year in Philadelphia.

My mother had two brothers, Ervin and Oscar. I never knew Oscar, but Ervin became a great favorite of mine. He worked as an engineer for a battery company and, on the side, enjoyed restoring an old car—a Model T—that ran on a rechargeable battery. Ervin married Louise, a delightful woman who had been a nurse in the army during WW II. Louise gave my wife, Ellen, and me her old army tent when we left Washington DC in 1965 to drive across the country with two children. Ervin and Louis had three sons, Dan, David, and Alex. Ellen and I became good friends with Dan and David and their wives and children when we lived in Philadelphia, while I was provost at the University of Pennsylvania.

My mother, as a girl, went to a camp for Jewish girls called Tripp Lake, where she achieved success as a champion swimmer. After graduating from Smith College, she went straight to the University of Pennsylvania and was determined to earn a degree in architecture. According to our family lore, she was not allowed to take the necessary courses in sanitation and plumbing at the University of Pennsylvania because she was a woman. Undeterred, after marrying my father in 1929 and moving to Cambridge, she studied at MIT and earned a degree in architecture. Unfortunately, the country was in a depression, and few buildings were being built, and certainly not ones designed by women, even those as extremely talented as my mother.

She didn't give up. Always interested in art, my mother went to the Fogg Museum of Art, part of Harvard University, and persuaded the director to let her work there for free in exchange for training in the new field of art conservation. A now legendary curator, Agnes Mongan, worked there, and with her help, my mother became an expert restorer of works on paper, one of the first in the country. She worked at the Fogg for decades and gained a national reputation in the field.

While at the Fogg Museum, she developed a technique of photographing through a microscope that enabled restorers like herself both to repair damaged works of art on paper and determine whether they were real or fake. She used the technique while repairing a famous engraving called "The Battle of the Nudes" by the Italian artist Pollaiuolo. The print had been purchased from a dealer for $25,000 and given to the museum by a Harvard professor and wealthy benefactor named Paul Sachs. Sachs viewed himself, at least as I learned the story, as a great expert in Renaissance art. In cleaning the print, my mother concluded that it was a fake and used her new technique to substantiate her discovery.

Her finding angered Sachs, who was embarrassed to have been tricked by a forger. He took the print back to the dealer, received the $25,000 he had paid for it, and gave the money to the Fogg so that my mother could write a book about art forgeries. She did write the book—I still have the manuscript—but it was never published. She believed the reason was that Sachs thought the book would put him in a bad light and blocked publication. Having read it, I suspect it simply was not good enough to be published. It certainly would have needed substantial editing. But my mother did write several articles about her work and was justly proud of her stature in a field that did not exist when she began at the Fogg Museum.

Her determination that "The Battle of the Nudes" was a forgery put her role at the museum at risk, but also cemented her reputation as a leading expert in the restoration of works on paper and in detecting forgeries. Of the many thousands of members of the association of art restorers today, she was one of the first ten.

My mother's talent and national reputation as an art restorer led to an exciting incident in her life. In 1942, when I was eight years old, she went to Fort Knox on a secret mission for the federal government. With guards watching, she and another expert rewove fibers of the original signed copy of the Declaration of Independence, which was being held there along with the nation's gold supply. It had been pasted on a board and, over time, had developed a tear. The mission was secret because—according to the story I was told—those in the government were afraid that a rent in the document would suggest a rent in the Republic. I knew about her trip, but as much as I wanted to tell my friends, I was sworn to secrecy.

Over a decade later, in 1953, the country was torn by anti-Communist sentiments fueled by Senator Joseph McCarthy, who claimed that the State Department was riddled with secret Communist agents. Richard Nixon made his reputation by echoing McCarthy's charges. He pointed to Alger Hiss as a top-secret Soviet agent who worked in the State Department. Hiss denied the charges under oath and was brought to trial for perjury. The key piece of evidence was the so-called "pumpkin papers" that an admitted former Communist, Whittaker Chambers, claimed to have received from Hiss after they were typed on Hiss's typewriter. Hiss was tried in 1949 and, after a hung jury, was tried again in 1950 and convicted.

As part of the appeal process, in 1950, a lawyer for Hiss named Helen Buttenwieser, who was also an acquaintance of our family, asked my mother to be an expert witness in the case and examine the "pump-kin papers" to try to determine whether they were typed on the Hiss typewriter. My mother agreed to do so despite the great potential jeopardy to her reputation by seeming to side with a man convicted of lying about his ties to Communism and the Soviet Union. FBI agents brought the documents to our apartment in Boston, where my mother examined them.

Ultimately, she concluded that they were forged, though the appeal by Hiss failed nonetheless. But the example that my mother set by doing what she saw as a civic duty despite the very real dangers to her reputation made a lasting impression on me. In her work on the Hiss case, she faced the certainty that some of her friends would be critical of her helping the defense in a high-profile criminal case involving someone accused of treason whom she did not know. But she did it because she thought it was the right thing to do.

The Hiss case was the last major professional assignment carried out by my mother. After that, she became increasingly recluse, lying on a sofa all day watching television—and drinking. Although I did not know it at the time, by the early 1940s, if not before, my mother became increasingly depressed and began seeing a physiatrist in Boston named Mandel Cohen. She saw Cohen at least once a week. At some point in the 1950s, she was diagnosed as manic depressive, now referred to as bipolar disorder. She was admitted twice to McLean Hospital near Boston for shock treatment. Alcohol abuse certainly exacerbated her health problems. My sister, Ellen, later told me of opening cabinets and finding dozens of empty bottles. I was not fully aware of her problems in my early years. But my sister, being four years older, was acutely conscious that our mother was an alcoholic. As a result of her illness, my mother became moody and difficult, especially toward my sister. She had neither the temperament nor the energy to spend time as a parent.

My mother's dark moods made it increasingly difficult for friends of my parents to have any social time with them. I later learned that my father's brothers and sisters were totally exasperated with my mother, but it is not clear that there was much my dad could have done. He stood by her and nursed her and watched as one by one, many, probably most, of their friends gave up on her.

Throughout those decades, my father never complained or showed less than complete love and caring support for my mother, bringing her meals, handling the household chores, paying the bills, and being both father and mother to his two children. Despite her depression and alcoholism, he always saw the remarkable in her. He never gave her or anyone else the sense that he was imposed upon and never apologized to others for her behavior or inactivity.

A letter from my grandmother to him, written on March 21, 1962, when he was fifty-nine, after Ellen and I were married, gives some clue to what he must have gone through in dealing with my mother.

> My very own darling William: I want you to know that I am constantly thinking of you and for you in these trying days, weeks, and months. Last evening I longed to take you on my lap enfolding you heart to

heart and hugging you, embracing you with my heart and soul, even while smiling, hiding my innermost self. I was penning words of wishes, hopes, and prayers for Aunt Ted's 90th, while I was really and truly pouring them out for you and your poor dear Evelyn, who on the advent of spring, March 21, came into this troubled world.

My children always asked me which of them I loved the best and my answer was invariably, "the one who needed me the most at that moment," and now so you. William darling, my most dearly beloved child, who must let me share your troubles and needs. I am enclosing a check of two thousand dollars towards Evelyn's hospital expenses.

There is more, but this gives a sense of how much anguish my father must have gone through. But he loved my mother—really loved her. I know that from some of his letters to his younger brother, Henry. Here is an excerpt from one written shortly after my mother's death. "She certainly had her problems during our 52 years together, but I wouldn't have given up a minute of the time we had together."

William Ehrlich was a kind and generous man who took great care of my mother, never suggesting that she was other than a wife whom he loved and would always support. He never—at least to me—suggested that he was other than fortunate to have her for his spouse. His sensitive heart, his patience, and his unfailing kindness have always inspired me.

3

The Best Education

Phillips Exeter Academy in the fall of 1949 was much different than it is today—only boys attended, there were few scholarships, and it lacked many of the current facilities. Nonetheless, I received a great education there—the best education of my life.

Entering Exeter as a "Lower Middler" or sophomore, I was placed on the edge of the lovely campus in a small, white frame home, called Sleeper House, that had been transformed into a dorm. Most of my classmates had already been at Exeter for a year and had signed up for housing in other, more desirable dorms. I soon found out why the Sleeper House wasn't anyone's first choice. It was considered one of the least desirable rooming choices on campus. Its housemaster (each dorm had a faculty member and his family living there) was a physics teacher with a sour disposition named Mr. Bickel. I soon learned to call him, behind his back, "Bickel the Pickle," My room was on the top (third) floor, and my roommate, Merton Minter, was from Texas and was also a "new boy." We liked each other and got along, but had little in common.

I quickly fell into the regimented rhythm of the school days—an assembly hall in the morning, then classes, then athletics in the afternoon, then study at night, with time out for meals in a common dining room and ample time for bull sessions, usually about girls.

I felt terribly lonely at first and cried myself to sleep for the initial few weeks, though I could not tell my parents, since it had been my idea to go to Exeter. During the first year, I felt very much an outsider for several reasons. Most of the other boys were returning students who knew each other. Many were from wealthy, but broken families. I can recall only one friend from my years before Exeter whose parents had been divorced. Divorce seemed to me an alien concept. A sizable group of boys were the social stars of the class, and I was never in their circle.

I also had trouble fitting in because I was not a particularly good athlete, and athletics was important at Exeter. I did try though. Not caring for team sports—football, basketball, baseball—I played tennis in the fall and spring, which I had learned at camp and had played at Browne & Nichols. In the winter. I ran the hundred-yard dash and the 440-yard race. But I was never good enough at either sport to make an Exeter varsity team. There was, however, one athletic highlight of my Exeter years: the time a friend named "Bats" (Bancroft) Wheeler and I made the school's tennis doubles finals. We lost, but the very fact that we reached the finals shocked the members of the varsity tennis team.

The third factor that separated me from others was that I was one of only a handful of Jewish students at Exeter. I never experienced anti-Semitism, but chapel was required on Sunday, and the hymns sung there were all Christian ones. Perhaps I could have gone to Jewish services in the town of Exeter, but the thought didn't occur to me. I do recall wondering how many of those around me really believed that Christ was the son of God. My own sense of God was, at most, some vague force that ordered the universe, and the notion that he could really be portrayed with human dimensions, let alone have a child, seemed absurd. (One of the particular pleasures I've had on visiting Exeter over the years is seeing that Jewish students are now encouraged to have Shabbat services on Friday nights, as well as services on Jewish holidays.)

That first semester, it seemed that all students not only knew each other, but were also smarter than I was. Even though I already had one year of French and two years of Latin, I was assigned to a first-year Latin class. My teachers must have realized that I would be unprepared for the academic rigor of Exeter. They were correct. My first Latin quiz—in a class that I had taken the year before—was stunning. The teacher, Mr. Galt, handed back the quizzes in order of their grades, announcing the grades, starting with the one with the top grade. I thought I had done quite well. Instead, it was the worst grade in the class. "D minus minus minus minus," Mr. Galt announced as he handed me my paper. "Ehrlich, you're only getting a barely passing grade because you're a new boy." Of course, I was mortified and held back the tears, while the rest of the boys in the class laughed. French and math were almost as difficult for me. I managed to get through French, in large part, because my teacher loved art, and I knew enough about art from my mother to steer most conversations around to the art scene whenever he questioned me.

Fortunately, things did get better. Much better. In the middle of my first year, Mr. Bickel left the house—but not the campus, unfortunately—and a new master, Colin Irving, father of the famous novelist, John Irving, took over, and I liked him enormously. Mr. Irving became one of my favorite teachers. He taught American history, which was my favorite course.

After that first rocky semester, I grew increasingly confident of myself in some classes, and over time, I became friends with lots of students, including my old childhood friend Chick (no longer Chicky) Kuhn. Even though he was a year ahead of me, we decided to room together the next year.

As my time at Exeter progressed, I continued struggling with the languages, science, and math courses. Science and math were always challenging, in large measure, I think, because I never found them interesting. Somehow the logic puzzles of advanced algebra and trigonometry, along with plain and solid geometry, never captured my interest. In those days, there was no effort to explain why we were learning these subjects or what possible use they could be. We learned formulas, but not the reasons behind them. The endless details required to master trigonometry, for example, left me numb. I envy the good fortune of current high school students who need not master a slide rule, but can use calculators and computers.

Science was not much better. The courses seemed to involve massive amounts of memorization, and I soon learned that this was not my strong suit. I invented all sorts of tricks to help me memorize the periodic table in chemistry and the essential points in biology—this was long before cell biology had come on the scene—but I never had my heart—and too rarely my head—in it.

In physics classes, at least I could be intrigued by some of the experiments, though much of the course was memorizing formulas. Unfortunately, it was taught by Mr. Bickel (the Pickle), whose typically cold and distant disposition did little to encourage me to learn. One day, as he was showing the class something about electricity, he handed me two wires and commanded me to hold them without letting them touch. Of course, like Curious George, I was intrigued to see how close I could bring the two wires together without them actually touching. As Mr. Bickel droned on and on, I brought the wires closer and closer. All of a sudden, a spark jumped from one wire to the other, not only causing a short circuit in our classroom but also blowing the fuses throughout the entire science building and plunging us into darkness. Of course, my classmates were thrilled, and they all cheered. Livid with rage at me, Mr. Bickel was forced to dismiss us. For a day, I was the hero of the class.

Although I never became a star in languages, math, or science, I moved to the top of the class in history and English. I loved those courses from the beginning and acquired a wonderful, deep, lasting love of reading and writing. Exeter, from my first days there, made me realize what a great world of learning was out there, ready to be investigated. Teachers demanded the most that each student could do, and I was stretched in ways that were never matched again in college or even law school.

Essential to my education at Exeter was the Harkness method and its application in history and English. (Today it is used in all subjects.) Twelve students sat around an oval table with a teacher. The teacher threw out the first question. From then on, students were expected to engage in a continuous discussion for fifty minutes and debate about the materials they read for class. This method tells you, as a student, that your learning is significantly up to you, and you have a key role not only in your own learning, but also in the learning of other students.

You have to be an active participant in that process. Through the Harkness method, I learned how to learn and to enjoy learning to a degree that I had never before experienced. Exeter enabled me to understand the pleasures of an inquiring mind.

English was a joy for me. My teacher was Mr. Lloyd, a pleasant man if not a particularly inspiring one. But I fell in love with nineteenth-century English literature in his classes, a love that has stayed with me ever since. We read Dickens, Eliot, and Hardy, along with Virginia Woolf, E. M. Forster, and more. We also read American authors, including Nathaniel Hawthorne, Edith Wharton, Mark Twain, and others. Each week, we wrote a theme about some aspect of one of our readings. I learned to enjoy not only reading great works of fiction but also writing about those works. My wife and I still regularly reread the novels I first met at Exeter, especially the works of Hardy, Eliot, Wharton, and Woolf.

I also started to write short stories at Exeter, which was a regular part of my English classes. I had actually begun to do this at Browne & Nichols under the guidance of Mr. Sindall. But I gained confidence as a writer at Exeter and learned to enjoy making up stories and writing them down. In small group settings, Exeter gave me a chance to write lots of stories. Each was returned with extensive comments and suggestions, and there were ample chances to rewrite and revise. One story put me in the position of a frustrated FDR speech writer, who complained that the president mangled the speech writer's prose. The writer drafted, for example, "The only thing we have to be afraid of is being afraid," and FDR changed it to "The only thing we have to fear is fear itself." This may seem a thin bit of humor for even a short tale, but when I came to Harvard, I submitted the story to *Lampoon Magazine*, and it was accepted. More about *Lampoon* later.

History was my other favorite subject—ancient, European, and US history all fascinated me. My teachers, Mr. Irving and the headmaster, Mr. Saltonstall—a good New England name and one of my favorite teachers—were excellent. I took Mr. Saltonstall's American history course in my junior year, although most of the other students were seniors. He was a particularly good teacher of history in an era when the great person theory of history was dominant. I read both ancient history and American history and everything in between in terms of great men—they were all men, I think—who shaped their times. In these history courses, I began to understand the qualities of leadership. Nowadays, of course, I realize the great-person theory of history is flawed because it's not only great men who shape history. Saltonstall, nonetheless, was an important early influence in my life. He became a good friend and mentor in my years after graduation. I much admired his decision to leave Exeter when the Peace Corps began in order to head a country Peace Corps office.

At the beginning of my junior year, Chick Kuhn and I became roommates in Knight House. Like other dorms, Knight House had a "butt room" in the basement where boys were allowed to smoke. Cigarette smoking was common, but I did not smoke until years later in college when I smoked a pipe bought at my father's store.

Mr. Atkins was the housemaster. This meant that he and his wife lived in the house in a suite of rooms, just as Mr. Bickel and then Mr. Irving had done in Sleeper House. Mr. Atkins, who was my math teacher, was a wonderful man with a lovely wife, and they treated the dozen or so students who lived in the house as colleagues in learning. I became friends with all those in the house, particularly Dick Jones, who became my roommate the next year. Mr. Atkins cared deeply for students, and we became close, even though I never excelled in his class.

This story illustrates his kindness. One day in the spring of my second year, when I was sixteen, my sister, Ellen, wrote me a letter, which had never happened before. She was a junior at Smith College, which she had chosen largely because our mother had gone there. In those days, it was expected that Smith women would be engaged before they graduated—yes, that was the expectation—and it meant that students were expected to have a steady boyfriend in their junior year. Ellen wrote that she was miserable because she did not have a boyfriend and was planning to leave Smith and "go away." At the time, my parents were away on vacation—in Bermuda, I believe—and were not available.

When I received the letter, I immediately went to Mr. Atkins for his advice. He said I must persuade my sister to stay at Smith at least until my parents returned. He told me to get on a train to Boston, and from Boston to take a train to Northampton, home of Smith College. My best chance of persuading her to stay, he said, would be to talk to her in person. He then let me call Ellen on his phone (there were no phones in students' rooms). I told her that I would be in Northampton the next day and not to do anything until we talked. Mr. Atkins then helped me figure out the train schedules, buy the tickets, and find a place in Northampton to stay. He may even have advanced me the money for my trip, though I am not sure of this.

I followed his wise advice. I talked for hours with my sister, who told me, in a rush of tears, that she felt our mother never paid any attention to her and, at the same time, held her to impossible standards. Ellen had followed our mother in going to Smith, and before that, went to Tripp Lake Camp, just as our mother had. Until then, I had no sense of how miserable she was in trying to do what my mother wanted—a life like her own—but always feeling rejected. My sister did continue at Smith and graduated in 1952, but she was never happy there. In the fall of her senior year, she met Melvin Gardner, who had graduated from MIT and was a handsome officer in the Army. They became engaged before Ellen graduated and were married the next year. Sadly, their marriage was not a happy one, though it resulted in four delightful girls—my nieces.

In my second year at Exeter, I took US history, and our main written assignment was a major research paper on some aspect of American history. I chose to write about Abner Kneeland, who was the last man in Massachusetts to be tried and convicted for the crime of blasphemy. He questioned the existence of God. He wasn't an atheist; he was an agnostic. But at that time, in Christian-dominated Boston—they were mainly Unitarians—that was considered blasphemy.

I spent much of Christmas vacation in the bowels of the Boston Library, reading old newspapers about Kneeland and his trial. In the last section of my paper, I compared Christian Massachusetts in the later eighteenth and early nineteenth centuries with then-current Jewish

Israel, focusing on the tensions involved in a Jewish state that, none-theless, wanted to be open and democratic. I recall how proud I was when my paper was one of those chosen for the Negley Prize. I still have a book that was given to me as a prize winner.

That second year was also my first introduction to crushes on par-ticular girls. Because girls were so scarce at Exeter and our hormones were all in high gear, much of our casual conversation was about them.

Exeter had a series of dances, one or two each semester. Sometimes girls were invited from all-girls boarding schools. We also had a dance to which we could invite a girl from out of town who would come and stay at the Exeter Inn. I invited a girl named Sylvia Teal, whom I knew when she was at the Buckingham School and I was at Browne & Nich-ols. Another girl I met at a dance was Judy Kaufman, who came from Pittsburg, and we began corresponding with each other afterward and into the next summer.

The summer after my junior year at Exeter, it was time to try some-thing new. Since my father had taken me sailing on his boat, "Folly," for years, I decided that I was a good enough sailor to get a job on a boat. I put an ad in *Yachting Magazine*, saying I was an experienced young sailor looking for a summer job.

My first offer was to join a crew sailing in the famous Bermuda race, but the job would have required that I miss all my final exams. Instead, I was hired by a man in Larchmont to take care of his boat during the week in Mamaroneck Harbor on Long Island Sound and to help him sail it on weekends and for a couple of weeks' cruise. His name was Lewis, and he owned a company that made women's nylon stockings. His burgee, or owner's flag, was a woman's leg covered in one of his stockings, to the shock of the society women who saw it. I was paid $35 a week and was to sleep on the boat and keep it clean when it was anchored. Since it was only forty-two feet long, this was not much of a job.

But Mrs. Lewis was a perfectionist, or perhaps she just wanted to prove that she was the boss. Every time she came on the boat, she ran her hand along the mahogany railing, then took out a handkerchief and wiped her hand as though it were dirty. We never got along. But

Mr. Lewis was the complete opposite. He soon realized that I had grossly exaggerated my knowledge of sailing, but rather than being irritated. He taught me continually when we cruised, and by the end of the summer, I was fairly competent.

We took a trip to Martha's Vineyard near the end of the summer. I slept on deck at night, except when it rained, when I curled up in the galley. But when we reached Martha's Vineyard, Mr. Lewis rented a room for me at a bed and breakfast. This was probably so I would be out of their way, but I had a wonderful week exploring the island with no obligations.

Judy Kaufman and I continued to write to one another that summer. She invited me to visit her in Pittsburgh, and I agreed, though I had never been that far on a train before, let alone taken any sort of trip to see a girl. I was convinced that when you visited someone's house, you were supposed to bring a present, so I went to a local gift shop and bought a little nut dish that I carefully carried in my hand on the train.

When I arrived in Pittsburgh, I was stunned to see a long, black car with a chauffeur, along with Judy, waiting to take me to her house. I had no idea that her father was one of the wealthiest men in the city, the owner of a famous department store that bore the family name. We drove up what seemed an endless drive, through lawns and gardens lined with trees, to their enormous house. We walked in, and Mrs. Kaufman met us in the enormous hallway. I presented my nut dish, nicely wrapped with paper and ribbon. She tore open a corner of the wrapping and, with one fluid motion, stuck it, still largely wrapped, in the drawer of a hall table. I was crushed.

The weekend went from bad to worse. Somehow, Judy and I had never contemplated what it would be like to talk for an entire day, let alone a whole weekend. I went home a little dejected, but realizing that being with a girl meant more than a dance and some talk at intermission.

During my final year at Exeter, I roomed with my friend from Knight House, Dick Jones. Awkwardly, another friend, Monty Dowling, the only Black student in our class, also asked me to be his roommate our senior year. I had already informally agreed to room with Dick but was worried that Monty would feel I was rejecting his request because he was Black. I finally told him that I had already committed to room with Dick, and I think he understood, though I was never certain and always felt conflicted about my decision.

Of course, my interest in girls continued that year. At a dance, I met a girl named Debbie Snover from Abbot Academy, and we began a torrid correspondence. At the same time, my roommate, Dick Jones, had a mad crush on a girl named Barbara who was at the Fine Arts Museum School in Boston. He had no idea how to write love letters to her. (His strengths were in the sciences, and he later became a doctor.) At his request, I started to write his love letters, as well as my own.

Things soon became complicated. I really enjoyed corresponding with Barbara more than writing to Debbie. Barbara had more spark, interest, and fun. I became convinced that when I went to college, I would no longer be obligated to defer to Dick regarding Barbara. And for a brief time, Barbara and I dated. Dick never knew this, and Barbara—I hope—never knew that I was the ghostwriter of his love letters.

During the fall of my senior year, 1951, it was time to choose a college. At the time, graduates of Exeter who did reasonably well could be assured of a place at any college in the country. Most went to Harvard, Yale, or Princeton. I applied to Swarthmore, which fascinated me because it offered an exciting intellectual environment and had the reputation of being among the best of its kind. I also applied to Harvard, which my father and two of my uncles had attended. (I did consider whether I would be better off at a liberal arts college away from Boston where my parents lived.) Harvard certainly had the strongest reputation at the time of any college in the country. In the end, I decided to go to Harvard. Swarthmore seemed too much like Exeter, while I hoped that, at Harvard, I would be stretched more.

With my next step secured, it was time to graduate and leave behind the best education I ever received. Why did Exeter have such a powerful impact on me? The three years were a twenty-four/seven experience. I knew when I arrived that I had to create my own sense of belonging if I was to belong. I had to reach out and make new friends and find new ways to learn in both curricular and extracurricular arenas. At Exeter, I was not an outstanding student. I had to learn to accept that reality and to take pleasure in what I could do well without being despondent about what I could not. I had been a star in the Browne & Nichols classrooms; that was not true at Exeter except for in history and English, and I had come to learn to tolerate that truth. And I made close friends, some of whom remained friends as long as they lived. One, Sumner Kaufman, was a roommate through college and then a fellow sufferer when we went to Army Reserve training together.

I do not think I realized until after I left Exeter what a remarkable band of teachers made up the faculty. They were a dedicated group of men—all were men—who committed their whole lives, not just nine to five, to the education of students, and from them, I learned the rewards of dedication to a job—to a calling. The following are words I said at an Exeter Assembly when I was invited there to speak in 2003. My words were a paraphrase of those Judge Learned Hand, my great mentor, said at Harvard Law School.

> More years than I like to remember I sat in this building on the benches where you now sit. They are newly cushioned now, but they were rock hard then, and they felt harder with each passing minute. I listened in Exeter classes, as you now listen, but more than that, I was quietly dissected by men, almost all of whom are now gone, including Saltonstall in history. I see his portrait to my left. What I got from them was not alone a love of reading and writing, of English literature, and of the history of our country, though I did get those as far as I was able to absorb them. But I got much more. I carried away the model of devoted teachers: patient, considerate, courteous, and kindly, whom nothing could daunt and nothing could bribe. The memory of those men has been with me ever since. Again and again, they have helped me when the labor seemed heavy, the task trivial, and the confusions indecipherable. From them, I learned that it is as craftsmen that we get our satisfaction and our pay. In the universe of truth, they lived by the sword; they asked no quarter of absolutes and they gave none. One can hope for no more than you go and do likewise.

All these factors and more made Exeter a special experience in my life. My wife, Ellen, and I have gone to reunions there. I have had the privilege of speaking at two assemblies before the whole student body. We have given every year as much as we could to Exeter and have left a gift to Exeter in our wills. But we can never really repay what I gained at that remarkable school. It was a great school then, and in every dimension, it is a greater school now.

4

Town and Gown

During my junior year at Exeter, my parents moved from their apartment on Beacon Street in Boston to a lovely house on Buckingham Street in Cambridge, about a ten-minute walk from Harvard Square. Even though they were nearby, both they and I wanted me to live in a student dorm. One of my best friends at Kennebec, Fred Willman from New Jersey, was also attending Harvard, and we decided to room together. We stayed roommates and good friends through all four years.

Fred and I had been asked what kinds of roommates we wanted, and we both stressed that we hoped to room with boys from backgrounds different from our own. When we arrived at Mower B-21, a three-bedroom suite on the second floor of one of the freshman dorms that line the Harvard Yard, we found that one of our roommates was Tom Burton, a quiet boy from the Midwest. The other was a Jewish boy, whose name I no longer remember, from Cheyenne, Wyoming, which had a tiny Jewish population. I learned later that other Jewish boys whom I came to know were also placed as freshmen with other Jews. The rationale, I'm sure, was that we would be more "comfortable," though neither Fred nor I were at all involved in Jewish activities during our time at Harvard. But the scars of bias were still there.

The shift to Harvard never seemed as difficult for me as it did for many of my freshman classmates. I had gone to Exeter with all its academic strengths and had already been away from home for three years. My freshman year was an exciting one in both academic and cocurricular terms. For the first time since the Lawrence School, my courses included girls and boys, for while Radcliffe was a separate college for women, its students took all their courses at Harvard.

At that time, Harvard had only recently adopted a requirement that freshmen take one course from each of three clusters of disciplines—the humanities, the social sciences, and the natural sciences. This new requirement was based on "The Red Book," a curriculum-planning effort headed by then-President Conant. At an institution that prided itself on being a meritocracy based on intelligence (though it was, in fact, some ways from that), Conant thought it essential that Harvard students have common academic experiences through these three core requirements. The experiences were not, in fact, completely common because the courses and their emphases differed within each cluster. But his rationale differed from the core Great Books curriculum at the University of Chicago, which was based on the view of Robert Maynard Hutchins (and Mortimer Adler) that the Great Books of the Western World were the foundation of our civilization. At least during my Harvard years, the university sought to have some of the very best faculty teach these general education courses, and I was fortunate enough to learn from them.

During my freshman year, I was not particularly challenged intellectually in some of my courses and was excited by others. We took four courses each semester, plus freshman composition. I looked forward to my humanities and social science courses, and with justification, because they were fascinating. But I was wary of the natural sciences requirement, recalling my experiences with science at Exeter.

The course that I chose in the humanities included the foremost Western political philosophers—Plato, Locke, Hobbes, Rousseau, along with Marx and some others—and was my introduction to these thinkers and their works. I have been engaged in the issues they raised ever since. Louis Hartz taught my social science course. He focused on the thesis of one of his great works, *The Liberal Tradition in America*, published a couple of years after I took his course. The thesis was that American politics has developed within a broad consensus based on Locke's principles. He argued that this happened, in significant part, because the US lacked a feudal past and did not have to overcome a conservative internal order, unlike the United Kingdom and other European countries.

To my surprise, my science course became one of my favorites over my four years at Harvard. It was taught by Bernard Cohen, the county's leading scholar on the history of science, and a young scholar named Thomas Kuhn (no relation to my friend, Chick Kuhn). Kuhn later became famous for his book, *The Structure of Scientific Revolutions*, one of the most influential books in the history of science written in the last half of the twentieth century. Cohen and Kuhn shared the lectures. We were introduced to the basic thesis of the book Kuhn was writing through a series of case studies of scientific revolutions, such as the ones led by Copernicus and Newton. In Kuhn's view, major advances in science occurred not through an accumulation of new facts and theories but rather by finding increasing anomalies in existing theories until those theories finally collapsed and were replaced by revolutionary new ones. This was a highly controversial thesis at the time, and it was exciting to find it played out in the case studies we read in the course. For the first time, I began to have some inkling of the scientific mind at work.

The other course I remember was a required composition course led by a graduate student. We had to turn in one paper of several pages each week. I had kept copies of the papers and short stories I had written at Exeter and turned a couple of them in for this class, only to find that the graduate student called them "juvenile," and I had to shift gears.

In retrospect, I owe that graduate student a lot because I focused on improving my writing after that, although I was not consumed by writing, as was my roommate, Fred Willman. He decided he would write the great American novel and took as many creative writing courses as he could. He wrote many pages of a novel but could never turn them into something that satisfied him. Unfortunately, his life from then on was marked by a frequent inability to do whatever he was working on in a way that satisfied himself. But at that time, he sparked my interest in American fiction, and while I soon concluded that I never could be a serious fiction writer, Fred introduced me to William Styron (*Lie Down in Darkness*) and Thomas Wolfe—all his novels—and many other contemporary writers. I recall the shock of recognition when Salinger's *Franny and Zooey* series first appeared in *The New Yorker*, along with his famous novel, *Catcher in the Rye*. We were bowled over by the power of his prose to mimic the feelings we shared. I cannot read either Salinger or Thomas Wolfe with any pleasure today. On the other hand, I remember finding Virginia Wolfe and E. M. Forster hard-going at Exeter, yet they are among my favorites in recent decades.

I campaigned to be president of the freshmen class, though I am not sure what led me to do this. In all events, I had a good time doing it, though I ultimately lost. As I mentioned in the previous chapter, a short story I had written at Exeter was accepted by *Lampoon Magazine*. John Updike was the editor in chief then and wrote and edited most of the prose and poetry. I then asked to join the editorial board of the *Lampoon*. Each candidate for that board was required to deliver piles of the magazine around the campus. A good friend and I were so upset by being turned down that we threw the copies in the trash. I consoled myself with the thought that membership was based on social standing as much as ability, as my friend, also Jewish, was likewise rejected. The experience did not stop me from continuing to write stories, and I took a creative writing course in my sophomore year.

As a freshman, I decided to translate my general interest in politics into action. That interest was fueled originally by my dad, who was always knowledgeable about political affairs even though he was never directly involved. My grandfather had been a staunch Republican, but my dad was a firm Democrat for all his life, and so was I. From the time of my first political memories, including Harry Truman's upset victory in 1948, I found the Democratic Party cared much more for the rights and interests of those in society who most needed help from the government. I thought FDR was a great hero, and Herbert Hoover represented the efforts of the rich and powerful to stomp on the poor. The fact that my parents were well-off and my grandparents had been rich did not seem a contradiction to me.

I began finding ways to support the Democratic Party on the local, state, and national levels. Over our undergraduate years, Fred Willman and I saw a good many Democratic politicians, including Harry Truman and Eleanor Roosevelt, both of whom visited the campus. We campaigned for Adlai Stevenson as freshmen and again as seniors. In my freshman year, I saw Stevenson drive by my window in Mauer Hall and later cried both times he conceded to Eisenhower. I was incredibly moved by what he said and how he said it.

After our first year in the Harvard Quad, Fred and I, along with Sumner Kaufman, my friend from Exeter, and Tom Burton and Chuck Rush, whom we met at Harvard, all moved together to a suite in Lowell House for the next three years. In each of those years, I was always active in House affairs. These were never burdensome, and they helped me meet several interesting people who came to speak at Lowell House, for one of the tasks of House officers was to shepherd distinguished visitors around. David Rockefeller was one of them. In the summer after my senior year, when Ellen and I were engaged, we went to New York for a friend's wedding and, on a lark, stopped in at the famous jewelry store Van Cleef & Arpels to look at wedding rings. A clerk took one look at Ellen's modest engagement ring and turned away, uninterested. Suddenly, from a back room, out came David Rockefeller, who had no doubt been buying baubles for his wife. "Hello, Tom," he said and visited with me for a few minutes. Suddenly, it seemed that half the store staff had swooped down to help us!

Fred Willman and I decided in our freshman year that the Young Democratic Club would be our main extracurricular activity, and we alternated president and vice president for our remaining years. One of my roles as Democratic Club president during my junior year was to invite outside speakers. James Michael Curley was no longer the mayor of Boston, but he was a political legend, having served four terms, including some time in jail during one of them. I invited Curley to speak at Harvard, which had never happened before. I persuaded Harvard to allow the event to be held at Sanders Theatre, the largest Harvard auditorium at the time.

I made the arrangements for Curley to speak through one of his assistants. We agreed that I would meet Curley outside Memorial Hall, which housed Sanders, at two forty-five in the afternoon so that we could go together backstage at Sanders in time for him to talk at three. By two thirty, Sanders was packed to capacity. I became increasingly nervous as two forty-five passed, and then it was three o'clock—still no Curley. Fred and I waited with a packed auditorium for him to appear. It had not been long since Curley had left jail, and Harvard students were eager to see and hear him, particularly because they assumed that he stood for everything that was not Harvard. We waited and waited, and finally everyone went home, thinking that the mayor had a better offer elsewhere. There were no cell phones then, of course. I raced to Harvard Square and called Curley's assistant.

"Why, he's with you," the assistant said. "We got your call this morning saying he should arrive at a building in Harvard Square, and you would go together to Sanders." The assistant did not know the name of the building, but when he described it, I knew—it was the Lampoon Building.

As I soon learned, a *Lampoon* editor had called the assistant, pretending to be me, and directed Curley to the Lampoon Building. There, Curley was welcomed and shown to a room where he could sit. The editor then left and locked the door so Curley could not get out. When my fellow Democratic Club members and I finally figured all this out and were able to release Curley, he was absolutely furious and went home. The *Lampoon* editors thought this was enormously funny. And, in retrospect, it was. But I was embarrassed and angry. It was bad enough to have been rejected by the *Lampoon* in my effort to become an editor. This was far worse. But I got over it.

Majoring in government was natural since I was so engaged in politics, and Harvard had a strong government department. (In retrospect, I wish I had majored in history and literature, both of which seem much more intellectually interesting to me now.) I particularly recall government courses taught by Samuel Huntington, a great analyst of American politics, who later became a personal friend. (His wife wore Ellen's wedding dress when they got married.)

Arthur Maas taught a course on how federal administrative agencies work. He was not a great scholar--his modest reputation was built largely on a book he wrote about the Army Corps of Engineers, titled *Muddy Waters*. But he was a wonderful teacher, with a probing, inquiring mind. He was endlessly helpful to his favorite students, and I was lucky to be one of those. In my junior year, tutorials were modeled on Oxford and Cambridge—one or two students met with their tutor and brought a paper on a book they had read for the week. Maas served as my tutor, and we read and discussed the papers. From him, I gained a real sense of collaborative intellectual activity at a high level.

V. O. Key taught a course on voting, which was the only quantitatively based course I took at Harvard. What a difference from today, when quantitative analyses dominate all the social sciences. The only weak link in the government department I recall was a professor named Cherrington, who taught a course on some aspect of government regulation. Merle Fainsod, a friend of my parents, taught an engaging course on Russian government. As was true of all government majors, I took a course on political theory from Professor Carl Friedrich.

Perhaps the most stimulating course was Arthur Schlesinger Jr.'s on American social and political history. At the time, his career was still very much in the shadow of his father—who was also a great historian, one of the first to take social history seriously—although Arthur Schlesinger, Jr. had already written a Pulitzer Prize–winning book, *The Age of Jackson*. He was a breathtaking teacher. He gave a sense of the sweep of American history in social, intellectual, and cultural terms in ways that had never occurred to me. I had thought of American history through its presidents. He examined the rise of different movements in American history, including the rise of populism in the time of President Jackson. While he certainly talked about Jackson, his focus wasn't on Jackson as much as the forces that led to the populist movement and how it developed. His course gave me a much richer textured sense of American life and history than I had before. I came to understand that ideas could shape American public policies. The notion that cultural forces, social forces, and economic forces could all interact and merge with political forces seems obvious to us now, but it wasn't clear then, at least not to a twenty-year-old, and it was a mind-popping experience.

Not all of my courses, naturally, were in government. Ellen and I took two art courses together, taught by Professor Deknatel, and I can still see slides from his lectures, which were held in the Fogg Museum auditorium. I took a course on analytic philosophy taught by A. J. Ayer, who was visiting Harvard and was a dominant philosopher at the time. I also took a course on the New Testament taught by Professor Buttrick because I knew nothing about it. Harvard offered me the chance to reach out intellectually in multiple directions, wherever my curiosity took me, and the teachers were reputably outstanding.

In all my courses, there was not a single teacher who was a woman. I do not remember a single Black or Latino faculty member. The most depressing part of that observation is that neither my soon-to-be wife, Ellen, at Radcliffe nor I thought this was troubling. Fortunately, some things have changed.

The only work I kept from my college days was a big folder of papers I wrote for various classes. Looking at them recently, I was struck by the extensive comments my teachers wrote in the margins and at the end of the papers. I also see that I received many Bs and some Cs. From reading those papers, I sense that grading was much tougher then than it is now, though it may also be true that Harvard students are brighter now than before.

In the summer of 1953, after my freshman year, I went to Europe with Fred Willman. We traveled on a ship to London and then proceeded in a whirlwind to visit England, France, Italy, Switzerland, and Spain, all in about eight weeks. We stayed only in places that charged less than $5 per night and spent no more than that per day on food. Less than a decade after World War II, $10 per day was ample for college students to travel, sleep, and eat in Europe. We went so fast to so many places that I have only faded snapshots in my mind of what we saw. The most vivid is a bullfight in Madrid. I was totally enamored of Ernest Hemingway at the time and thought *Death in the Afternoon* was one of the greatest books I had read. Today, I cannot read any Hemingway except his short stories, and the idea of a bullfight is disgusting. But then, the experience was alive and real.

The Korean conflict was underway during my undergraduate years, and I joined the Army Reserves after my sophomore year to avoid being drafted. One of my roommates, Sumner Kaufman, joined as well, and we went together to a National Guard unit one night a week and two weeks each summer for the following six years. In that time, I rose from being a private to the rank of corporal and disliked the entire experience.

While at Harvard, our summer camps were at Fort Devens in central Massachusetts, and later at a base in New Jersey. Most of the officers seemed to be seeking a holiday from their wives. They delighted in showing "blue" movies to the enlisted men. Many of the soldiers were seeking to escape from drab lives working at grocery stores and gas stations. My unit commander was a postman.

My worst experience in the Army Reserves happened one summer when my unit was out on maneuvers. The sergeant in charge of the unit ordered me to "take cover" in a bunch of bushes. "But, Sergeant," I said, "I can see from here that those bushes are full of poison ivy, and I am acutely sensitive to poison ivy." The sergeant immediately responded, "I don't give a shit about poison ivy. Get your ass into those bushes." The next day, I was covered, head to foot, with an acute case of poison ivy and had to spend almost a week in the hospital.

Most importantly, in terms of my army experience, it taught me a life-changing lesson in empathy. I came to care—really care—about the men I trained with. They became my buddies, spending endless hours with them, drilling and doing KP (kitchen patrol), peeling potatoes. On maneuvers, we crawled together on our bellies, cradling our rifles in our arms. Real bullets flew overhead.

The army taught me I could really care about people with different backgrounds than mine, and that caring became important to my sense of who I was and how I wanted to relate to the world around me. That life lesson has stayed with me.

I enjoyed a busy social life at Harvard, including the regular mixers, which brought girls from Radcliffe and Wellesley together for dances with Harvard boys. I had dates with girls from both colleges until I met and fell in love with the right one—Ellen. She was a student at Radcliffe and came from one of the finest public high schools in America, New Trier High in Winnetka, a Chicago suburb. We knew each other in our sophomore year, both because we were both majors in government and had many classes together and because Ellen was dating one of my good friends, Jody Steinberg, who lived in Kirkland House.

One day, I was walking out of Bertram Hall, a Radcliffe dorm, where I had been visiting another girl, when I saw Ellen, and we started talking. Ellen was born in Chicago and grew up in Glencoe, Illinois. For the next three hours, we talked about our lives, our hopes, and our dreams. Ellen and I both think we also talked a lot about God, though we cannot be sure. We strolled down to the Charles River and kept talking and talking as we walked along it. And we never stopped.

I found Ellen a combination of loveliness, intellect, and humor, unlike anyone I had ever known. She had—and still has—a voracious curiosity. Every question she asked, when answered, was followed up by another question. When I got back to Lowell House, I called Jody and said I would like to take Ellen on a date, and asked if he would mind. Fortunately, he said he would not object. I don't know what I would have done if he had resisted.

My roommates knew that I was smitten and, for my birthday, gave me a five-cent coupon good for "coffee with Ellen." Our friendship quickly ripened into love. (Ellen says she went home after our Charles River long conversation, called her parents, and said, "I met the man I'm going to marry." Her father replied, "Take a deep breath, lie down for a while so you can regain your senses, and call back in an hour. Your mother will be home then.") We spent much of each day with each other, including a number of classes that we took together in government. We soon became a steady couple.

The following summer, Fred Willman, Chick Kuhn, and I decided to drive out west together, working our way across the country. We offered to drive Ellen to her home in Glencoe, Illinois. Her parents agreed, but only if we went by way of Buffalo, New York, so we could stay overnight with her cousins, the Sidney Maisels, instead of sleeping outside in sleeping bags, as we planned to do for the rest of the trip. The notion that there was something improper about a girl staying overnight with three boys sounds silly today, but it was very real then. (Ellen and I had previously gone together for a weekend to the Harvard Forest, where we had stayed together—unknown, of course, to her or my parents.) By the time we arrived in Glencoe, I was a mess—covered from head to foot with poison ivy—and Ellen was itching as well. Ellen's mother, Topsy—her given name was Irene—and her father, Oscar, met us at the door. Oscar took one look at us both and exclaimed, "Ellen, didn't I tell you to stay out of the bushes!"

I fell in love with Topsy and soon knew that Ellen would become just like her mother as she grew older. Ellen had all her mother's energy, enthusiasm, and love of life and took great interest in people from all backgrounds. Like Topsy, Ellen also had the ability to make everyone feel at ease. I liked Oscar as well. He was a kind, gentle, and thoughtful advisor who never pressed his perspective. "If each of you go twothirds of the way whenever your views diverge," he told me, "You will be okay." He was right, though I cannot claim to have always followed that counsel. Ellen and I became engaged in the spring of our senior year. What a blessing!

During that same year, one of my friends wanted to be married in the Harvard Chapel but was denied because he and his bride would have a Jewish ceremony. I was incensed—more so than my friend—and wrote a letter expressing my outrage to then-President Pusey, who had taken over from President Conant after my freshman year. I also asked for an appointment to see the president.

After being ushered into his office, I expressed my view that Harvard and its facilities should be open to all, regardless of religion. Pusey replied that Harvard was founded as a Christian College, and though it no longer had exclusive ties to Christianity, the church was still a Christian Church, and only Christian ceremonies were permitted. I asked whether he thought a Jewish ceremony would damage the church, but he just responded, politely but firmly, that it was Christian—period. Since then, this policy, like so much else, has fortunately changed.

My most important writing experience at Harvard was my senior honors thesis, which became the longest work I had written up to that time. I told Professor Maas, who served as the "tutor" for my thesis, that I wanted to write about the impact of public opinion on public policymaking. I thought it was a good way to explore American democracy in both theoretical and practical terms. I was fascinated by how much did and should public opinion shape political decisions and how much those decisions did shape public opinion. Maas suggested that along with my theoretical analysis, I examine a massive survey of family farmers done by the Department of Agriculture. At the time, it was the largest such survey ever done by the US Government Department of Agriculture. It was called the Family Farm Study. Literally tens of thousands of farmers in the 1930s were brought together in various town-hall groups around the country to discuss their views on the future of small farms and the role of the government in that future.

I spent two weeks at the end of the summer before my senior year living in Washington with my aunt Polly and uncle Bob and studying in the bowels of the Department of Agriculture's thousands of pages of microfilmed records of those town halls. Insofar as I could tell, they had never been reviewed before. The records included all the data from the survey. As the time to return to Cambridge approached, it became clear that I could not possibly finish examining the data in time.

I had the idea of going to the office of my congressman and asking staff members if they would borrow the entire set of files—two huge boxes—and let me have them for a short while. I explained that the survey had been done in 1935, and in the intervening twenty years— it was then 1955—no one had ever even looked at the material. "Of course," was the answer. One telephone call and the boxes were mine. I promptly shipped them to Cambridge. It was only sometime late in the next spring, with my thesis just about done, that I received a frantic call from the congressman's office seeking to retrieve the records, which I returned.

The thesis became a study of the ways public opinion generally, and surveys particularly, impact public policy. In retrospect, it was an audaciously big topic, but the challenge taught me much about writing a sustained piece of prose and helped shape my passionate conviction that active, knowledgeable involvement by people of every social and economic level is essential to the sound working of American democracy.

Over the course of my senior year, I read widely in political theory about my thesis topic. I ambitiously started with Aristotle and Plato and worked my way up to the clash between Walter Lippmann, who thought that public policies were best left to experts, subject only to the decisions of the ballot box about those officials who choose the experts, and John Dewey, who thought that citizen involvement in all aspects of public-policy making was essential. This was my first engagement with a philosopher, Dewey, who became a key figure in shaping my own opinions about both public policymaking and education. Much of my later writings about civic responsibility and higher education are rooted in my support of Dewey's philosophy.

Maas went over draft after draft, full of helpful suggestions at every stage. My thesis won the Eric Firth Prize for the best essay on the subject of the ideals of democracy. I was pleased that the prize money was just enough to cover the cost of hiring a typist to type it. A few years later, I found an article by a Harvard graduate student who lifted—with inadequate attribution—my research for his own use.

In the spring of my senior year, I sought a Rhodes Fellowship. In hindsight, it was good fortune that I was not chosen. The decision came down to one of my classmates and me, and the chief of the judging panel told me afterward that the other student was chosen because he had less educational advantages coming into Harvard than I did, which was certainly true. Studying for two years at Oxford or Cambridge would have taken me away from Ellen for two years, and that would have been a terrible mistake. Furthermore, it is not clear to me that the education I would have received there would have better prepared me for what turned out to be my careers.

Long before my senior year at Harvard, I knew I was going to law school, and I did not consider any school other than Harvard. By reputation, it was a great school. I applied and was accepted at Harvard Law School.

My mother insisted that Ellen and I not get married until after my first year at law school, which was a mistake, but we grudgingly acquiesced. This was, in part, because my parents would still be paying my tuition, and while Ellen would get a job after graduation, it would not pay enough to make us self-sufficient. It was also true that my mother was seriously ill then, and I did not want to cross her.

At this time, I became further engaged in local politics when one of my government professors, Robert Wood, asked me if I wanted to write speeches for a Democratic candidate for Massachusetts governor named Foster Furcolo. I had done well in the professor's classes, and he knew I enjoyed writing. For three months after I graduated, I wrote dozens of speeches and followed Furcolo as he traveled back and forth across the state. This was my first in-depth experience in practical politics, and I loved it. Furcolo was Italian American from Springfield, while at the time, Democratic politics in the state were dominated by Irish Americans, including the Kennedys. As I traveled with Furcolo, writing speeches for him, I learned about political pressures from the ground up. I recall being particularly struck by the hard-scrabble life of those I met in South Boston rallies. I saw firsthand the power of ward politics. Ward bosses took care of their constituents, and their constituents rewarded them with their votes.

Furcolo won the primary, and then the general election. While I worked for him, Ellen worked part-time for Professor Maas and one of his colleagues, doing research on a project about river basins. She also entered Harvard Graduate School of Education to get a teaching certificate. After a year, with her certificate in hand, Ellen taught fifth grade in Lincoln, Massachusetts.

I was pleased to end my college career by graduating Phi Beta Kappa and Magna Cum Laude. Ellen graduated Magna Cum Laude as well. In retrospect, I wish that I had been more of an explorer, taking additional courses in more fields outside my comfort zone. But since then, I have tried to make up for that failure by reading widely in history and English literature, both of which I much enjoy.

Harvard was an incredible learning experience for me over four years. I was lucky enough to be able to do what I've later come to see as enormously important: successfully merging the curricular with the extracurricular, which for me, was politics. I learned later that a rich cocurricular experience was an important goal for higher education and that separating academics from lived experience was a mistake. At Harvard in the 1950s, I was blessed to have both. Most important of all, Ellen and I fell in love.

5

Marriage and Law Lessons

I lived in a Harvard Law School dorm for my first year of law school and saw and talked with Ellen almost every day, sometimes more often, although we were not living together.

I loved law school from the start, unlike most of my classmates. In retrospect, the whole curriculum seemed designed to preclude learning for many students, except that the students were bright coming in and could learn despite the design. All the classes were large—150 or more students. The sole approach was to assign a cluster of appellate court cases, and then each day, day after day, professors called on one or more students—without advance warning—to engage in what was called a "Socratic dialogue" but more often resembled an inquisition. The goal was to train us to think like lawyers, which meant taking a problem, breaking it into its component parts, analyzing each part, and then putting it back together again. I did a lot of writing, analysis, and speaking. That was when *One L*, if you remember the book, was prominent as an example of, "Look to the right of you. Look to the left. One of you will not be here next year."

I found this process fascinating and fun—two adjectives that most of my classmates would have found absurd. The effort was intensely intellectual on the one hand and, on the other, applied to a finite body of text—appellate court opinions. Even the course in property—which spent an entire semester on early English (sixteenth to seventeenth century) land law—was stimulating, though I would be bored by the subject today. Part of my enthusiasm, no doubt, was that the teachers were exciting—Casner in property, Sacks in civil procedure, Hart in criminal law, Fuller in contracts, and Keeton in torts. The fact that I can remember all their names and details of their classes, unlike my undergraduate curriculum, of which I remember only the high points, shows that they were powerful teachers.

My favorite was contracts, and one of my teachers was Lon Fuller, who was considered the preeminent scholar in the field. More important, he was a moral philosopher. A year after my class with him, he wrote a famous response to the British philosopher H. L. A. Hart on the relation of law and morality. I delighted in the framework of rules and procedures, based on evolving precedent, along with legislation and administrative rule-making that made up the legal system. I also enjoyed discussing when the rules of contracts (or other fields) needed to be overcome by a moral imperative that contradicted the rule. A prime example is when a contract is not enforceable because it calls on one party to commit a crime or because the terms of the contract are too harsh. Fuller was masterful in infusing our discussions of legal cases with both law and morality.

Reading a law case about a particular set of facts in dispute and then seeing how a judicial opinion resolved it captivated me. The challenge was always to change a fact or two and see if the reasoning in the case had to be modified. Going from factual to theoretical was a mode of thought that I found natural, much more so than going from theory to practice. This must be one reason I struggled in math and science when I learned theorems and then applied them to problems without ever understanding the why of the theorems.

Like Harvard College, no women were on the faculty. There were only a few female students in my class. The dean at the time, Erwin Griswold, later US solicitor general, met with them once a year in his office. Ruth Bader Ginsburg was in our class and a friend of mine. She told me that the dean had said to them, "You're taking the place of a man."

We did not have exams until the end of the spring semester, except for a practice test midway through the first year. No one knew how much learning was actually penetrating our brains. We knew that each of us would be ranked, from 1 to 526—a truly barbaric system—but none of us had any clear idea of where we were on that spectrum. For the first part of the year, I felt like I was engaged in a process like turning on a radio and trying to find the right channel. There was a lot of static and then voices became clear, only to return to static from time to time. Without feedback, all students believed the worst about their capabilities, and I certainly was no exception. Fortunately, Ellen and I were to be married in June, and that forthcoming event was much more important to me than class standings.

I was surprised and delighted when two letters arrived the same day, one saying that I was fifteenth in the class and the other that I was one of twenty-five new members of the *Harvard Law Review*. I later came to realize that the rankings were absurd—only fractions of fractional differences in grades separated those who were chosen for the *Law Review* and many others. Once one became a member of the *Law Review*, professional doors opened in every direction that would otherwise be closed.

Much more importantly, Ellen and I grew in our love for each other and our eagerness to be married. I understood more deeply the extraordinary strengths of her person and personality. I also came to more fully appreciate her ability to find something interesting— really interesting—in almost everyone. This meant she quickly attracted friends who became lifelong friends wherever she was— another quality that has lasted our lives together. And she was brilliant. She graduated Magna Cum Laude from Radcliffe, which could be said to prove this. But more significantly, she was wise in making our life decisions with me in ways that deepened our commitment to each other. Ellen has such a warm and caring personality that she soon started cracking my Boston reserve and, I think, made me a more interesting person as a result. She knew how to make mundane chores fun when we did them together. We each grew, of course, during that year and every year thereafter. But from the start, we were committed to growing together and to using our complementary abilities to that goal.

Ellen and I were married at the home of her aunt and uncle, Janie and Gene Adler, in Highland Park, Illinois, on June 18, 1957. About sixty people were there—her close relatives, all my aunts and uncles, and many of our Radcliffe and Harvard friends. It was a beautiful day and a beautiful wedding. Ellen surprised me by wearing a white wedding dress—I thought she had previously rejected that idea. We were married by Rabbi Siskin, head rabbi of the temple Topsy and Oscar attended. Ellen's cousins Helen and Bob Adler gave a wonderful swimming/ice cream party for us, and there were other festivities as well. At the party the night before the wedding, Oscar played the piano, and we all sang songs written by Ellen's uncle Teddy and by my father and Uncle Richard.

Ellen's parents had given us our first car, so after the wedding, we drove into Chicago for our wedding night at the Drake Hotel. It was interrupted in the early hours of the morning by a knock on the door. "Fruit man," was the voice at the door. Friends had sent a basket of fruit, and the hotel delivered it at about two in the morning. From then on, whenever there is a knock at the door at an awkward moment and we do not know who it is, we exclaim, "It's the fruit man!"

We drove the next day to Martha's Vineyard, where I had rented a room at Blueberry Hill Inn, which friends recommended. I had called the owner, Mr. Lewis, and explained that we would be on our honeymoon but did not have much money, and he immediately quoted a low rate. When we arrived, we found that we had a whole cottage to ourselves, thanks to his thoughtfulness.

After a wonderful week, we drove to Cambridge and our apartment on Frost Street. We had a living room, bedroom, and kitchen on the first floor, and we spent much of the summer painting the walls and even putting a new linoleum floor in the kitchen. I can still feel my embarrassment one hot July day when Hedy Kuhn, the mother of Chick, and a close friend of my parents, walked past the front door—open to catch any breeze—and found me in my undershorts, on a ladder, painting the ceiling. She had brought a German Postexpressionist print as a wedding present and couldn't leave until she told us all the details of its provenance.

Ellen was preparing to teach fifth grade in Lincoln, Massachusetts, that fall while I continued writing speeches for Governor Foster Furcolo. He tried to persuade me to stay on in the job, at what seemed like an incredible salary—$10,000 per year—but I knew I needed to finish law school. Meanwhile, Ellen and I entertained friends in our apartment with fondue parties, along with bananas foster, various after-dinner drinks, and other dishes that are long gone from our cuisine. No wine then—too expensive! Ellen became a terrific cook, using lots of recipes from her mother. We lived simply and had fun, though I spent too much time working on the *Law Review*.

Membership in the *Law Review* meant that I had to start working on the *Review* several weeks before my second year at law school began. Ellen soon learned to hate Gannett House, home of the *Review*, because it seemed I was always there.

In my second and third years of law school, I spent most of my time on *Review* work and found the majority of classes less challenging than those in the first year. This was primarily because when one learned, and relearned, how to "think like a lawyer," there was not nearly as much sparkle as before. Once I knew I was near the top of the class in the first year, it was not much of a challenge to stay there.

I did have some classes that were exceptions: an antitrust seminar with Carl Kaysen, for example. The best was advanced corporations, taught by Abe Chayes in my third year. Almost the entire course was devoted to legal issues involving dividends, a cluster of concerns that was certainly not of much importance then and became useless in subsequent years. But Chayes was such an exciting teacher that the subject matter was irrelevant. We called it "the case of the month" club because we spent class after class spinning out a seemingly endless series of hypothetical questions that took off from the base of a single case. Fortunately, I enjoyed those verbal games and was good at them. Along with three or four others, out of a class of a hundred or so, I engaged in exchanges with Chayes in class and after class, while the rest of the students listened in benumbed boredom.

The *Law Review* was a wonderful experience for me, and I learned a great deal about legal analysis in the process. *Law Review* work consisted of a series of increasingly difficult assignments, starting with reading advance sheets, newly decided cases printed in paperback form before publication in bound volumes, to identify interesting decisions for possible written comments, writing memos about those cases, and writing short case comments to a full note about some new development in the law. I wrote a note in my first year on the antitrust issues involved in "concerted refusals to deal"—what should happen when two or more companies refuse to do business with other companies without a formal agreement to do so. At least three times, we also proofread every word in every one of eight issues of the journal, and we also cite checked every reference at least three times. The *Law Review* published a form book, called the "Blue Book," and each citation had to be in exactly the form dictated by the Blue Book. Occasionally, long arguments erupted when the proper form was unclear. I proofread so much that I still sometimes find myself correcting printing errors in text.

It involved intense, close textual analysis, and it was the first time I did such analytic work. I think a leader has to know how to do that kind of work for 5 or 10 percent of his or her reading time. The other 90 or 95 percent can be spent skimming through a vast quantity of stuff. The trick is to identify quickly what must be read carefully. It's the difference between reading a murder mystery and reading a poem or recipe. You can't whip through a poem. I have been a fast reader for most of my life, but that experience at the *Law Review* taught me how to stop—I don't want to say I always do it at the right times—and do a very close, careful reading. I learned a lot from that experience.

In my third year, I was chosen by graduating editors to be an article editor of the *Law Review*, which meant that, along with a fellow editor, I chose all the articles. The notion that two students should decide among dozens of submissions by distinguished law professors and others seems absurd, but that was and still is the practice. After the articles were accepted, we had no qualms about insisting on extensive revisions. I can still feel my embarrassment when I returned an article on labor law to Archibald Cox, later of Watergate fame, and corrected *hod carrier* to *hog carrier* because I had never heard of the term. He laughed and told me that a *hod carrier* was a type of construction worker.

At the time, the Harvard Law School was dominated by the school of thought that viewed deep skepticism as a virtue and judicial activism as a sin. The skeptical mindset led naturally to the view that process was all-important, since one could never be absolutely certain about any substantive judgment. Supreme Court Justice Felix Frankfurter, former Harvard Law School professor and leader of the "process is sacred" school, was revered. Hugo Black and William O. Douglas, also on the Supreme Court, were viewed as scoundrels. It was many years before I gained a different perspective and realized how important an activist court could be, as witness *Brown v. Board of Education.*

In my second year, I took a required course taught by Professor Albert Sacks called "The Legal Process." He and Professor Henry Hart had just developed its radical design, which focused solely on how legal decisions were made, particularly apart from litigation, not on the results of those decisions. For the first time at law school, judicial decisions were not the main material we read. That single course had the most substantial impact on my legal thinking. A key premise of the course was that most of the legal system is made up of various rules, procedures, and practices that do not involve the courts, at least directly, and most of the time, people obey those rules, at least at some instinctive level, because they know that society needs rules. Most of the time, for example, we obey speed limits not because we worry that a cop will catch us if we don't but rather because we think it is the right thing to do. The course was taught for several decades, and I taught it at Stanford Law School, but Hart and Sacks never published the course materials because they could not bring themselves to say that the process of preparing those materials was finished.

After my second year of law school, Ellen and I decided to try San Francisco for the summer. My sister was living in Menlo Park, and we thought we might want to live on the West Coast. I was offered a summer job with the then-largest firm in the city—Pillsbury, Madison, and Sutro. We lived in an apartment on Green Street and had a fun summer, though it ended in a dispute about the apartment that left a sour taste in our mouths.

I was given a range of interesting projects on which to work—this was my first real law job. One was to write a memo on whether the firm's client, a giant seed-producing company, could maintain a property interest in its seeds after they were planted in the ground by buyers on credit, with the hoped-for result that if the buyers failed to pay, the crops could be seized.

I enjoyed the summer but knew that a mega-firm like that one was not for me. I came to know two lawyers at the firm who had spent their entire adult lives on a single Standard Oil antitrust case and would continue on that case for decades. Again, not for me. I also recall that Mr. Sutro took me under his wing, which was fun. But it was not fun that he kept criticizing his own son, also a law student, in my presence, and asking him why he could not have done what I did. Not a happy situation.

In the fall of my third year, Ellen and I needed to decide where we would go after I finished law school. Life in the same city as my mother had been sufficiently difficult for us that we were clear we would not stay in Boston. We wanted to go someplace big enough to be a big city, but small enough so that we could be part of the whole.

Where? I knew at the time that I wanted to teach law—combining my interests in teaching and law. I admired many of my teachers, starting with Mrs. Scattergood and continuing to Harvard College and Harvard Law School. Over time, I came to realize I wanted to be some type of teacher. By that point, I knew I wanted to end up as a law teacher. I thought it wise, however, to spend a little time first learning what lawyers actually did so I would know what my students would be facing. I also wanted to practice with some friends from law school. Three others on the *Law Review* had a similar idea, and we decided, in effect, to apply together. Such a collective approach was unheard of in that era, and I have never learned of another group to adopt a similar strategy.

The firm that seemed best to us was Foley, Sammond & Lardner (later Foley & Lardner, now with eleven hundred lawyers in twenty-four offices). At the time, there were just forty lawyers working at offices in Milwaukee. Ellen's parents were in Chicago, so we would be near them. She also had relatives in Milwaukee, Mitzie and Clarence Jung. The firm offered among the highest salaries in the country at the time and, even more importantly, would let each of us work in the legal areas that interested us. I wanted to do a little of everything—trials, corporate work, and so forth—and was assured that this would be possible.

I also appreciated that the firm had Jews and non-Jews, which was not true of many firms across the county. In fact, when I was considering a firm to work for, one of my father's Boston Jewish friends said I had to work for Minz, Levin, and Cohen because I would not be comfortable at any but a Jewish firm. A bit later, I had a call from the hiring partner at Ropes & Gray, the most prestigious law firm in Boston, asking me to come and work for the firm. "You see," confided the hiring partner, "Jim Vorenberg has left to teach at Harvard, so we have a place for you." He meant that since a Jew left the firm, there was now a position for another Jew.

The founder of the Milwaukee firm, Leon Foley, was a lovely man whose daughter was a psychologist. At her urging, the firm gave every prospective associate a daylong battery of psychological tests to determine the likelihood that we would stay in Milwaukee and at the firm for the rest of our careers. You didn't have to be very smart to figure out what the right answers were. Are you going to go out drinking on the town, or are you going to stay and play canasta with your wife? (Ironically, we all passed the test, but only one of us—Bill Kiernan—eventually stayed at the firm.) I was still reasonably sure I wanted to go into law teaching if I found the right opportunity but did not say this at the time.

Then the unexpected happened. A law school professor and assistant dean named Livingston Hall, whom I knew only slightly, called and asked if I would like to apply to be a law clerk for Judge Learned Hand. At the time, Hand was eighty-seven years old and the country's most respected jurist outside the Supreme Court and, many would say, including the Supreme Court. He had been a federal judge for more than fifty years, most of that time on the Second Circuit Court of Appeals in New York, the most influential court in the country apart from the US Supreme Court. He had written more than two thousand opinions and had shaped the law in literally every area of federal law, civil and criminal. Ellen and I talked it over and quickly decided that this was the chance of a lifetime. A clerkship offered an excellent opportunity to work with a judge close up and personal and see how that judge operated for a year. And this judge was the best.

I went by train to New York for my interview with Judge Hand. I assumed that a recommendation by Dean Hall assured me of the position—and it did.

First, however, we moved our small cluster of belongings to Milwaukee and stayed for much of the summer with the Jungs while I studied for the Wisconsin bar. This was not known as one of the most difficult exams, but I would have felt mortified if I had failed, so I studied extremely hard and passed.

I began working much of each day at the law firm of Foley, Sammond & Lardner, where I got a terrific education in the practice of law. It was brief, but as promised, I learned something about everything. Along the way, I learned some lessons about myself.

One of my initial assignments during my first month was to meet with a client of the firm, a couple who wanted to set up a new corporation. I knew that this was no more complicated than typing in the name of the new corporation on a form supplied by the Wisconsin Secretary of State, listing the corporate officers on the form, and then filing it with the Secretary of State's Office. I ushered the couple into a conference room, listened while they told me that they wanted themselves to be the president and secretary of the corporation, and to list their names on the form. "I will be delighted to do that, Mr. and Mrs. Smith," I said with some pride, and when they were gone, I proceeded to instruct a secretary to list Mr. Smith as president and Mrs. Smith as secretary, as they had asked me to do. I then sent the form off to the Secretary of State for filing. I had just completed my first solo task as a lawyer and was feeling overly proud of myself.

A few weeks later, I was filling out an internal law-firm form to explain how my time should be charged, and I saw a notation for "Mr. and Mrs. Smyth: formation of new corporation." I suddenly realized, of course, that I had misspelled what I thought was the simplest surname. In my desk, waiting for the couple to come into my office again, I had a certificate of incorporation with the wrong spelling. The only way to change this under Wisconsin law was for the couple to sign a form asking for an amendment of the certificate. This, of course, would mean they would know exactly what had happened.

Oh, God, the first thing I do, I have messed it up completely. I messed up one of the simplest, most basic things I could do. What am I going to do? I was in a total panic and can still feel the sweat rising on my face. After an agonized hour, I picked up the phone and called the Wisconsin Secretary of State. Given the prestige of my law firm, he answered the phone without delay, though I had never met him.

I confessed exactly what had happened. "I'm a brand-new lawyer, and I've just done something stupid. I hope you can think of some way to help me."

After a long silence, during which I was increasingly uncomfortable, the Secretary of State finally said, "Why don't you come up here this afternoon with the certificate, and we will see what we can do." I drove from Milwaukee to Madison and came to his office. When I was ushered in, he closed the door and asked me to give him the certificate of incorporation. He handed me back a new one with the names of the officers and incorporators properly spelled. He did not have to inform me that what he had done was quite beyond his legal authority. Perhaps I only delude myself to think he did not only a charitable act of great kindness but also a moral one. At the least, I hope this is true. In all events, during subsequent years, I have often thought of this incident when I have been in positions of authority and subordinates have made mistakes through lack of care and attention. I hope I have followed his example.

At the end of the summer, I took a year-long leave to be a law clerk for Judge Hand. The firm wanted to keep my name on the letterhead with a reference to Judge Hand, but the judge absolutely and rightly refused. Ellen and I found a small apartment in Bronxville that was owned by a Sarah Lawrence professor—a great expert on Martin Buber—who would be on leave.

I was excited about my next steps. Years of education had prepared me and paved the way for a career that was becoming increasingly meaningful as it gradually came into focus. Now it was time to work alongside great mentors in public service who would soon teach me.

Ellen and Tom walking down the aisle at the wedding of grand-daughter Bridget Ehrlich to Tyler Bellenfant, October 2023. Photo courtesy of the author.

Ellen, about age six.
Photo courtesy
of the author.

Tom about age ten, a loyal Red Sox fan, and his friend, Christopher Eliot.
Photo courtesy of the author.

Marion and Adolph Ehrlich, Tom's grandparents. Photo courtesy of the author.

Ehrlich family in 1948: Tom's grandparents, parents, and his aunts, uncles and their children, at the annual Beverly, Mass., gathering for Adolph Ehrlich's birthday. Photo courtesy of the author.

Tom's parents: Evelyn and William Ehrlich. Photo courtesy of the author.

William Ehrlich and Frances Ehrlich, Tom's stepmother. Photo courtesy of the author.

Ellen's parents: Irene "Topsy" Rome and Oscar Rome. Photo courtesy of the author.

Ellen and Tom's sister, Ellen Gardner. Photo courtesy of the author.

Tom and Ellen's children: Elizabeth, Paul, and David. Photo courtesy of the author.

Tom and Ellen's children and their spouses: Hillary Ehrlich, Peter Dumanian, Paul Ehrlich, Elizabeth Dumanian, Maureen Ehrlich, and David Ehrlich. Photo courtesy of the author.

David and Maureen and their daughters. Casey, Reilly, Hannah, and Brigid, along with Tyler Dellenfant, at Brigid's wedding to Tyler. Photo courtesy of the author.

Elizabeth and Peter and their children, Jay with his wife, Rachel, and Kate with her husband, Conor Kelly, and Grant. Photo courtesy of the author.

Paul and Hillary and their children, Henry and Benjamin. Photo courtesy of the author.

Ellen and Tom with their great-grandson, Simon Dumanian. Photo courtesy of the author.

PART II

LEARNING

6

Craftsmanship and Calling

Ellen and I greatly enjoyed our year in New York City, starting in September 1959. In the first week of my clerkship with Judge Learned Hand, who was eighty-seven years old, I sat at a desk a few feet from his in the magnificent, paneled room that was his chambers at the Foley Square Courthouse. "I want you sitting next to me so we can discuss the cases," he said. Soon after I started, Ellen came into his chambers, very pregnant. Judge Hand took one look at her and asked, "Young lady, don't you know about birth control?" To our great joy, David was born not long after.

Ellen and Judge Hand developed a real affection for one another. Some time later, when his birthday was coming, we noticed that the pillow on his couch exploded in feathers when he lay down for his daily nap. Ellen made a new pillow cover, and I snuck the pillow home the night before his birthday so that she could sew the cover around the pillow. The next afternoon, the judge lay down for his accustomed nap. Soon I heard a loud bellow, "Who de-feathered me?" I rushed in to explain, and he was delighted.

"My best present ever," he concluded.

Our son, David, was born in October after we made several practice runs to the White Plains Hospital. Since Ellen and I have brown hair, and he was a redhead, everyone asked, "Where did he get that red head?" The real answer was that both my grandfather and Ellen's had red hair, so we should not have been surprised. After growing tired of responding with those facts, our answer to that inevitable question became, "Green stamps." At the time, customers at certain grocery stores were rewarded with "green stamps" that they could paste into special books. After you filled five or six books, you could send them to the Green Stamp Company for prizes—an early version of Frequent Flyer Miles.

Ellen and I soon traveled around New York City and visited West Point and other places of interest, all with David in tow.

Judge Hand came to his chambers on most days. He was involved, however, in only a third as many cases as those judges who were not "senior"—a status any judge could assume after a certain number of years on the bench. But he wrote either the majority opinion or a dissent in every case he heard. As a result, he wrote as many opinions as other judges.

A typical day with him went like this. After we each read the briefs concerning a case and heard the oral arguments, he asked me to argue one side, and he urged opposing views. Sometimes we then switched sides. Judge Hand moved back and forth from the facts of the case to the law as possibly applied to those facts, making arguments and countering them. Every day, those exchanges were tutorials, one-on-one, with nobody else around, from an extraordinary mind. His thought processes were inextricably linked to his writing, for he wrote and rewrote eight, ten, and sometimes more drafts of an opinion, all in longhand on a pad of paper with a board to hold it up.

Judge Hand was my most important mentor in terms of his impact on how I think about analyzing problems and seeking their solutions. I was never a judge and never wanted to be one because I felt the intellectual life of a judge was too passive for me. But Judge Hand's ability to think through an issue, see it from multiple perspectives, and examine and reexamine his premises, as well as their application to the dispute at hand, set a standard for me. Though I could never emulate it, it was always my North Star.

Judge Jerome Frank was one of Judge Hand's close friends as well as his colleague. When Judge Frank died, a copy of *Essays of Schopenhauer* was found in his chambers with the following words underlined in red, and "L. H." marked in red next to them. "On the wisdom of an old man: Constantly finding new uses for his stores of knowledge and adding to them at every opportunity, he maintains uninterrupted that inward process of self-education." The lines mark with precision one of the qualities that made Judge Hand great—an "inward process of self-education." By self-education, I mean not merely a continued effort to devour more knowledge on all subjects, though this was certainly true of Judge Hand. The process was also one of constant reevaluation of ideas.

Judge Hand never examined a case without reexamining all the principles, no matter how basic, that were argued or that might be used to support a position. He began at the beginning, often with enormous effort, and, without predeciding the result, work toward it. He often told me that "uncommittedness" was the essential quality of a good judge. That quality was evident in no one I have known more than in Judge Hand. It was, however, only a part of his "self-education," for the process also required an impartial viewing of alternatives, no matter how strong the preconceptions.

Judge Hand believed that the ability to withhold commitment can exist only in the skeptic, one for whom doubt dispels all absolutes, and he was a supreme skeptic. Perhaps his favorite quotation to me was that of Oliver Cromwell, who told his soldiers on the eve of battle: "I beseech ye in the bowels of Christ, think it possible that ye may be wrong." That sentence, he once told me, should be placed on the entrance of every courthouse in the county. He believed that a judge must try to decide between conflicting values without imposing his own values. He often said that the only absolute of our government is that there are no absolutes.

Judge Hand told me that not having been appointed to the Supreme Court was the biggest disappointment of his life. Felix Frankfurter was, he thought, the only great judge on the Supreme Court. He was withering in his comments about judges he did not think measured up to his standards, and he was also sharply critical of those he called "the sacred four" Supreme Court Justices: Black, Brennan, Douglas, and Warren. He thought they were making social policy rather than applying the law with necessary restraint, especially when considering whether to declare a state or federal act or practice unconstitutional. Judge Hand repeated to me often that "what goes around, comes around," and predicted that one day, a majority of Supreme Court Justices would be as conservative as the then-current majority was liberal, and they would make social policy as well. It had happened before, he said, in the early New Deal era, and it would happen again. His prediction has become a reality today.

Justice Oliver Wendell Holmes was the judge he most admired, "Never a word too much," he told me. In one of his essays in honor of Justice Holmes, he referred to "the Society of Jobbists," which admires "honest craft, gives good measure for its wages, and undertakes only those jobs which the members can do in proper workmanlike fashion." I don't know whether I would be allowed to join, but Judge Hand taught me to aspire to membership.

Judge Hand often mentioned an incident when he met Justice Holmes on the street and offered to share a taxi. When Justice Holmes left the taxi, Judge Hand called after him. More as something to say than anything else, he said, "Goodbye, and do justice." Justice Holmes shot back, "Never say that to me. I don't do justice; I just follow the rules." Judge Hand always tried to "follow the rules."

The apparent significance of a case in the public eye was never a factor in the care with which Judge Hand examined a controversy. We spent many days, for example, considering and debating a case with the following facts. A defendant in a criminal case was indicted for forging a check and for knowingly trying to cash a forged check—these are two separate crimes—in circumstances that made it clear that the defendant could only have knowingly tried to cash the forged check if he had also forged it. He denied both of these offenses. The jury found him guilty of trying to cash a forged check but not of forging a check.

On appeal, the public defender representing the defendant argued that since the defendant was found not guilty of forging a check, his conviction for knowingly trying to cash a forged check should be reversed. The public defender said it was logically impossible for him to have done the crime for which he was convicted while being innocent of forgery.

Judge Hand and I knew that juries do not always behave logically. Indeed, we assumed that when the jury started deliberations, some jurors argued for innocence and some for guilt. So, the jury probably decided to compromise and find the defendant guilty of one crime but not the other. This would arguably not have been a problem if the defendant had been found guilty of forging a check and not guilty of knowingly trying to cash a forged check. But the jury did the opposite. What to do? After days of legal research, I could not find a case on point, nor was one cited by counsel on either side.

Ultimately, Judge Hand decided to uphold the verdict, its illogic notwithstanding, and in doing so, he established a precedent. He concluded that the appellate process should support a jury's decision, even when it cannot be logically defended, as long as a reasonable hypothesis can be drawn about what probably occurred in the jury deliberations. Judges were required to be logical, he concluded, but juries are not.

Over the nine months that I clerked for Judge Hand, I wrote no more than a few paragraphs that were included in his opinions. Unlike other judges on the Court of Appeals for the Second Circuit at the time, he did not ask his law clerk to draft his opinions. I only wrote the occasional comment to the judge in a memorandum that might find its way into his opinions.

Though I did not draft opinions for Judge Hand, I was fortunate that several other judges on the Second Circuit Court of Appeals asked me to do so. One of the wisest was Judge Sterry Waterman from Vermont, who was also one of Judge Hand's good friends. I particularly recall a case that was of no great legal interest, but affirmed the conviction of the mobster Frank Costello, nicknamed "the Prime Minister of the Underworld."

Another case I worked on for Judge Waterman involved a brand-new judge on the court, Judge Henry Friendly, who was also a friend of Judge Hand and someone whom Judge Hand encouraged the

Eisenhower Administration to appoint. Friendly was finally chosen in 1959. By happenstance, Judge Friendly's daughter was one of my wife's closest friends, and Ellen and I joined Judge Friendly and his family for dinner a number of times during that year.

I learned a lesson, watching Judge Friendly, in how easily one's reputation can be quickly altered. Superb craftsmanship is important, but it is sometimes not enough. Friendly came to the bench with a reputation not only as one of the smartest lawyers in the country, but also as a great expert in railroad reorganizations, an arcane field of the law. One of the first cases on which he wrote an opinion dealt with a complex railroad reorganization. Friendly's lengthy opinion was an erudite masterpiece of craftsmanship. Just a few days after it was issued, however, the federal government, which was a party to the case, filed a motion to dismiss on the grounds that the case should have gone directly to the Supreme Court. Friendly was acutely embarrassed when he realized he had completely missed this point. Others had missed it too, but he was the expert in the field and not modest about his expertise, and the misstep galled him.

Judge Hand had a wonderful sense of humor. He knew virtually every Gilbert and Sullivan lyric and sang them to me frequently. He loved limericks too; the dirtier, the better. I'll quote one of the cleaner ones, which he used to show me the distinction between "broken" and "breached" in our discussion of a contract case. It also underscores the care that he took to teach me the elements of style:

> There was a young lawyer named Lance
> Who contracted to buy some red ants.
> But the contract was broken
> When soon he felt pok'n
> The ants in his breached underpants.

He also made up an array of off-color limericks. His elderly secretary was named Mundane, and this is what he wrote:

> There was a fair lady named Mundane
> Who found she could never refrain
> From stepping out just a bit

For a pee or a shit
Whenever her bowels gave pain.
"Oh why," said her boss with a shout
"Must it always be that you're out?
Is your bladder so weak
That you must take a leak?"

Judge Hand also loved toys and once commandeered a toy truck that was an exhibit in a patent case, and rode the little vehicle with sheer delight around the halls and to other judges' chambers, laughing all the way.

Being a Jew, Judge Hand knew I would be interested in the background of the time he wrote to President Lawrence Lowell of Harvard when Lowell proposed a quota of 15 percent on the admission of Jewish undergraduates. Hand responded in a letter that soon became public, as he knew it would. He wrote that he was prepared to assume the accuracy of the claim that there were many "insensitive, aggressive, and ill-conditioned [Jews] whose presence causes much hostility among the Christians." But even if accurate, Hand said, this did not justify a quota. Universities like Harvard, he wrote, were centers of learning, not social clubs, and students should be chosen only on the basis of their scholarly credentials.

In other realms, as well, Hand was a firm opponent of the antisemitism, sometimes implicit, sometimes explicit, that was widespread in the halls of power and among many of those around him. When the American Jewish Committee asked Hand to address its annual meeting on "the principles of civil liberties and human rights" in 1955, he responded with an address he titled "A Fanfare for Prometheus." It is a wonderful statement of his views, deeply rooted in his essential skepticism. In it, he says, "It is only by trial and error, by insistent scrutiny and by a readiness to reexamine presently accredited conclusions that we have risen, so far as in fact we have risen, from our brutish ancestors; and I believe that in our loyalty to these habits lies our only chance, not merely of progress, but even of survival." Sound advice for us right now, when ideological certainty is so troublesome a part of public discourse.

Judge Hand taught me by example to try to achieve the highest order of craftsmanship. He stressed that a good judge must be a master of the craft. He or she must be able to comprehend the complexities of a problem in its entirety, make a tentative judgment about its resolution, analyze each component part, and then fuse the matter back into a coherent whole that will not only resolve the immediate controversy but also provide guidance for the future.

He also stressed the importance of pride in doing a job correctly, primarily for the satisfaction of doing it well as a craftsman rather than for the applause of an audience. None of us needs to be so noble as to ignore public reaction. But I learned from Judge Hand that if the approval of others is the primary fuel that motivates your work, your judgment is inevitably flawed.

Over the the half-century since I clerked for Judge Hand, I have come to disagree with many of his judicial decisions and some of his judicial philosophy. At the time, Harvard Law School had been a place of deep conservativism about the social role of judges in making decisions. Most of my professors there agreed with Judge Hand that judges were there to apply the law, but not to apply their own moral or ethical judgments and that the people were represented in the legislature. That perspective, steeped in a commitment to the craftsmanship of judicial work, taught me a lot.

It took me a long time to see that other perspectives, particularly in constitutional law, are sometimes more persuasive. The most striking example I recall is that Judge Hand was very dubious about the Supreme Court decision in *Brown v. Board of Education*. To me, that decision was one of the greatest judicial opinions of my lifetime. But I continue to be committed to the belief that one should always be wary of moral absolutes. Some people, I recognize, will bridle at that statement. "What about honesty, compassion, and other basic moral values?" they ask. "Are they not absolutes?" In a sense, of course, they are. But in the sense that Judge Hand taught and I learned, such moral precepts have real muscle only when applied, and in their application, thorny problems can arise.

After my clerkship with Judge Hand, we stayed in touch through the mail. A passage from one of his letters still fills me with pride. "You helped me all the time so much that I do not believe that without you, I could have carried even the small weight I undertook."

At the end of my clerkship in 1960, Ellen and I headed off for a few weeks in England, Denmark, and Greece. Ellen's mother and father babysat for us—and David came down with chicken pox just before we left! Ellen's parents gave us $3,000 to buy furniture, and with the gift came advice to go to the best furniture store in Copenhagen, Illums Bolighus, for our purchases. We had already picked out an apartment on North Wilson Drive in Milwaukee with two bedrooms, a living room, and a kitchen. We went to Illums with the apartment floor plan in hand and spent a couple of days picking out the furniture. We bought everything for the dining room (a rosewood table, breakfront, and eight chairs), for the living room (sofa, chairs, and tables), for the bedroom (bed and tables), and a desk, all for $3000. And we are still using most of that furniture today.

I remember little of the trip except for our time in Greece. We not only visited Athens and had a wonderful time there but also drove through the Peloponnese, where we ran into an army convoy and were briefly terrified that war had been declared. We also took a six-day cruise through the Greek Isles, which was truly spectacular, including stops at Mykonos, Patmos, Delos, and Rhodes.

We returned to Milwaukee and again stayed with the Jungs until our furniture made it through the St. Lawrence Seaway to our apartment. We were thrilled, and I sat at the desk the first night, thinking about how lucky we were. Unfortunately, I had a cup of tea at the desk and used the top of a blue box to keep the tea warm while I did some chores. When I returned, I put the box, top down, on the desk. When I picked it up the next morning, a deep blue stain was left on the desk, and I was devastated. Fortunately, a furniture repair man made a house call and, with a little stain and filler, eliminated most of the problem, though sometimes I think of that little crisis when I sit at the desk.

We quickly made friends in our apartment complex, including Mort and Bea Weintraub, who were still our friends until he died some years ago. David played continually with two little boys, one blond and one brunette. Two of our closest friends there were Maggie and John Pomfret, with whom we also stayed in touch for over forty years. John was then a reporter for the *Milwaukee Journal*, and Maggie was an accomplished painter. They left Milwaukee about the same time we did to go to Washington, DC, where he became a labor reporter for *The New York Times* and then Washington Bureau Chief for that newspaper. Barbara and Herb Franklin also became and stayed good friends until they also went to Washington, where both practiced law.

Meanwhile, I resumed duties at Foley, Sammond & Lardner. I was assigned to the corporate division, working particularly with Mr. Lardner. I was tasked with going to Chico, California, to sell an olive ranch Mr. Lardner's sister owned. It was early fall 1961 and very hot, and there was no air conditioning at the ranch. At the end of four or five days and after eating many, many olives, we closed the deal. I was given a five-gallon jug of raw olives as a parting gift. I was so sick of olives by then that I threw the jug out the window as I drove around the first curve after leaving the ranch.

I was still in the Army Reserve in Milwaukee in the summer of 1961, and President Kennedy, faced with an escalating crisis with Khrushchev in Berlin, called up a number of reserve units. On September 15, I was due to complete my six years of Army Reserve service—one night a week and two weeks in the summer. I knew that if I were called up, I would sit in a Berlin barracks for a year, waiting while nothing happened. Would my discharge come through in time, or would the usual army delays doom me to a wasted year? Fortunately, I asked my Congressman for help and was officially discharged on September 15.

We were always busy with work and family in Milwaukee, but I did take time to sail a boat owned by a friend who had gone to work in Washington. Mort Weintraub was a much better sailor than I, and he was captain while I crewed. One day, we entered a race from Chicago to Green Bay, Wisconsin. We sailed the boat down to Chicago Yacht Club the day before the race began and tied up at a buoy, with a small rowboat for our use. Mort, who weighed at least 250 pounds, got into the rowboat after I did, and it immediately started to fill up with water. We sat there as the water rose around us, with the fancy Chicago Yacht Club members around us watching and laughing. Mort and I were angry and embarrassed, and our ire sparked us to win the race, even though we were the smallest boat in our class.

Ellen and I then sailed the boat by ourselves around Door County in Upper Wisconsin. She was pregnant with our daughter, Elizabeth. One day, we were docked in a little harbor when a twelve-year-old boy asked if he could join us for a sail. He was so eager that I agreed. However, no sooner did we get out into the bay than a squall came up. I quickly untied the main halyard and handed the end to the boy.

"Just hold onto this while the sail drops," I ordered. "Don't let go!"

But, of course, when the wind really started to blow, he got scared and dropped the halyard. We made it back into the harbor without trouble using the engine. When the storm had passed, I knew someone needed to go up the mast to retrieve the end of the main halyard. I couldn't do it because Ellen was not strong enough to raise me in the bosun's chair. So, she got in the chair and, with her legs wrapped around the mast, slowly made her way up, with me pulling as best I could. The worst part was when she had to crawl around the spreaders. After that, her interest in sailing took a steep decline.

I soon became restless at the firm. I spent most of my time helping clients I did not particularly like and doing tasks that did not interest me. The firm did give me every opportunity to try new responsibilities—I argued in a trial, helped in a Wisconsin Supreme Court constitutional law case, and carried out many other assignments. The case involved whether it was constitutional for public-school buses to pick up parochial school students and drop them near their schools, as long as they did not deviate from their regular routes. We argued that this violated the constitutional separation of church and state and won. What a contrast to today, for the US Supreme Court has upheld much more substantial state support for parochial schools.

After a year, I knew in my heart and much of my mind was not in my work. Knowing I wanted to teach law someday, I applied to

Northwestern Law School on a lark and was offered a job. After mulling it over, I thought I wasn't quite ready yet, and it was best to stay on at the law firm and gain more experience. In retrospect, I'm convinced that someone was watching over Ellen and me when making that decision, for it helped to ensure that things would work out in the long run for us, personally and professionally.

In the early spring of 1962, I was working in my office when Ellen went to hear a talk by Abram Chayes, my former favorite law-school teacher, who had actively supported John F. Kennedy during the campaign. When Kennedy won, Chayes gained an appointment as legal adviser in the State Department, a position he had sought. He had taken a leave of the faculty for the two-year limit imposed by Harvard. After the talk, she went up and introduced herself.

"I've been wanting to get a hold of Tom to come be my special assistant," Chayes said to her. "Why doesn't he come to work with me?" This was the second of two fortuitous events that changed my professional life. The first was the invitation to become law clerk for Judge Learned Hand. The invitation from Chayes was equally transformative in my career.

When I returned home, Ellen reported the conversation. Despite the lower pay, she thought it would be a great opportunity to join the Kennedy administration. I had been moved and inspired by his inaugural address.

I was cautious, however, thinking that despite my restlessness, it might be too early for me to shift professional gears. I talked to one of my good friends in the firm, a young partner named Alan Taylor, who was involved in banking law. He urged me to stay at the firm until I was made a partner. Then, he assured me, I could leave with the knowledge that after my public service, I could come back.

Not long after, Taylor was offered the position of general counsel to the comptroller of the currency, and he wanted desperately to accept it. I had no idea what the comptroller of the currency really did, but Taylor thought it was the best job he could possibly have. He went to the head of the firm, Leon Foley, and asked for a leave to go into public service and a subsidy since the job paid much less than his current compensation. Mr. Foley told him he was welcome to leave the firm, but if he did, there would be no guarantee that he could come back, and he certainly would not receive a subsidy from the firm. Taylor turned down the position. "I just can't afford to leave," he told me with some anguish.

Don't mess around. Get out of here. Suddenly, it was clear that if I stayed at the firm, I would always believe, like my friend, that I could never afford to leave. My firm pay would inevitably exceed a government or teaching salary.

I decided then that I would never let myself be in a position where I could not leave a job. Years later, when I was dean of Stanford Law School, I recalled that decision often when young partners in big law firms confided their anguish along these lines. "I have made my goal in my professional life, but now that goal doesn't seem important to me. Rather, I feel trapped—my high pay precludes me from doing anything else. But I am miserable in my firm. Is this really all there is to my professional life?"

I would respond, "No, there is much more if you have the courage to resign from the firm. Become a legal-services lawyer for low-income people or a public defender or a lawyer in a public-interest firm." Sadly, too often, the young lawyers said they could not afford to do that.

The harsh reality of my friend's dilemma made it clear that I should join Chayes. After waiting several months while the FBI processed my security clearance, I became his special assistant. None of my friends in the firm, let alone the partners, could understand why I was leaving. Realizing that I would be forever trapped in golden handcuffs if I did not escape, I walked away from the practice of law and have never looked back.

7

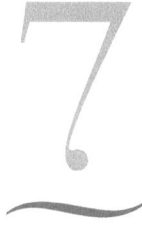

What You Can Do for Your Country

We rented a house in Washington, DC, on Faraday Place, a block or so off Wisconsin Avenue. Mr. Sclarantes, the owner, catered State Department functions. I arrived before Ellen and the children to check out the house. Opening the door late at night and turning on the lights, I was shocked—scores of cockroaches scattering in every direction. I was too shaken to sleep for hours. But over time, we found ways to eliminate the cockroaches and turn the house into a good home for our family.

It had taken some time for my security clearance to go through at the State Department, the first of perhaps a dozen such clearances I received over my career. Each involved a full-field investigation by the FBI, taking several months and thousands of dollars of taxpayers' money.

I reported for work on what became known as Cuba Monday, October 22, 1962. Abe Chayes called me and Andy Lowenfeld, his other special assistant, into his office almost as soon as I arrived. Abe explained that Soviet missiles had been sighted in Cuba and that the president was going to speak to the nation that night, declaring "a quarantine of Cuba." He told us that it was our job to prepare a defense of the quarantine that would withstand scrutiny in terms of international law. I had never taken a course in international law and knew nothing about its precepts. Chayes had also never been involved in the field. Yet, somehow, we seized our assignment with enthusiasm.

From ten o'clock that morning until four the following afternoon and for many days thereafter, Lowenfeld and I worked with Chayes on a memorandum explaining the legal basis for the United States's action. Chayes had some of what I call a "white-paper complex." He was brilliant, but had a hard time writing a first draft. He was a superb editor, theoretician, and analyst. After we talked through the issues involved and how to handle them, Lowenfeld and I wrote a "sacrificial" draft, and then he revised it. Over time, the draft went through many revisions. We went back and forth doing this for different documents relating to the quarantine as part of our defense under international law.

We quickly steeped ourselves in the legal rules that applied to nations in times of peace and in times of war. A key legal step in the Cuban Missile Crisis was to refer publically at all times to the US action as a *quarantine* rather than as a *blockade* because a blockade is an act of war under international law. The president and his advisors wanted to minimize the Russian claim that the United States was engaged in an act of war while effectively preventing further Soviet missiles from reaching Cuba. The quarantine label had been proposed earlier by the deputy legal adviser, Leonard Meeker, who participated in the first White House meetings dealing with the crisis because Chayes had been away.

Others saw the US response strategy differently. Some leading US foreign-policy experts, including former Secretary of State Dean Acheson, urged the president not to worry about international law, but instead bomb the missile bases in Cuba without delay. He and other advisers argued that if a legal argument was needed, the United States should simply claim it was acting in self-defense. The United Nations Charter is clear that its terms do not limit "the inherent right of individual or collective self-defense if an armed attack occurs." Acheson and those supporting his position claimed it was a legal technicality that no actual "armed attack" had occurred because it might occur at any time. Fortunately, wiser judgments prevailed, led by then-Attorney

General Robert F. Kennedy. Llewellyn Thompson, who had been ambassador to Russia, told Kennedy a strong legal argument was important when dealing with the Russians.

We concluded that promoting a policy to ensure that the United States acted in collaboration with regional allies would strengthen the persuasiveness of its actions to other nations outside the region. The legal case we made was rooted in a proposed action by the Organization of American States (OAS), which included twenty countries, and from which Cuba had been excluded. A key OAS treaty (the so-called Rio Treaty) provided that the OAS members were obligated to assist any American state "to meet armed attacks against" that state and "to deal with threats of aggression against any of them." In a critical OAS meeting, Secretary of State Rusk himself presented the US position that the secret buildup of nuclear missiles in Cuba constituted a "threat of aggression" within the meaning of the Rio Treaty and, therefore, triggered a necessary response in support of the quarantine. The governing body of the Rio Treaty voted eighteen to zero to support the US position.

The United States made a compelling two-part legal case to the United Nations. Adlai Stevenson, as the US ambassador to the United Nations, made a dramatic showing of the extent to which Russian missiles were actually on the ground in Cuba and could quickly be used to attack America. The United States was thus faced with "a threat of aggression" within the meaning of the Rio Treaty. The second part was that the United Nations Charter expressly provides that "nothing in the present Charter precludes the existence of regional arrangements or agencies for dealing with such matters relating to the maintenance of international peace and security as are appropriate for regional action," provided they are consistent with "the Purposes and Principles of the United Nations." Our carefully crafted legal case made clear that the Rio Treaty established just the type of "regional arrangement" referred to in the UN Charter, and the quarantine, supported by that regional arrangement, was consistent with the UN's "Purposes and Principles."

The designation *quarantine* and the legal case we prepared to defend the US action were key steps toward our country's ultimate success in persuading the overwhelming majority of countries within the United Nations to reject the Soviet position and support the United States. The United States was viewed as not engaged in armed intervention on its own, but rather as joining a multinational effort to head off what quickly might have become World War III. The legal argument we made was not determinative, of course, but it was an important part of the US case in terms of both the United Nations and the worldwide court of public opinion.

After a tense week in which nuclear war seemed—and actually was—a real possibility, the Soviet Union backed down and agreed to withdraw its missiles from Cuba.

The Cuban Missile Crisis was an example of how the public interest was ultimately judged by a wise president and shaped in legal terms by a resourceful legal adviser. It also illustrated that an effective lawyer in government will not simply defend the public policies made by other officials, but will also be directly engaged in helping to decide those policies.

With the successful conclusion of the Cuban Missile Crisis, I hoped US policymakers would see the advantages of multinational actions and that unilateral military interventions by the United States would be a thing of the past. Unfortunately, I was wrong. The US invaded the Dominican Republic on the thinnest possible legal basis in 1965, and the Vietnam War quickly escalated after that with more tragic consequences.

For much of the next six months, I spent considerable time on various legal aspects of our policy toward Cuba, including our increased efforts to isolate that country from interactions with the US and other Western countries. In retrospect, I think this policy was a profound mistake. We would, I believe, have been in far better shape in terms of our military position, as well as our leadership in the Americas, if we had sought to strengthen economic and political ties with Cuba from the time of the revolution led by Fidel Castro. But, of course, I was not making the key policy judgments at the time.

I was assigned the role of legal counsel for the State Department in negotiating the sale of Polaris nuclear missiles to the United Kingdom, which had been agreed to by President Kennedy and British Prime Minister MacMillan. This was the first sale of nuclear missiles to any foreign government, and the negotiations at the Pentagon were cloaked in great secrecy. The US negotiating team was headed by a full admiral, assisted by numerous other Defense Department officials, including someone from the general-counsel's office, and by various State Department officials. We met over several days.

At the outset, the admiral in charge of the US team said, in effect, "Let's agree that no transcript of the negotiations will be kept so that no one will feel inhibited about speaking. In short, no records will exist until we have the final text of an agreement covering all aspects of the sale." The British agreed, everyone put their pens on the table—no computers then—and the negotiations proceeded.

At the end of the second day of negotiations, everyone else had left the room where we were meeting in the Pentagon except the lawyer from the Defense Department and me. A sailor came in, ducked under the table around which we had all been sitting, and pulled out a box from which he extracted several recording tapes. It was instantly clear that a secret taping machine had been recording all our discussions. I turned to the Defense Department lawyer and told him the recording violated the commitment of all meeting participants not to keep a record of the proceedings. "Oh, don't worry about that," he told me. "The British will never know."

But I did worry about it. I hastened back to the State Department and told this story to Chayes. He immediately called Secretary Rusk and urgently asked for an appointment. A few minutes later, we went up to the Secretary's cavernous office on the seventh floor, where I repeated my tale to Rusk. While Chayes and I were still in his office, Rusk picked up a special phone that connected him directly to Secretary of Defense McNamara. Rusk told McNamara my story and said it was unacceptable for the United States to violate its word to our closest ally. McNamara did not wait to hear his colleagues' side of the story but instantly agreed that the recording would be suspended and the tapes destroyed. The Polaris Sales Agreement was eventually finalized and signed on April 6, 1963.

Ellen and I shared some wonderful experiences connected to my job. The most memorable was seeing President and Mrs. Kennedy at a ball at the Waldorf Astoria on May 22, 1963. It was like watching the king and queen when the Kennedys came down a grand staircase and into the ballroom led by Louis Armstrong, playing his trumpet held high.

Later that fall, I heard Kennedy talk to a group of senior officials in the State Department. I was included, not as a senior official but as the assistant to the legal adviser. We all stood as the president walked into the drab State Department auditorium and up to the podium. I do not recall his exact words, but I do remember that he began by thanking us for our civic work and spoke eloquently about the importance of public service. The words of his inaugural speech came to my mind: "Ask not what your country can do for you, but what you can do for your country." I felt he was talking directly to me, and I felt ten feet tall and proud.

Our daughter, Elizabeth, was born in March of that year in Georgetown Hospital, and she was a beautiful redhead like her brother. We quickly found that two babies were more than twice as much work as one. Ellen handled most of that work, though we both were sleep-deprived for months.

Our son David had a wonderful, independent personality almost from birth, not unusual in eldest children. But he was also eager to do far more mischief than his two siblings. Ellen and I had only the counsel of Topsy—which was wonderful—and Dr. Spock (our "baby bible") to follow. David soon declared his independence and, in tandem with a neighborhood boy, who was his age, got into all sorts of trouble. One day, for instance, the two boys cut all the flowers in the garden of our lovely next-door neighbor, Mrs. Eliopolous, and gave them to Ellen as a gift. Neither Ellen nor Mrs. Eliopolous was pleased. On another occasion, the oil man came in his truck to fill our tank for the winter. When the tank was full, the oil man drove away, forgetting to put the top back on the pipe to the tank. David dragged the garden hose over to the tank, shoved it in the hole and turned on the water, pretending he was doing just what the oil man had done. It was only when the water sank to the bottom of the tank and doused the furnace flame that we realized what had happened.

We spent a cold night before the oil man could return, drain all the oil and water out of the tank, blow-dry the tank, and then fill it up again with oil, this time being sure to put back the tank top. We were then presented with a monstrous bill for all the work. I argued that the oil man had left what is known in legal language as "an attractive nuisance," and as a result, the oil company was responsible. After some tense moments, that argument prevailed.

While working for Chayes, I had many extraordinary opportunities to serve as a lawyer representing the United States, even though I was not yet thirty. I was engaged in international arbitrations and drafting treaties and other agreements—all responsibilities far beyond what I could have found in any private firm.

For example, I assisted Chayes in an arbitration with France that involved a dispute over international aviation rights. The United States and France had a treaty on aviation rights. The treaty provided that US air carriers could fly from the US to Paris. We argued that the treaty allowed those carriers to stop in London to let some passengers leave and other passengers join the flight. The French claimed that the treaty allowed only nonstop flights. The matter was arbitrated before the Arbitration Tribunal in Geneva for nine days in September 1963. I helped Chayes write the brief and then prepare our oral argument. We had a wonderful time there and won the arbitration.

The real beneficiary was Pan American Airways, then the giant of international air travel. To celebrate, the Pan Am legal counsel, Norm Seagrave, took Chayes and me to Pere Biers, then one of the few three-star restaurants in the world. (It is now two stars.) The restaurant is in the tiny town of Assez-sur-Passez, and we ate in the lovely garden. I recall my amazement that any dinner could cost well over $50—it was a true feast, topped off by brandy from the time of Napoleon.

Then came the assassination of President Kennedy on November 22, 1963. Like so many others, I can still picture the moment I heard the news. I was sitting in the senior officers' dining room on the seventh floor of the State Department with my Aunt Polly. We heard the terrible news on a loudspeaker, and the whole room went silent. We were all stunned. Suddenly, life had stopped, and we had to be with people we cared about. I just stood up, said a hurried goodbye, and went home to be near Ellen and our kids. And cried. Ellen and I took David to Pennsylvania Avenue to watch the funeral procession. (Elizabeth was too young.) I held David high on my shoulders so he might glimpse the horse-drawn funeral coffin, though he had no idea of what he was seeing. It was very moving. Ellen and I both cried.

Lyndon Johnson came soon afterward to speak to the same group of senior State Department officials that Kennedy had. He was accompanied by the next two people in line for the presidency: seventy-one-year-old John McCormack (the Speaker of the House) and Senate Pro Tempore Carl Hayden, who was eighty-six years old. Hayden was drooling.

My God, here are the two guys who are in line to be president, I thought. Of course, the possibility of assassination was much on my mind. President Johnson spoke, and in contrast to President Kennedy, he was not particularly forceful or eloquent. I felt not ten feet tall but five foot eleven and a half, which was my actual height. It was depressing. I didn't have any idea at the time that Johnson would be much more effective than Kennedy in getting his domestic agenda passed by Congress—the Great Society legislation and the Civil Rights Acts of 1964 and 1966.

President Johnson appointed the Warren Commission to investigate the assassination of President Kennedy. I was the liaison from the State Department to the Warren Commission. My task was to select which State Department documents concerning Lee Harvey Oswald and related matters should be sent to the Commission. For weeks immediately after the terrible day when Kennedy was shot, I pored over every document I could find that related to Oswald. Since he had spent time in Cuba and was married to a Russian, rumors were swirling that a Communist conspiracy was involved and that Oswald was simply a pawn. In the end, the Warren Commission concluded that Oswald acted on his own. Though books appear regularly to dispute that judgment, I am convinced that the Commission was right.

Shortly thereafter, I traveled to Panama to defend before an international tribunal the US actions in the wake of riots in the Canal Zone
on January 9, 1964. The violence erupted over the tearing of a Panama-
nian flag that students were trying to raise in the Canal Zone. Three
days of riots followed, in which the US military was called in to assist
the Canal Zone Police. Twenty-two Panamanians and four American
soldiers had been killed.

I was sent to defend the United States, along with Joseph Califano
from the Defense Department. (He later became secretary of Health
and Human Services in the Carter administration.) For a week, we
interviewed witnesses and prepared an analysis of what happened and
why. We also presented the US position to a commission of jurists from
the Organization of American States that was sent to do an inquiry.
That experience convinced me that the US would eventually have to
relinquish sovereignty over the Canal Zone, an issue that became a
major controversy when Jimmy Carter was president.

Chayes also put me in charge of legal representation for the assistant
secretary of state for security and consular affairs, Abba Schwartz,
who soon became a dear friend. He was a longtime mentee of Eleanor
Roosevelt, who helped him gain the position. Under his leadership, the
US immigration laws were liberalized, and many of the harsh restric-
tions against non-European immigrants were lifted. Not surprisingly,
Schwartz ran afoul of the conservative forces that backed Senator
McCarthy, including the longtime head of the Passport Office, Frances
G. Knight.

Schwartz was called to testify before both the House Un-American
Affairs Committee and the Senate Internal Security Committee. (The
staff head of the Senate committee had the wonderful "everyman"
name of Sourwine.) My job was to help him prepare his testimony
and get him ready for the Congressional hearings. I peppered him
with tough questions, as I knew Congressional committee members
would do. Schwartz stood up to both committees in controversy after
controversy about visas for alleged communists and other alleged
misdeeds. In 1966, he abruptly resigned, worn out from his battles. It
is hard to overstate the sense of dread that thousands of Americans

felt because these Congressional committees threatened their civil liberties.

One day Secretary Rusk called me to his office. I was smoking a D. P. Ehrlich pipe at the time and shoved it into my pocket, only to find it burned a hole right through. Somehow, I managed to put out the fire and clean up the mess before arriving at the secretary's office. He told me he suspected that the head of security in Schwartz's office, Otto Otepka, was bugging the office and leaking secrets to the Internal Security Committee and the Un-American Activities Committee. He told me to fly to London immediately and interview two persons who had worked as security officials in Schwartz's office before transferring to security positions in London.

I caught the next plane and went immediately to the embassy to grill the persons. I questioned them separately and together for over eight hours.

"You must have bugged the office," I said to each of them. "That's how they got the classified information Otepka knew about. How did you bug the office?" They told me in countless different ways that they didn't bug Schwartz's office. I thought I was being very smart by coming at the question from one angle, and then another angle, and then another.

After returning to Washington, I reported to Rusk, "As far as I can tell, they didn't bug the offices." Forty-eight hours later, I got a call from a lawyer saying, "Two foreign-service officers would like to come to see you." I agreed.

The men came in and admitted, "We didn't bug the offices. We tapped the phones. We didn't lie. You just didn't ask the right question." At Harvard Law School, my classmates and I gained from Chayes the ability to examine problems closely and from all sides. Most of all, we learned that the hardest part of any analysis is knowing what questions to ask. If you know the right questions, he taught us, the right answers will eventually follow. If you fail to identify the right questions, no amount of insight or intellect will help you find the right answers. In this case, I had forgotten his teaching and was not wise enough to ask the right question. I relearned a lesson that I subsequently never forgot.

In a few situations, I was called on to represent the US Government even when I thought its policies were completely wrong. The most significant involved a 1964 case before the US Supreme Court, *Herbert Aptheker et al. v. the Secretary of State*. Mr. Aptheker was a US citizen and prominent historian. He had been denied a US passport because he was a member of the Communist Party. Under the terms of the Subversive Activities Control Act, he was prohibited from applying for a US passport, without which he could not travel abroad. Aptheker claimed he had a constitutional right to travel abroad, which could not be abridged by US officials implementing an act of Congress.

Chayes had wanted to argue a case before the Supreme Court for some time, but only the Justice Department could authorize a government official outside the Justice Department to do so. After some time, the Justice Department turned to Chayes to represent the United States in defending the Congressional statute. We both personally thought that the Subversive Activities Control Act was unconstitutional in authorizing the denial of a US passport to Aptheker. But we also thought that the case, since it arose under a statute that was approved by Congress and signed by President Truman, should be adjudicated by the Supreme Court, with the lawyers for the US Government making the best possible arguments for the statute's validity. On this basis, Chayes and I fashioned the strongest legal arguments we could, while personally hoping that the Supreme Court would decide for Aptheker, as it did, by a vote of six to three. We felt we had properly defended the public interest and that the Supreme Court rightly decided that interest.

After I spent two years working with Chayes, his leave from Harvard Law School came to an end in the spring of 1964. He left DC and returned to Harvard. My time working for him gave me extraordinary opportunities to learn and grow; he was one of the great mentors in my life. Although Chayes had shifted from Cambridge to Washington and from professor to government official, he was still a wise teacher, and I remained his student after I joined him as his special assistant. Among the many lessons I learned in the years I worked as special assistant for Chayes was the importance of being prepared. Before each meeting, we discussed what was expected to happen, what might happen even though it was not expected, and how best to handle even remote contingencies.

Chayes also taught me that while we "worked for" the Secretary of State, the American people were our clients, and our civic work required a degree of independence of judgment that should not be overruled even by the Secretary of State. On many issues such as the Cuban Missile Crisis, Chayes worked directly with the president and his chief national security advisers in the White House. In theory, Secretary Rusk might have fired Chayes if their judgments had clashed too sharply. But this course would have had its own set of risks, particularly if Chayes had chosen to air publicly whatever caused the rift. In fact, Rusk—who started law school but never finished his legal education—had great respect for Chayes, a view that was reinforced by Rusk's deputy, Under Secretary of State George W. Ball, who was a renowned international lawyer with many years of experience in the field.

Chayes was a particularly good mentor for me after Judge Hand. Chayes was an activist and would never have been comfortable as a judge whose professional responsibility was to react to the claims of adversaries. Chayes wanted to create law in the furtherance of social justice, while Hand was deeply skeptical of those with that mindset. But both of them were committed to the belief that their roles were to serve our country and its interests as best as they were able.

Over the years, I have found myself much closer to Chayes in my views of law, including the roles of law of serving society. Chayes opened my mind to think more broadly and deeply than I had before about how government work—and all civic work, for that matter—can serve the public interest.

8

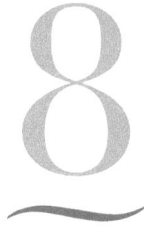

Vietnam and Dominoes

When Abe Chayes announced that he would have to return to teaching at Harvard or lose his tenured position there, I immediately decided I wanted to work for George W. Ball, who had been at the State Department since the outset of the Kennedy administration, first as Under Secretary for Economic Affairs, and then as Under Secretary, the second-ranking person in the State Department after Secretary Rusk. I admired Ball more than anyone in the State Department because he was a superb statesman in every sense. I had written a number of memoranda for him and knew he was the best craftsman of policy and words in the State Department. I could not forgo the chance to work for him if he would have me. Ellen agreed that staying in Washington for one more year would make sense if my working for Ball was possible.

I went to Ball's chief assistant, George Springsteen, and asked whether Ball would hire me. I was somewhat wary because I knew that Bayless Manning, a former Yale law professor and a friend, had briefly worked for Ball on a project for the NATO alliance to jointly own a fleet of nuclear submarines—a "multilateral nuclear force"—and Manning had crossed swords with Springsteen several times. Manning left to become dean of Stanford Law School, but not before Springsteen made his life miserable.

Surprisingly, Springsteen readily agreed to check whether Ball was interested in hiring me. Ball soon called me to offer a job writing policy analyses and speeches for him. (In my later years, I joked that I spent the first half of my career writing speeches for other people to give and the second half of my life giving speeches that other people wrote.)

Throughout the next year, I had a roller-coaster experience as a writer and aide for Ball. He had a superb prose style and taught me a lot about writing. I never wrote a single piece of prose for Ball that he did not revise by at least a few words, with one exception. That was, ironically, a short introduction to a volume titled *A Practical Guide to Effective Writing* (Random House, 1965). The guide was written by a retired government official who taught writing to others in the government. The substance of what I wrote in that guide was based on lessons I learned from Ball:

> I was taught to believe that the statement of an idea is no less important than the idea itself. Clarity of expression can never replace thought, but no thought can be expressed with full force unless it is clearly stated. Few of us can write gracefully, but all of us can write intelligibly. Yet I have observed both in private and in public life that many papers are written to conceal ideas—or the lack of them—rather than to communicate any thought or purpose.
>
> Those who take pleasure in words and the meanings of words enjoy their use. They find satisfaction in the plain statement of a complex problem. But this virtue seems lacking in the authors of many papers that, over the years, have crossed my desk.
>
> I am dismayed at the inability of people in all walks of life, including the Government, to express themselves. They cross swords with syntax in almost every sentence. They apparently regard the conception that a sentence should have a subject and a predicate as outmoded, if not subversive. I persist in my simple faith that the unadorned declarative sentence is one of man's noblest architectural achievements. But it is also one of his rarest.

Sometimes, Ball drafted, and I edited. More often, he edited my drafts. Either way, we worked together as a team. He had a distinctive voice, a pattern of putting together words and phrases unique to his mind and pen. He cared deeply about words and the meaning of words. His bibles, like Judge Hand's, were Fowler's *Modern English Usage* and

The Elements of Style by Strunk and White. Ball enjoyed finding the right word for a particular point almost more than knowing whether the point was right.

Ball taught me much about foreign affairs. He had a remarkable ability to concentrate on key issues in American foreign policy and to bear down on those issues with intensity. He believed passionately that the future of the United States depended primarily on a close partnership with a united Europe and with Japan. The major enemy was the Soviet Union, and the partnership was essential, primarily through NATO, in defending our vital interests. Other matters could be important, but this was the top US priority. He did not want the US to lose sight of the big picture in its foreign policy or to be diverted to less significant concerns.

On one of the trips to Europe when I accompanied Ball, we spent a day talking with Jean Monet, the great architect of the Common Market. I gained an understanding and commitment to the European-American alliance. Ball was much less concerned about relations with developing countries, but not because he lacked compassion for those needing help from the United States. He was strongly supportive of giving that help. Rather, he was concerned that the United States not be diverted from its main foreign-policy objectives.

Ball insisted that I attend many meetings with him. As a result, I observed and learned from leaders from various parts of the US Government who were connected to US foreign policy. One that stands out was about an explosive crisis in Cyprus. Intercommunal violence between Greek Cypriots and Turkish Cypriots flared in 1964 despite UN peacekeeping operations. Though the island is small, its strategic location was critical because of a NATO military base located there. Archbishop Makarios was the president of the government and a constant thorn in the side of the United States. He delighted in verbal attacks on the United States and in threats to limit our ability to use Cyprus for our defensive purposes.

I often sat in on intelligence briefings for Ball and Rusk by members of what was termed the intelligence community. At one of these meetings, representatives were present from the CIA, the Defense

Department, the National Security Agency, and the State Department. Ball chaired it. Someone from the CIA said, "Wouldn't it be convenient if he were out of the way?" We all knew what he meant—if Makarios were assassinated, then we wouldn't have this problem. He went on to suggest that this could be done in such a way that there would "be no US fingerprints."

Suddenly, Ball stood up, all six-foot-four and 250 pounds of him looming over everybody. "The United States of America and its government do not do assassinations," he declared loudly, looking at the official. After a long moment, he sat down, and the discussion resumed. I was struck by the force of his words, setting a clear marker of where we stood on that moral issue.

When I started working for Ball in June 1964, the United States had military advisers in South Vietnam, but our country had not committed to a significant troop buildup. The war was going poorly for South Vietnam and the US, however, and President Johnson was considering sending large numbers of troops. General William Westmoreland was head of all US troops there.

In early August 1964, an apparent attack by North Vietnam occurred on a US ship in the Gulf of Tonkin. I worked closely with Ball in drafting a resolution authorizing the use of force against North Vietnam, which Congress rapidly passed. The Department of Defense reported the attack to the president and the State Department and claimed no doubt about what had happened. We learned only later, however, that the attack was misreported, and the intelligence from the Defense Department about the incident was significantly off-base. McNamara would not have supported retaliation, he later said, if he had known the actual facts.

The Gulf of Tonkin "incident" increased pressure from Secretary of Defense Robert McNamara to send more US soldiers to Vietnam, and he was supported by Secretary Rusk and President Johnson's National Security Advisor, McGeorge Bundy. Bill Bundy, brother of McGeorge, was assistant secretary of state for Far Eastern Affairs and another advocate for escalating the war. Bombing was the key, they claimed—it would destroy the Viet Cong's military strength and demoralize its forces.

Ball was the only senior official who strongly opposed increasing our forces in Vietnam. At the end of World War II, he had been part of a team that studied the impact of US bombing on the German war effort, and he (along with John Kenneth Galbraith) concluded that bombing—at whatever level of intensity—had relatively little impact. For example, when the Allies hit a ball-bearing factory, the Germans just went on building tanks but stopped using ball bearings in them.

Over the course of the year I worked for Ball, I helped write a series of lengthy secret memoranda to President Johnson, spelling out the strongest case we could for why escalation was a mistake and why the United States needed to extricate itself from South Vietnam. These documents were so sensitive that usually only four copies existed: one for the president, one for Rusk, one for McNamara, and one for Ball. They were responsible for ensuring that no other copies were made. This was, of course, long before the era of the internet and even before rapid copy machines were common, so secrecy was much easier to maintain than it is today.

Ball organized an informal group of State Department offices who shared his views and possessed great expertise in Vietnamese and Chinese history and politics. The major argument made by the pro-escalation advocates was that Communism, backed by China, would roll over Asia "like dominoes" unless the US stopped it in South Vietnam. These advocates claimed that the Chinese were supporting North Vietnam as a first step in what would become a massive strategic power shift. President Johnson became persuaded by Rusk, McNamara, and a group of generals, along with McGeorge Bundy, that this argument was correct. Johnson did not want the dominoes to fall on his watch as president. He felt that the Vietnam War could derail his Great Society program and the War on Poverty unless he acted decisively by sending all the troops the Pentagon generals wanted. I had the opportunity to watch McNamara presenting the arguments about Vietnam in meetings. He was a supremely able advocate—confident to the point of arrogance—one of the best I've seen in terms of marshaling facts and figures to present a case.

But Ball was equally effective. He made the case—forcefully and, in my view, more persuasively—that this domino view was the wrong big picture. He argued that vital US interests were not at stake in the conflict between North and South Vietnam. On the contrary, our vital interests focused on Europe and Japan, and that was where the future of our broader foreign engagement really lay. The ancient enmity between China and Vietnam meant that Vietnam would never agree to be under Chinese domination any more than it would agree to be under US control. The Cambodians and Laotians were equally unlikely to do other than resist any attempts to invade them. Ball argued that the North Vietnamese had ample reason to view South Vietnam as part of "their" country and that the Government of South Vietnam was so corrupt that it was unable to mount a serious resistance movement.

In Ball's view, South Vietnam was a diversion because the US had no dominant interests there or in its survival as a country. For that reason, he thought that the US involvement in the escalating war between North and South Vietnam was a mistake from the outset. The French defeat in Vietnam illustrated the difficulty of fighting the Vietnamese on their own territory. Ball thought we should learn from the mistakes of the French and not get entangled in a war we could never win. He was convinced that America's foreign-policy interests required our prompt withdrawal of military personnel from South Vietnam.

While our country moved inexorably to heightened military involvement in Vietnam, President Johnson did a miraculous job of moving important legislation through Congress to promote the Great Society and do battle in the War on Poverty. I came to see that the domestic agenda that had stalled under Kennedy was taking off like a rocket under Johnson. He had an inspiring vision for the country, what it could be, and how it could ensure that all people had a decent meal, a place to live, an education, and health care. He believed all of this was possible in a democratic and capitalistic country that took care of everyone. Because I worked for Ball, I went to meetings with Bill Moyers, White House press secretary, and others and saw glimpses of this change going on and thought, *Wow, this is amazing, wonderful, and important.* While the Camelot glitter of the Kennedys was gone, the country was rapidly moving forward toward a more just society. The Civil Rights Act of 1964, the Voting Rights Act of 1965, and the Great Society Movement were all making a powerful difference.

Ball liked Johnson and was intensely loyal to him, so in public, Ball never publicly indicated his deep reservations about US involvement in Vietnam. Those reservations were not rooted in any lack of concern about the rights of the Vietnamese or the devastation that the US would inflict on North Vietnam. He viewed the North Vietnamese leaders as bad people; he also regarded those in South Vietnam as little better.

To the president's credit, he always encouraged Ball to state his views, even though he was a minority of one. And Dean Rusk was equally supportive. Ball, in turn, never said publicly what he constantly repeated privately—in his view, the war could not be won. The Viet Cong were simply too determined to succeed in what was "their" country, and the costs of the war, even if victory were possible, were simply too high in the projected number of US casualties.

During that time, I learned an important lesson about dealing with reporters. Since living in Milwaukee, Ellen and I were close friends with John Pomfret, the White House reporter for *The New York Times*, and his wife, Maggie. We were scheduled to have dinner at their home one Saturday night, but at the last minute, I could not come because of an issue concerning the Vietnam buildup. Ellen innocently told our hosts that I was detained in a meeting with Ball at the Defense Department. With a seasoned nose for a good story, John immediately guessed that a rumored US attack on North Vietnam was underway and called his newspaper colleagues to track down the story's details, which they did. No one knew that Ellen was the immediate cause of the leaked story, but we learned a valuable lesson. Good reporters may also be good friends, but when they smell a story, their journalistic instincts will trump friendship.

One of my last experiences working for Ball in 1965 was to take a top-secret plan for ending the war to Saigon to learn the reactions of our ambassador to South Vietnam, former general Maxwell Taylor, and the deputy ambassador, Alexis Johnson.

Ball had prepared a lengthy memorandum detailing his plan in the fall of 1964, waiting for the right time to present it to the president. "Timing is everything," Ball frequently told me. The right time came in the spring of 1965 after a White House session at which the president told Rusk and Ball the results of a Honolulu meeting between McNamara, Taylor, and the US military leaders. That group unanimously urged the president to authorize sending a massive increase in US troops to South Vietnam. Ball strongly responded to the president that such a step should not be taken without considering other options. The president said he would give Ball "until tomorrow morning" to come up with a settlement plan. In response, Ball sent his memorandum to the president the next morning.

In summary, the memorandum stressed Ball's conviction that the US could not continue to bomb North Vietnam and use napalm against villages in South Vietnam without damaging the US's status in the world. And the American people would not accept a significant increase in US casualties. Given those realities, Ball proposed a ceasefire, the establishment of a coalition government, and a general amnesty for all Viet Cong who wanted to return to the north. An international commission would police the ceasefire. Most importantly, the United States would withdraw its troops from Vietnam when the coalition government was in place.

The president read the memorandum and then met again with Ball. Bill Moyers soon told Ball that the president was very interested in the plan. Ball knew he needed to gain the support of Taylor and Alexis Johnson, for they would have to persuade the South Vietnamese government to accept the plan. Ball sent me to make the case directly to those two men and Westmoreland.

Ball told me on a Friday afternoon that I was to leave on Sunday for a secret mission to Saigon, where I would present the plan to Taylor and Johnson. I was recovering from the flu and felt terrible. The next day, I felt even worse after going to the State Department medical center to get about six shots that ordinarily were to be given over a period of weeks.

On Sunday afternoon, with the plan in a locked briefcase, I rolled on to Pan Am 1—a flight that went, with many stops, around the world—still reeling from the flu and the shots. I drank two stiff Scotches and water and fell asleep for the next fourteen hours. At the time, State Department employees flying for more than twelve hours straight were permitted to fly first class, and that is what I did. By some miracle, when I woke up in Bangkok, I felt fine.

I had told only Ellen about the trip. The night I departed, there was a formal dinner and dance at the State Department, and we had long planned to go. Ellen went with Lee Marks, a close friend and former assistant to Abe Chayes. Marks sent Ellen an orchid, and both had a wonderful time. At one point, Ball asked Ellen to dance. He said in a voice that others could hear, "Oh, too bad Tom had to go off to Vietnam and couldn't be here, but now I can dance with you." Stunned, she thought she could keep a secret even if he couldn't.

In Bangkok, the Ambassador's personal plane was waiting for me at the airport. I was soon in the back seat of a two-seater fighter jet, ears crackling from the sudden changes in altitude with no pressurized cabin. The pilot told me we would have to fly low over parts of Laos to escape possible detection from enemy radar, and that's what we did. It was a frightening experience to know that just below us—what seemed only a few hundred feet—were soldiers with guns who would be thrilled to shoot us out of the sky if they could.

Fortunately, we landed in Saigon without incident. It was just ten years after the French had been forced to leave, and their influence was everywhere. The city seemed like a huge military base superimposed on a once-lovely French town, with tree-lined streets and large villas.

We drove straight to Taylor's residence. Taylor met me at the door and ushered me into his study, where Alexis Johnson was waiting. None of their aides were present. Ball had cabled Taylor that I was coming and told him the reason for my visit, so he and Johnson were prepared. But I don't think they expected a thirty-year-old to walk through the door.

Taylor and Johnson were polite and listened for an hour or so as I outlined the essence of Ball's plan. Alexis Johnson seemed somewhat supportive. But I sensed that Taylor—who had previously been a four-star general and chair of the Joint Chiefs of Staff—listened to what I had to say only because Ball was my boss as well as theirs. I concluded by saying, "Please read this document, which makes the case, I think, powerfully and persuasively. I'll go to sleep for a couple of hours."

When I woke and had a shower, Taylor, Johnson, and I had lunch. Again, I sensed that Johnson might be supportive, but Taylor was firmly against it. "No one in Washington," Taylor began, "seems to understand what we need is more troops, and if we have more troops, we can win this war." He went on to make clear what I had already suspected—that he was totally and unalterably opposed to the plan. He thought it was a formula for surrender, something that American military forces had never done and should never do. Our honor was at stake, he said, and, no less important, at stake was the freedom of millions everywhere who would be subjected to Communist domination if this domino fell. He was determined that the war must be won and that this would be possible, though only with a substantial increase of US ground troops. This was a *real* war, and the way to win a war was to blast and blast and blast the enemy with bombs and then crush its forces with superior strength on the ground.

I came back from Saigon shaken by what I had heard from Taylor. I had known his position beforehand; it was the same position held by Rusk, McNamara, and the two Bundys. But I had not realized what a war zone was like, nor had I been surrounded by the realities of war I had witnessed in Saigon—guns, wounded soldiers and civilians, and constant danger.

Unfortunately, my trip failed. After I returned, Taylor and Johnson sent Ball a long list of questions, going over the issues we had discussed. Although Ball answered those questions, every other senior official advising the president was adamant that more US troops were the only answer. The president accepted their judgment.

Virtually every day in the last months of 1965 that I was with Ball, he reviewed bombing proposals from the Defense Department to help ensure that they met guidelines that had been established to minimize South Vietnamese civilian casualties. I knew now firsthand that the likelihood of avoiding those casualties was zero. We were killing innocent people. Some of them, of course, really cared about who was in charge of their government. A few might even have been willing to die for a government that was not controlled from the North. But most South Vietnamese wanted simply to go back to their lives of peace when they could grow rice, raise children, and not worry whether bombs would obliterate their lives.

In urging US troop withdrawal from Vietnam, Ball was a great international lawyer arguing his case for the public interest before the chief judge on the issue: President Johnson. And Ball was as brilliant an advocate as I have ever seen in action. Johnson listened carefully to him. He took seriously the arguments that Ball was making. But the president ultimately came to rely on McNamara and the generals on the one hand, and McGeorge Bundy and Rusk on the other, and to view Ball as a devil's advocate.

By the time I left Ball to start teaching at Stanford Law School in June 1965, it was clear that Ball would not succeed. In the summer and fall of 1965, the US troop buildup continued at an accelerating, alarming pace.

During that year of public service, I came to admire Ball as a morally forthright public official with a brilliant intellect and a superb writer. History is clear that on the issue that concerned him the most, Ball was absolutely right. Tragically, as we know, it took almost a decade of war, more than fifty-eight thousand American lives were lost and even more Vietnamese casualties, before his courageous, determined—and sometimes lonely—stance was vindicated.

Ball and I stayed close friends in the years after I left my role as his assistant. At my request, he came and spoke at Indiana University when I was president there. He stayed on at the State Department until 1968, when he became US ambassador to the United Nations.

Looking back, Vietnam was a series of tragedies. The worst, of course, were the needless deaths and destruction caused by the war. On a much less important plane, in my view, if President Johnson had followed Ball's advice, he would now be viewed as one of the great presidents in American history.

9

Horizons West

Washington had been a great adventure and a chance to engage in public service. It was much less wonderful for Ellen, as I traveled a lot and left her alone with our two children. We made good friends, but Washington is not an easy place to plant roots, and it would never be our permanent home. It was, once again, time for a change for both of us.

In 1965, I was convinced that my next career step would be teaching law. Further, I had spent time analyzing how international law was generally taught in law schools—by studying judicial opinions, just as with other legal subjects. I learned through my State Department experience that international law was actually made primarily by treaties and other international agreements and by the actions and inactions of governments. Only rarely were judicial options involved. The International Court of Justice and other international judicial bodies issued only a handful of decisions each year, and most of them did not deal with center-stage issues in public international law.

On that basis, I planned to prepare a new set of materials based, in large part, on issues I had worked on over the past three years—political problems such as the Cuban Missile Crisis and the controversies regarding the island of Cyprus and the Panama Canal, and economic crises such as tariff fights and the aviation arbitration with France. Only a few judicial controversies in US and international courts would be part of these materials.

I sent out feelers to Yale and Stanford Law Schools, the latter because my friend Bay Manning was now dean and had encouraged me to apply. Fortunately for me, the former dean of Stanford Law School, Carl Spaeth, was the only international law teacher on the faculty, and he taught just one seminar. The Stanford law faculty wanted someone to teach public international law and did not seem put off by the fact that I had not even taken a course in the subject.

Ball tried to persuade me to stay in the State Department for another year. He took me to a NATO meeting in Paris, where we stayed in the city's most elegant hotel, the Plaza Athénée. We ate superb dinners—my first experience with bouillabaisse—and I had lots of free time to explore, including visiting art galleries and purchasing a watercolor, which we kept for many years until I gave it away when we left Indiana University.

I received an attractive offer to become the research director for the 1968 presidential campaign, which President Johnson and his staff were planning. *Gee, I won't have this chance ever again, and it would be so exciting.* I went to former Supreme Court Justice Abe Fortas, a friend of my aunt Polly, for advice. He encouraged me to take the job, underscoring that I might never again have the opportunity to be involved in a presidential campaign in which I would help shape major public policy positions in every arena. But a more potent and galvanizing realization kept intruding: *I've got to get started and teach.* Since Lyndon Johnson decided not to run in 1968, it was lucky I didn't accept the offer.

Despite Ball's efforts, Ellen and I agreed that it was time to move and establish roots for our family elsewhere. Bay Manning offered me a salary of $16,000, and we settled on $17,500, with the understanding that there would probably be no increases for a while. Even though Ellen had never seen Stanford, we felt this was too good an opportunity to forgo. It was a great chance—a small school with a supportive faculty and several mentors, Manning and Spaeth particularly, ready to help.

We decided to camp our way across the country and went to the Blue Ridge Mountains in Virginia for a test run. My aunt Louise Seltzer, who had been an army nurse in World War II, gave us her old canvas army tent, complete with a center pole and heavy pegs. Meanwhile, we traded in the small English car we had owned since our Milwaukee days for a new Dodge Dart with a roof rack so the tent could easily be strapped on top. After purchasing four sleeping bags and a Coleman stove at an army surplus store, we were ready. The test run in the Blue Ridge Mountains worked well.

Our friends held a big farewell picnic party for us, complete with songs and poems. Ellen and I started a custom at that party that we have often repeated in the years that followed. We gave each couple a brown paper bag containing two or three paperback books. The rule we established was that anyone could trade any book, but we would not take them back. So, we managed to divest ourselves of scores of paperbacks while our friends enjoyed trading books with each other.

We set off for the West Coast in the summer of 1965 after our furniture had been packed and shipped. Ellen and I had rented a house sight unseen with the help of the only couple we knew at Stanford, Ruth Franklin—a Radcliffe classmate of Ellen's—and her husband, Mark, a Stanford law professor. We first drove nonstop to Chicago, stayed for a bit with Ellen's parents, and then went on, stopping in a series of state and national parks.

All went well for most of the trip. Ellen had the great idea of bringing a little present—a toy car or a puzzle—for each child each day, and they eagerly looked forward to present time. Each had one side of the back seat, with an invisible line running through the middle that they could not cross.

Our only real problem finding a campsite over the ten-day trip was in Nevada, where we drove mile after mile of desert with no campgrounds in sight. Finally, we saw a sign for Murphy's Magic Springs, and ten miles later, we pulled into a patch of weeds with cows munching nearby. Pitching the tent, as we did every night, we cooked dinner on the stove and soon were asleep. We were abruptly woken the next morning by a cow sticking her head in the tent and mooing loudly.

Half asleep, we stumbled outside, only to find ourselves surrounded by cow pies, which we managed to avoid as we carefully moved to the car.

Soon, we were camped at Yosemite, not nearly the tourist attraction then that it later became. In the adjacent campsite, a guy with a beard taking lots of pictures taught us how to make tacos. He introduced himself as Ansel Adams, who was later the most famous nature photographer of that time, but then, he was relatively unknown. We waited in Yosemite until our furniture was about to arrive and then drove into the Bay Area. I was stunned by four lanes of traffic going down Route 101 from San Francisco to Palo Alto, little realizing that the traffic was just a trickle compared to what it would become during our years in California.

Our first California house was on Hilbar Lane. A couple living nearby, Anne and Jack Schlaefli, had two boys, Robert and Scott, one of whom was David's age, and later a girl, Dawn. We became good friends; Jack and I shared duties leading the PTA at Green Gables School, which David attended.

The house was fine, but after eleven years of marriage, Ellen and I wanted to stop paying rent and start gaining an equity interest in a home. We found a lovely small home on Walter Hays Drive, in the same neighborhood as Hilbar Lane, with excellent schools. We bought the house for $33,500. We knew we needed to remodel it to fit our needs—the first of several redos of the house over the next four decades. We added a fourth bedroom and a study, a wall in front, and a breakfront between the entryway and dining area. The renovations cost about $18,000, including landscaping—what a bargain compared to today's prices!

We quickly made many friends, most not connected to Stanford. We met a number of couples initially through our kids, whom we stayed in touch with after our children grew up. These included the Schlaeflis, who remained close friends, although they later moved to Southern California and then Texas. Another set of special friends was Elaine and John Freeman—John was Ellen's first date in Chicago, and his parents were good friends of Topsy and Oscar. The Freemans had followed us to California, sending us a telegram in advance saying, "Wither Thou Goest." We had great times together.

Our third child, Paul, was born in February of 1967, two years after we arrived in California, when we were well settled in our new home. Many of our friends, like our parents, stopped with two children. We didn't debate having a third child and were confident it was the right step.

Ellen and I felt we knew a lot about child-rearing when Paul arrived in Stanford Hospital, certainly more than we knew before. I had planned to be in the delivery room and was excited about the prospect since that had not been allowed during the birth of either David or Elizabeth. When Ellen started to have contractions, we rushed to the hospital and called our doctor. Ellen was moved into the labor room. Paul was born so quickly that the doctor had not even arrived, so he was delivered by a resident in the labor room after I had been shoved out the door. Fortunately, all went well. But when the bill came, it included a hefty amount for the delivery room. I protested that we didn't use that room or benefit from a doctor. The hospital prevailed and, since Paul was healthy, I stopped protesting.

Amid the ongoing excitement and energy of making new friends, renovating the house, and welcoming a new child, I began teaching at Stanford Law School. When I walked into my first class, contracts, in the fall of 1965, I had never received even five minutes of instruction on how teachers should teach or how students should learn. I had never taught a class. I had no experience in teaching. A fellow teacher, Byron Sher, gave me a copy of his notes for the course, which was my only aid.

Further, as I mentioned, I had done extremely well in my contracts class at Harvard Law School. This meant that the concepts in the course came easily to me. It also meant that I could not understand why most of my twenty-four students were having a hard time understanding those concepts. It took me some time to realize that while the concepts were simple to me, they were often bewildering to students, just as many concepts in math and science had been bewildering to me at Exeter. I knew I was not doing as good a job teaching as I wanted to, and I struggled to do better. At my request, a new friend at the law school videoed three of my classes, and I watched the videos carefully. Over time, I learned how to break the difficult concepts into their component parts and talk through each part with students rather than just plunging into appellate court cases, in which knowledge of the concepts was assumed.

Decades later, when I started teaching at the Stanford Graduate School of Education, I learned there was no course at the school on teaching and learning in higher education. I offered to teach the course and spent most of a summer reading everything I could on teaching and learning. Time and again, I tried to help my students in that class avoid the mistakes I had made in my first contracts class.

Each student in the first year at the law school took one course in a small section of about two dozen students for the fall and spring semesters, while their other courses were larger. My contracts class was one of those sections. By spring, Ellen and I had bonded with most of the students in the class; we were not far apart in age. We had invited them to our home for a meal soon after the course began in the fall.

After the first rocky weeks, that first year of contracts felt like I was taking an extended voyage with a small class of eager students, and we had a truly exhilarating time together. On the last day of class, the students surprised me with a picnic in a state park. Since then, I have taught hundreds of classes, but rarely have I connected so joyously and totally with an entire group of students.

Of all those students, we became closest friends with Steve Walters and his wife, Mabsie. A year later, we asked them to stay with our three children for six weeks while we went to Chile so I could teach a group of Chilean law professors how to engage their students in active learning rather than just lecturing. (Today, I can't imagine leaving very young children for that long—but we did.) Michael Wright was also a student in that class, and he and his wife, Pam, became good friends as well.

I taught contracts for several more years and added a then-required course in legal process, using the very mimeographed materials by Professors Hart and Sacks that I had studied as a student at Harvard Law School.

For my international law course, as I had planned, I had the hubris to develop a brand-new course built around materials based mostly on my experiences in the State Department and unclassified memoranda and other documents I had taken with me when I left Washington, DC. I had just come off the battlefield, so to speak, and I wanted to expose students to the issues public international lawyers faced then.

Franticly, in the fall semester of my first year, I developed eight problems—two involving issues before courts, three concerning international economic matters, and three relating to international political crises. I drew on virtually everything I had done over the past three and a half years, from October 1962 to June 1965. Perhaps basing a course on my experiences alone was a bit risky, but fortunately, the 150 students were intrigued by the opportunity to wrestle firsthand with real issues rather than abstract hypothetical ones.

At this time, I started writing a lengthy law review article on the international law issues relating to the island of Cyprus. As Ball's assistant, I had been deeply engaged in those issues and had thought hard about them. I used the range of legal concerns surrounding the island to explore a series of questions about the roles of international law when force is involved. I also had a second article in mind on the legal issues concerning passports, which I believed had not previously been covered in any law review.

Meanwhile, Abe Chayes and Andy Lowenfeld made plans to spend most of a summer month in Palo Alto while we developed an outline for a book, *The International Legal Process*, using my materials for the international law course as the starting point. We each agreed to prepare a third of the chapters, which we outlined that month. Over the next year, we passed back and forth hard copies of drafts—no internet connections then.

By the next summer, we finished a rough draft of the entire book and again spent several weeks together reviewing it page by page. Fortunately, Chayes and Lowenfeld enjoyed coming to California. Chayes had arranged for Little, Brown to publish our book, and the following year, we tested it in paperback form, with several other law teachers using it as well. Unfortunately, the total royalties from the three-volume work—about $10,000—were eaten up by the costs of that test paperback.

I had been out of law school for five years before I came to Stanford, and I started as an associate professor without tenure. Three years later, in 1968, the faculty voted for my promotion to a tenured position as professor. I was told afterward that it was the shortest faculty meeting on record. I was delighted.

Almost immediately after I was promoted, Dean Bay Manning asked me to lead a complete review of the law school's curriculum and co-curriculum. I agreed and asked an assistant dean at the school, Tom Headrick, to join me. For most of the next two years, we were heavily engaged in a searching look at almost every aspect of the law school. We conducted extensive interviews with every faculty member and the senior staff, and out of the interviews, we created an agenda of possible ideas for reshaping the curriculum and student activities. We then formed a score of task forces, each focused on one of the suggested key ideas. We tried to arrange the process so that everybody with a good idea was in charge of an effort to design a program that implemented the idea.

After about a year of planning, we prepared an agenda of nearly two dozen new initiatives. We then discussed each initiative with each faculty person, making it clear that any idea could only succeed if the others were supported. In this way, we built coalitions for the whole package of reforms. We then scheduled four faculty meetings, at which each idea was discussed, revised, and discussed some more, all without votes. At the final faculty meeting, all but one or two of the initiatives were adopted.

The curriculum revision was quite radical for its time. It included a number of active clinical experiences. Students had the opportunity to spend their entire third year in a full-time internship, which included a series of reflection papers and regular consultations with faculty about what the students were doing. Working on the curriculum revision also gave me a chance to think more deeply about what was going on in the transfer from thinking like a lawyer in the first year into the second and third and how to make the whole law school experience cohere in a better way. It was the first time I realized that law school should be two years, not three.

The curriculum revision was also my first experience with academic politics. I learned on the job that if I put enough pieces on the table that potential partners wanted and made it a condition of their getting their piece that they had to support the other pieces, we could have a mosaic that actually worked. This was invaluable preparation for the political dimensions of leadership.

In 1969, Harlan Cleveland, then president of the University of Hawaii, asked Dean Bay Manning and me to design a new law school for that university. We had known Cleveland from our State Department days, for he had served as assistant secretary for International Organizations and then ambassador to NATO during the Kennedy and Johnson administrations.

After a few visits, it became clear that Hawaii's legislature would not fund a first-rate law school. I then had an epiphany—one of the few really original ideas I've ever had about higher education. I proposed that students from Hawaii spend the first two years of law school at a mainland institution and their third year at the new University of Hawaii Law School. Since most of the students went to the University of Hawaii as undergraduates, this would have the advantage of exposing them to a much broader set of experiences than would otherwise be possible. Then, I proposed that the new Hawaii Law School should focus on just the students' final year, freeing them to specialize in, for example, native land claims, government issues, or other matters particular to the islands. This approach would enable the new school to hire just nine to twelve faculty members in two or three clusters and achieve world-class academic excellence in those clusters.

Manning and I wrote up the plan, and the faculty and Cleveland were enthusiastic. Cleveland said the plan was brilliant. However, within minutes after we started to explain the plan to the Hawaii Legislature, I knew it was doomed. The legislature did not want young Hawaiians leaving the islands to go to law school. An innovative school was the last thing its members sought. They wanted a law school just like those on the mainland, and if they could not have that, then a pale shadow of such a school was far better than some new model. A year or two later, Mike Heyman, a friend of mine and later dean of Boalt Hall, Chancellor of UC Berkeley, and then head of the Smithsonian Institute, prepared a new plan that gave the Hawaiian Legislature what it wanted.

In 1969 and 1970, I was increasingly drawn into law school administration through my work on the curriculum revision and other projects. Two other clusters of efforts soon surfaced and occupied my time and attention. The first was university politics. My closest law school friend and colleague, Herb Packer, had taken on the job of vice provost under the then-provost, Richard Lyman. Packer was in charge of a massive examination of undergraduate education called the Study of Education at Stanford (SES), and I agreed to head one of about a dozen task forces. My focus was on study abroad, and I spent about eighteen months reviewing Stanford's multiple programs in Europe.

SES needed to go through a discussion, revision, and approval process. The subcommittees of the SES came up with a series of recommendations, and Packer wanted to be sure they were not simply the lowest common denominator, but had some real bite as well as a consensus to support them. He knew the proposals in each SES report needed faculty approval to have legitimacy, but there wasn't any vehicle to gain that approval. There was only an unwieldy Academic Council of nearly one thousand faculty members with a nine-person Executive Committee. Fortunately, the Executive Committee was headed by a very wise man named Kenneth Arrow, a winner of the Nobel Prize in Economics. Equally fortunately, Packer was also on the Executive Committee.

Impelled by the forthcoming SES—and more generally, the need to have some group that could act on behalf of the faculty—Packer proposed the formation of an Academic Senate, one that was big enough to be representative but small enough to be deliberative. He wanted one that could effectively represent the faculty in its schools. Arrow and the rest of the Executive Committee of the Academic Council concurred, and—after a good deal of discussion—the Stanford Academic Senate was created in 1968.

I was one of those elected to the new Academic Senate, and after a year, I became one of its two vice-chairs. That role taught me about the rest of the university, and I became much more involved in trying to protect the university as a whole.

It was a bad time at Stanford. Protests against the bloody, seemingly unending war in Vietnam became increasingly strident on campus. Led by an English professor named Bruce Franklin—a science-fiction specialist who was expelled in 1972—there were regular sit-ins and marches. A good deal of physical damage was done to the campus, including firebombing the offices of former president Wallace Sterling. In 1971, eleven law school students were arrested when they blocked the entrance to the San Jose draft board. I used to jokingly say that I spent my years in the State Department trying to get the US out of Vietnam and spent my early years at Stanford trying to get students out of jail for protesting about the Vietnam War.

Those were very tough years. The students didn't have to turn in exams on schedule. The protests were disruptive of the educational enterprise, and too many students left Stanford without a decent education.

The Academic Senate met thirty-one times in thirteen months to deal with a number of matters, including SES (which resulted in many close votes) and, yes, parking. But most of our meetings were related to the explosive situation on campus. The very first meeting—after the organizational session in September 1968—dealt with a temporary policy on campus disruptions, which was endorsed. Two weeks later, the second meeting focused on what to do about the Reserve Officers' Training Corps (ROTC). This was a lightning rod for great concern about what our armed forces were doing and also about classified research on campus, including at Stanford Research Institute, which was part of the university. We deliberated: Should we keep the Institute? Should we abolish it? Should we keep it with limitations? In April 1969, students protesting war-related research on campus occupied the Applied Electronics Laboratory. The Academic Senate voted to part company with Stanford Research Institute, which became a separate entity named SRI.

Just think about it—a new system of faculty governance, which was inevitably somewhat fragile because it was brand new and untested, had to be tested by fire during those early years with issues that went to the very heart of the university's existence. The new system actually worked. It was an amazing feat. I felt so fortunate to be involved. The experience helped me understand the university world outside of the law school. Suddenly, I benefitted from an intense set of tutorials on a wide range of issues faced by the Senate and, therefore, the university. I felt I had an opportunity and an obligation to learn about those issues so I could make reasoned judgments.

A new president, Kenneth Pitzer, former president of Rice University, was chosen in 1968 but soon showed that he was completely unable to deal with the tumult sweeping over the campus. Pitzer was a chemist and seemed to be guided by the view that if one bit of evidence was contrary to his current course of administrative action, the action must be reversed. Like an experiment in chemistry, one wrong finding meant the whole approach was wrong. However well this mode of action had worked for Pitzer in a laboratory, it was a disaster in trying to lead a university. In less than two years, Pitzer had been reduced to a bowl of jelly, unable to decide anything, let alone stick to a decision. He was a weathervane.

Those were tumultuous years, especially after the invasion of Cambodia in 1970. Without the Academic Senate and Lyman as provost to provide some semblance of governance, the university would have been in a lot more trouble.

Finally, enough was enough. I went to the trustee executive committee with a small group of faculty leaders from the senate to tell them our view that Pitzer was a disaster and that the university's future was at risk. I am sure the trustees heard the same message from other quarters of the university as well. To their credit, they acted promptly and decisively, and Pitzer resigned within a matter of weeks. He went to the University of California as a distinguished professor of chemistry. Fortunately, Lyman was chosen as president. To the extent that the university was being led at that time, Lyman had been in charge. He was a tough and forceful decision-maker, but he was fair and deeply imbued with what I thought were the right academic values. Over the next ten years, he led the university with great distinction.

Just about the same time that Pitzer resigned, in 1971, Manning announced that he was leaving the deanship. He told the faculty at a meeting at his house, the first faculty gathering of the new academic year. His wife, Margery, whom Ellen and I liked enormously, learned of his decision at the same time as the faculty. Soon after, Manning also told his wife that he was leaving her for the wife of a law student—a major scandal. He became the head of the Council on Foreign Relations in New York.

Almost immediately, many on the law faculty told me they wanted me to be dean, though I was only thirty-six at the time. Was I ready to be an academic leader? I had written a fair amount during my time as a professor, which I really enjoyed. I also liked teaching. I was learning, however, that I probably wasn't the kind of long-distance runner who could stay on as just a teacher if I had the chance to pursue other interesting opportunities. I loved my time in government and had recently considered going back to Washington. Until I worked with Manning and acquired experience as vice-chair of the Academic Senate, I didn't think I could be a university administrator. Now, it sounded like an interesting challenge.

I spoke with a faculty friend, Joe Sneed, who had gone to Duke to be dean there before going into the Nixon administration and then becoming a federal judge. Joe warned me not to become a dean because he feared I would get bored with the job after a while, and then I would have nowhere to go professionally. I had confidence, however, in my ability to find another professional path if I did eventually become restless. I saw the deanship as a great opportunity to engage in what I call "institutional architecture"—determining where an institution should be going and helping shape its future accordingly. That challenge and opportunity would be my next step.

PART III

LEADING

10

Institutional Architecture

When Richard Lyman became president of Stanford, he told me there would be a full search for a new law dean, for it would not be fair to me to do otherwise. He said I would need the full support of the law faculty to be effective as dean, and that support would be possible only if the faculty had been directly involved in the search. He also made clear that he expected me to be chosen. And I was.

I became dean in the late spring of 1971, the seventh dean of the law school, and the youngest Stanford dean at the time. The most important among a new dean's goals is usually academic—strengthening teaching, research, or both. When I became dean, I had just led a major revision of the curriculum, so that part of the academic enterprise was already in strong shape.

At that time, Stanford Law School boasted a first-rate faculty and student body, but they were housed in a second-rate building. In 1971, the school still occupied part of the original Quad—the facilities Leland and Jane Stanford built in the 1890s. Very little had been fixed in the preceding eighty years, and it was a mess. The facilities were, to put it gently, inadequate. The library was inadequate. The classrooms were inadequate. Stanford sought to join the ranks of the best law schools, but its financial support and facilities were far behind those of its competitors.

My predecessor, Bayless Manning, recognized this pressing problem and spearheaded an extensive process to design a new set of law
school buildings. The university trustees had approved an excellent
site for the buildings near the academic center of the campus. Manning had thought about a fundraising program to gain the necessary
support but had left before a penny had been raised. The annual Law
School Fund raised less than $100,000 per year.

Being dean of Stanford Law School then was not a complex administrative job. In six or eight months, I could have learned what I needed
to know about administering internally. But I couldn't do that during
my first year because I had to focus most of my time on external fundraising. And I had never been a fundraiser, so I had to learn. That was
not my preference, but I felt I had no choice. As he departed, Manning
gave me a list of faculty members he said either had or could get offers
from leading law schools elsewhere and would probably accept those
unless the new facilities were built.

This would be the first capital fundraising campaign in the history
of Stanford Law School. Fortunately, I had a crash course in fundraising from the able head of the Stanford Development Office, Kenneth
Cuthbertson. He became a superb tutor for me as well as a close friend.
I knew that $12 million was needed to build four new buildings that
would be positioned in the form of a quadrangle. One of Cuthbertson's
first pieces of advice was to include funds to endow faculty positions
and student scholarships in the capital campaign. The school had only
a very modest endowment.

In total, with the approval of the Stanford president and trustees, I
set a campaign goal of $16 million, the equivalent of about $120 million today. I hired the necessary support staff and launched a capital
campaign within months of being chosen as dean. I quickly learned
the essential lesson that people give to people. I had to spend a great
deal of time individually with potential donors until they developed
confidence not only in Stanford Law School but also in me as a person
and leader.

The Development Office had a list of potential large donors, which
was my starting point. Surprisingly, few of those on the list had attended

the law school, but each had some strong tie to Stanford and the field of law. Manning had prepared several fancy publications about the proposed new buildings, but I knew I had to make the pitch in person. And so I did, over and over again, for the next twelve months.

Although the law school lacked wealthy donors among its alumni, it did have a Board of Visitors that advised the dean and included a number of influential men and women across the country. These included Warren Christopher, who later became secretary of state; two subsequent justices of the Supreme Court, Sandra Day O'Connor and William Rehnquist; Shirley Hufstedler, a Ninth Circuit Court of Appeals judge, and later the first secretary of education; and several other leading judges. They were extremely helpful in the fundraising campaign.

Almost immediately, we had several lucky breaks. The Lucy Stern Estate donated a couple of million dollars. Several long sessions with a recluse named Fred Richman brought another couple of million dollars for a classroom building. The Kresge Foundation agreed to fund an auditorium building. We also received a large gift from the Cooley family for the courtyard. And so forth. By late spring of 1972, we had raised $9 million for the new buildings, as well as another $7 million for scholarships, faculty support, and other needs.

Our first capital campaign was indeed going well, but we still needed another $3 million before we could begin constructing the new buildings. John Crown, then a judge in Chicago, had gone to the law school. I knew that his parents, multimillionaires in Chicago, were looking for an appropriate memorial for another son, Robert, who had recently died. The deceased son had no connection to Stanford, but that did not seem important. Rather, Colonel Crown, as he was known, wanted a prominent memorial. What could be better than our buildings? I could even promise to name the largest building, the library, after Robert Crown. Unfortunately, John Crown told me that naming the library would not be enough. His father would want Stanford to change the school's name to the Crown Law School. I knew Stanford had a firm rule against naming schools for individuals. (The rule was broken in 2022 when John Doerr gave $1.2 billion to transform the School of

Earth Science into the Doerr School of Sustainability.) I hoped I could figure out something to handle the naming issue, and John Crown arranged a meeting for me in his father's office. I carried a scale model of the building on my lap all the way to Chicago and then into Colonel Crown's huge office.

He wasted no time and immediately asked me how much money I needed. He didn't blink when I said $3 million, which would have been among the largest single gifts Stanford had ever received at the time. In exchange, I told him an idea that had come to me on the plane—we would call the entire complex of four new buildings "Crown Quadrangle." Just as Michigan Law School—one of the best in the country— was known as "Cooley Quadrangle," Stanford Law School would be known as "Crown Quadrangle." I promised him that all our stationary would include "Crown Quadrangle" and the library would also bear his son's name. Thinking about it for only a minute, he reached out and shook my hand. "Done," he said. And that was it. I walked out of his office with the promise of $3 million.

With the money in hand, the next four years were spent finishing the design and then construction. An excellent Chicago firm, Skidmore, Owings & Merrill, completed the design. The contracts for the new buildings were signed in 1973, followed by construction. I hired a full-time construction manager to help ensure our plans made sense and were followed in the construction of the buildings. Then the blueprints were slowly translated into concrete reality—literally concrete, which was the main construction material.

A half-century later, the buildings still hold up well and are among the best on the Stanford campus. A few mistakes were made—the lack of an obvious entrance being the most troubling to me. During construction, I had several struggles with the vice president of facilities, who thought the designs were too opulent. He fought with me about the size of the faculty offices and also about the wooden shutters that had to be custom-made. But I held my ground, insisting that the faculty offices were the counterpart of science-faculty labs, and since I had raised all the money for the buildings, they would be built according to our plans.

John Merryman was one of my closest friends among the law school faculty. He was an expert in contemporary art and wrote about and taught popular courses on art and cultural property. Merryman headed a faculty committee overseeing the interior decor to make sure the colors and furniture were attractive. He also arranged for the loan of several dozen stunning artworks by leading contemporary artists The loan came from the Los Angeles fine-art printmaking company, Gemini Prints.

With Merryman's help, we received a spectacular Barbara Hepworth sculpture on a long-term loan for the front courtyard. The loan came from the industrialist Norton Simon, who was married to the actress Jennifer Jones. Simon invited Merryman and me to his Pasadena home for dinner to discuss the loan. I could not keep my eyes off the beautiful Jennifer Jones.

Merryman and I wanted to commission a work of art to celebrate the new law school buildings. We went to New York together to visit art galleries familiar to Merryman. We considered a number of options and commissioned the abstract expressionist Robert Motherwell, who graduated from Stanford, to prepare a large and stunning collage to hang in the entryway to the Crown Library. Merryman arranged for a fine print to be made from the collage, which we gave to donors to the building, along with a poster from the collage as well.

Finally, again with Merryman's help, I arranged for the Stanford University Press to publish a volume of legal essays by law school faculty to celebrate the law school's new home and the scholarship that would be produced there. I asked every member to write one of the essays, and most of them did. My essay was on international law and the use of force.

The buildings were finished in the spring of 1975, just in time for commencement. I insisted we hold the ceremony in front of the new buildings because I wanted the graduating class to feel connected to the school's new home. At about one o'clock on the Sunday morning before commencement, I received a call from Gerry Gunther, a faculty member, biographer of Learned Hand, and good friend. He had just left the school where he had been working and saw that vandals had spray-painted graffiti all along the building behind the sculpture and on the sculpture itself.

Oh, brother. Every dean has challenges, I thought. My mind flashed to when I was reading the records of the first Stanford law dean. He used to go around the law building each night removing light bulbs lest they be stolen. Not everything was easy for deans in the good old days, and they certainly weren't now.

I immediately decided that the ceremony would go on and that we would not let thugs destroy what we had worked so hard to build. Though it was the middle of the night, I called the director of physical facilities and asked him to have the best available sandblaster come at dawn the next morning.

"But it's Sunday," he complained. "We can't get anyone until Monday at the earliest."

"We can if money is no object," I replied, "and it's no object."

Sure enough, a sandblaster started working at six the next morning. Meanwhile, I had alerted John Merryman, and he, an art historian named Albert Elson, and some graduate students, cleaned the sculpture. By nine forty-five, just as the students were lining up for the commencement ceremony, the last bit of graffiti had been removed.

We beat the little bastards, I remember thinking. And we did.

The new Crown Quadrangle was a complex of four linked buildings: the open-stack Robert Crown Library and faculty office building, the six-hundred-seat Kresge Auditorium, the FIR classroom building, and the James Irvine Gallery of meeting rooms and faculty and student lounges.

To commemorate the completion of the new law school buildings, we held a week of celebration, beginning with a visit and an address from President Gerald R. Ford on September 21, 1975. We were able to arrange this because one of the members of the Board of Visitors was a major fundraiser for Republicans generally and President Gerald R. Ford in particular.

The visit of President Ford had its own set of challenges. The Secret Service insisted on posting guards with machine guns on the roofs of all the new buildings facing the courtyard where Ford would speak. The speech was a ticketed event, and without my knowledge, the Santa

Clara Republican Party got hold of a bunch of tickets to give its members. I insisted that an equal number of tickets be given to the local Democratic Party.

Ford was not a great speaker, but he gave an excellent talk. Further, at my request, he met with twenty law students to answer their questions before the talk, with only Secret Service agents and me watching. Though Ford had pardoned former President Nixon and the Vietnam War was escalating with the draft in the minds of many, Ford connected with the students extremely well.

Two days of celebration activities followed, including tours of the new buildings, exhibits showcasing the history of the law school, an alumni banquet, class reunions, seminars on future trends in different areas of the law, panel discussions on the legal profession, a law school musical revue, receptions for emeritus professors and deans, and the formal dedication of Crown Quadrangle.

The purpose, of course, was to celebrate an important event in the school's history: the move to our new facilities, the first set of buildings expressly designed for legal education at Stanford. The celebration was also intended to give our alumni and other friends of the school a sense that those new buildings were their school, that although we moved to new quarters, the school's goals—to provide the best in legal education and legal scholarship—were still the same.

More than one thousand alumni returned to the school for the week of celebration, a considerable share of the law school's 5,500 living alumni. The celebration was also a culmination of my efforts to encourage our alumni to feel proud of their law school as it was changing and getting better—not to believe they were being left behind. Alumni of every campus I know often feel their alma mater was frozen in amber the day they graduated. It is important to their continued support that they stay connected. I had been reaching out to alumni since I became dean, speaking at alumni events nationwide. Since I could not visit every alumni club quickly, I even commissioned a movie about the law school and its faculty and students so alumni who saw it could be proud of what was happening at their law school. The movie was not very good, but it served its purpose.

Deepening relationships with the alumni supported one of my overarching aims during my tenure as dean—finding ways to bridge what seemed to me a gap between legal education and practicing lawyers. A key role for alumni was helping ensure that the school was not isolated from the practice of law. We developed ways to gain guidance through the Board of Visitors, alumni leadership conferences, and other activities. Individual alumni became a prime source of ideas about what should happen at the school and how to improve what we were doing.

Of course, part of the role of alumni was financial support. The law school faced ongoing financial challenges because it was a small, private, expensive institution. Fortunately, our financial support steadily expanded during my term as dean. I became convinced that if we continued to do the job that we were called on to do—excel in legal education and legal scholarship—then the financial support would continue to come from our alumni, most of whom cared about Stanford Law School and about maintaining its leadership position.

For example, we raised funds from some alumni for students who wanted to go into public service. Having served in the administrations of Presidents Kennedy and Johnson, I felt strongly that public service was a noble calling. John W. Gardner, a Stanford trustee, the founder of Common Cause, and secretary of the Department of Health, Education, and Welfare under President Johnson, encouraged me to find ways to facilitate our graduates choosing to enter public service. Within the first week or so of my becoming dean, Gardner came up to me while I was walking across campus.

"Tom, do you know that only a tiny handful of Stanford Law School students are going into public service?" he asked. "What are you doing about it?" Not, "What are you going to do," but "What are you doing about it now?"

"Gee, John," I replied, "You know I just started here as dean." But he was right. Only a few of school graduates went into public service. We needed funds to help ensure that the loans students had to repay for their law school education did not preclude them from public service. With support from two alumni, Myles Rubin and Victor Palmieri, we developed a fellowship program that forgave student loans for those going into public-service positions.

Apart from a new home for the law school, my most important priority was to make certain that we kept the faculty we had and recruited new, outstanding professors. The parting gift former dean Manning had given me—a list of faculty members with offers from other leading schools—made this a priority. I knew having decent facilities was a key to retaining them, but we also needed endowments for faculty positions. Fortunately, our fundraising campaign exceeded its goal for endowed faculty support.

For example, in 1973, a new endowed professorship was established—the Lewis Talbot and Nadine Hearn Shelton Professorship of International Legal Studies—in honor of the late parents of Talbot Shelton, a Stanford alum who was then vice-president of Smith, Barney & Company, Inc., New York investment bankers. His donation was matched by funds from an earlier grant from the Ford Foundation to help support chairs in international studies.

A central concern to me was diversifying the faculty. When I became dean, no women or people of color were on the faculty. It was all white men. It's hard to wrap my head around those facts now. We had three open faculty positions, "billets" they were called. I told the faculty that we had to hire at least one female faculty member and one faculty member of color in that group of three. Otherwise, I would not recommend anyone for an appointment. Fortunately, we hired the school's first woman faculty member, Barbara Babcock, in 1972. As director, she had brought distinction to the Washington Public Defender Service and had taught one of the first "Women and the Law" courses at Georgetown and Yale. Babcock stood out for her teaching abilities and what she had done in the Public Defender's office. She was also brilliant. Professor Michael Wald had taken a leave from teaching at Stanford Law School in 1971 to work with Babcock and her team at the Public Defender Service. When he returned, he urged me to hire her.

It quickly became apparent to everyone that Babcock was a terrific addition to the faculty. Babcock brought invaluable practical legal experience and a commitment to clinical education at Stanford. She made it easier to hire more women on the faculty and was a path-breaker on many levels.

That same year, we also hired Stanford's first Black faculty member, William Gould, a renowned labor law scholar and practitioner. He later became chair of the National Labor Relations Board (NLRB). Gould argued (and later won) *Stamps v. Detroit Edison*, one of the first racial discrimination employment cases in the country. His clients, Black workers at Detroit Edison, had been forced to accept lower-paying, unskilled jobs, regardless of their qualifications. Gould was a visiting professor at Harvard Law School in 1971 when we recruited him. He taught the first employment discrimination law seminar at Stanford. We reconnected when Ellen and I returned to Palo Alto in 1995. Bill became one of my close friends.

On April 30, 1974, Babcock and Gould joined Gerald Gunther and me in welcoming retired Chief Justice Earl Warren, who spoke informally before a capacity crowd in Annenberg Auditorium. The student Law Forum had invited Warren to visit the school to commemorate the twentieth anniversary of *Brown v. Board of Education*. He passed away a few months later.

Increased diversity in the student body was another key goal. Students were admitted based on their college grades and their scores on the Law School Aptitude Test (LSAT). To be chosen, students had to do well in both. Recommendation letters, no matter who the authors, had little weight. Before I became dean, the school had developed a plan that essentially enabled admission of African American and Latino students who had either a high LSAT score or college grades competitive with those of admitted students. We created a free summer session to help these admitted students acclimate to the law school. The result of these steps was a significant increase in students of color.

Not all faculty members were pleased with the steps to enhance the diversity of the faculty and students. A small group was vocal in urging that affirmative action had no place in hiring faculty or choosing students. Fortunately, most of the faculty joined me in successfully making the case that the faculty we hired and the students admitted were well-qualified and that the law school community benefited substantially from diverse backgrounds.

Most of the faculty were excellent scholars and teachers. Unlike many other parts of Stanford University at the time, the law school stressed the importance of teaching and research. But when I became dean, I realized that three or four faculty members were well below a standard of excellence in teaching and had done no scholarly work for years.

I had control over faculty compensation and could refuse to give them raises, as I did despite their regular complaints. But should I move to try to have them fired on the grounds of inadequate performance of their faculty duties? That was tempting because it would have opened up billets for new faculty. But insofar as I could tell, no faculty in the university had been fired on this ground, and I knew an effort to do so would be so controversial that the rest of my agenda would grind to a halt.

Yet the situation made me extra cautious in promoting untenured faculty. Most of the tenured faculty agreed, and we rejected several assistant professors. My experience dealing with this issue at the law school helped me at the University of Pennsylvania as provost and Indiana University as president. I adopted a "when in doubt, don't" stance regarding promotions to tenured positions. If, in retrospect, the rejected person became an outstanding scholar and teacher, that person would probably have found another position. If not, the decision would have saved millions of dollars that would have been paid for a lifetime of compensation. The decision would also have left the chance of choosing someone better open.

I had problems with some staff members, as is true in every organization. I discovered that one of the assistant deans had taken what he called an "alumni trip." It was a trip to the California Republican State Convention that had nothing to do with our alumni. While I was pleased to have an active Republican on the staff—because I had a strong Democratic background—it was obviously not acceptable to lie on the forms that he had filled out. I told him he would have to resign.

I believed it would be wise for me to tell David Packard, who helped create Silicon Valley and was a leading Stanford alumnus, about this situation since he was a prominent Republican in California politics, and the staff member had been an actively involved Republican as well. I naively thought that when I met with Packard, he would say, "That was the right thing to do, and I am glad you did it." Instead, he just looked at me and growled. And growled. Finally, I got up and left. Clearly, he wasn't all that happy to lose an up-and-coming leader in the California Republican Party.

I enjoyed being dean. I could have gone on for another decade and felt I was doing useful things for the law school and enjoying it. As Joe Sneed predicted, however, I was getting bored. By 1975, I had visited every law alumni society. We had redesigned the curriculum. We had a new set of buildings. We had begun diversifying the faculty and had an aggressive affirmative action program underway to attract students of color. A number of leading law scholars had joined the faculty. We strengthened ties with the alumni. The school had also taken other important—though less visible—steps. There were things to do, of course, and there always would be. But I had done the main things I had set out to do and was ready for a new professional opportunity.

A conference and a new friend helped me to appreciate the acute need to enhance civil legal services for Americans living in poverty. This led me to seek a position helping to meet that need. The State Bar of California sponsored the conference. As Stanford Law School dean, I had tried to look over the horizon at the needs of lawyers in the decades ahead so that I could help shape legal education to meet those needs. I decided that a conference of lawyers from a wide range of perspectives could enhance my and others' understanding of future demands on the legal profession and how best to meet those needs.

With help from two members of the school's Board of Visitors, Warren Christopher and Stuart Kadison, I persuaded the leaders of the California State Bar to host the conference. We called it "Law in the Future: What are the Choices?" I was the conference editor and commissioned a set of papers that would be the focus of conference discussions and then recommendations. One of the papers underscored the need to enhance civil legal services for the poor with a sense of urgency that caught and kept my attention. Exchanges at the conference highlighted that need.

I met my new friend, Clint Bamberger, at a meeting of law school deans early in my years as dean of Stanford Law School. He was then dean of the Catholic University Law School. I admired him greatly, particularly because before becoming dean, he was the first director of the White House Legal Services Program, part of President Johnson's War on Poverty. In that role, Bamberger had been a champion of free civil legal services for low-income people. He also successfully brought a case before the Supreme Court, arguing that prosecutors were constitutionally required to reveal evidence that might be favorable to criminal defendants.

Bamberger told me he would have a sabbatical, and I invited him to spend a semester at Stanford. During that time, he and his wife, Katherine, and Ellen and I became the closest of friends. He often talked to me about his civil legal-services work and helped me realize that a legal problem that might be only a nuisance for those with financial means could be a disaster for poor people.

Learned Hand, speaking at the seventy-fifth anniversary dinner of the New York Legal Aid Society, concluded his extemporaneous remarks with this aphorism, "If we are to keep our democracy strong, there must be one commandment: Thou shalt not ration justice." I had become increasingly troubled that justice was rationed in America. I did not know of any more important task for the legal profession. If I could, I wanted to help.

When I learned in 1975 that a new federal agency, the Legal Services Corporation, was established to enhance civil legal services for low-income people, I immediately thought it might be the next right step for me.

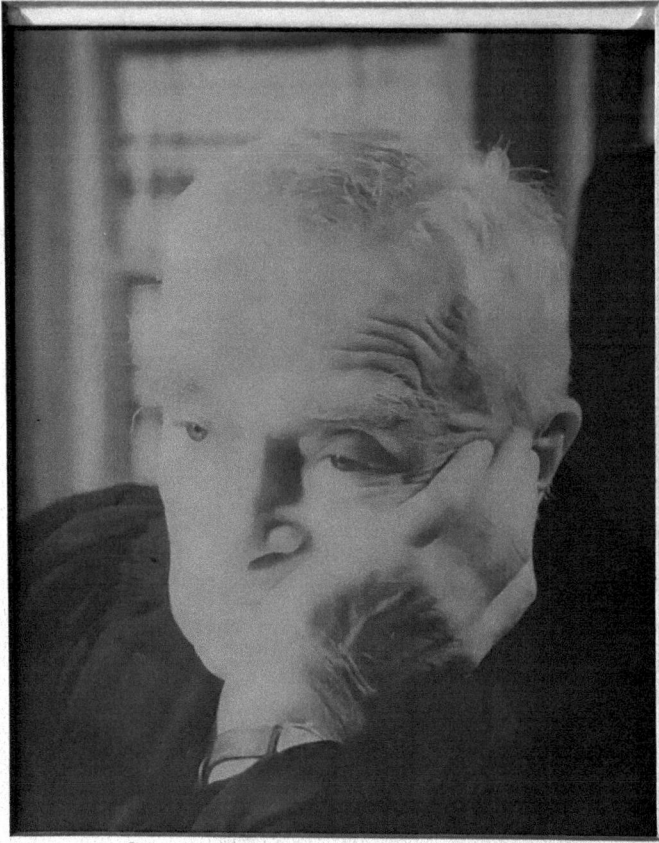

Judge Learned Hand with the inscription: "To Thomas Ehrlich, Who, far more than he realizes, has been my support and my comfort for the past eight months. May 26, 1960." Photo courtesy of the author.

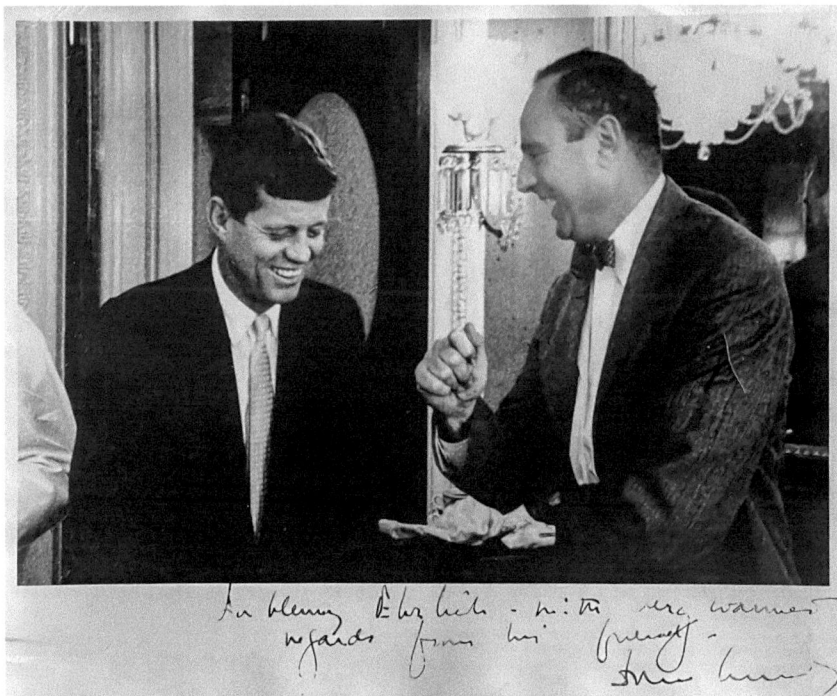

Tom's uncle Henry Ehrlich and President Kennedy with the inscription:
"For Henry Ehrlich with my warmest regards from his friend, John Kennedy."
Photo courtesy of the author.

To Tom Ehrlich
with best wishes,
Gerald Ford

To Tom Ehrlich
with best wishes
Dean Acheson

To Tom Ehrlich
With admiration
and affection
George W Ball

President Johnson, Dean Acheson, and George W. Ball. Photo courtesy of the author.

Tom with former Stanford Law School Deans Bayless Manning, Carl Spaeth, and Marion Kirkwood. Photo courtesy of Stanford Law School Archives.

Tom showing alumni a model of Crown Quadrangle, the proposed new Stanford Law School buildings. Photo courtesy of Stanford Law School Archives.

President Ford at 1975 dedication of Crown Quadrangle, with Tom and Ellen and their children. Photo courtesy of the author.

Ellen and Tom admiring a present from the Stanford Law School faculty on Tom's departure as dean. Photo courtesy of Stanford Law School Archives.

Initial staff of the Legal Services Corporation with Tom. Photo courtesy of the author.

Initial Board of the Legal Services Corporation with Tom. Photo courtesy of the author.

Tom testifying before Congress on Legal Services Corporation budget.
Photo courtesy of the author.

Senator Ted Kennedy and Tom. Photo courtesy of the author.

With Best wishes to Tom Ehrlich

Jimmy Carter

Photo signed by President Carter with Tom after Tom's appointment as president of the International Development Corporation. Photo courtesy of the author.

THE WHITE HOUSE

WASHINGTON

February 26, 1980

MEMORANDUM FOR

        DIRECTOR, INTERNATIONAL DEVELOPMENT
        COOPERATION AGENCY

SUBJECT: IDCA Policy Statement

The IDCA Policy Statement that you sent me is a sound
agenda for United States efforts in international development over the coming year. I hope that you will move
vigorously to fulfill this agenda, and to carry out the
development policy coordination that is required. I also
look to you to take the lead in two particular tasks:

    (1) developing coordinated Executive Branch positions
on the Brandt Commission's proposals, in time for use in
preparations for the Venice Economic Summit, submitting
disagreements to me for resolution;

    (2) preparing, prior to our fall budget decisions, plans
for improving the effectiveness of major development assistance
programs, both bilateral and multilateral, giving priority to
programs that will raise significant budgeting or legislative
issues in FY 1982.

Jimmy Carter

Tom— You are the boss. Act boldly re bureaucratic coordination and efficiency. I'll back you up. Keep me informed re problems & progress. J

Memorandum signed by President Carter with this handwritten post-
script approving Tom's initial policy statement for the International
Development Cooperation Agency: "Tom, You are the boss. Act boldly
re bureaucratic coordination and efficiency. I'll back you up. Keep me
informed re problems and progress. J" Photo courtesy of the author.

To Tom, with my deep admiration and sincere thanks for your compassionate and dedicated work, for all the disadvantaged peoples of the world, during our years in office together, *Jimmy Carter*

Watercolor print signed by President Carter: "To Tom, with my deep appreciation and sincere thanks for your compassionate and dedicated work, for all the disadvantaged peoples of the world, during our years in office together. Jimmy Carter." Photo courtesy of the author.

Tom and his mother in Tom's University of Pennsylvania provost's office. Photo courtesy of University of Pennsylvania Archive.

Tom teaching a class in his University of Pennsylvania provost's office.
Photo courtesy of University of Pennsylvania Archive.

University of Pennsylvania president Sheldon Hackney and Tom at university commencement. Photo courtesy of the author.

Cleo Laine and John Dankworth, two of Ellen and Tom's favorite musicians, with Walter Annenberg, University of Pennsylvania trustee, and Lee Annenberg, at the University's Annenberg Theater. Photo courtesy of the author.

Tom's investiture as president of Indiana University. Photo courtesy of Indiana University Archives.

Tom speaking to Indiana University Faculty Council. Photo courtesy of Indiana University Archives.

Tom presenting Indiana University budget to State Ways and Means Committee. Photo courtesy of Indiana University Archives.

Audrey Hepburn and Tom at Indiana University Sigma Tau International Distinguished Lifetime Award Ceremony. Photo courtesy of Indiana University Archives.

Ellen and Tom in front of Bryan House with Becky, their golden retriever. Photo courtesy of Indiana University Archives.

Ellen and Tom at an IU basketball game.

Terry Clapacs and Tom in front of Indiana University Student Memorial Union. Photo courtesy of Indiana University Archives.

Herman B Wells and Tom in front of portrait of Andrew Wylie, first president of Indiana University. Photo by Garrett Ewald.

Tom with Ira Harkavy receiving a Campus Compact award in Tom's name. Photo courtesy of Campus Compact Archives.

Tom with students and faculty from Illinois State University at American Democracy Project meeting. Photo courtesy of American Association of Colleges & Universities (American Democracy Project) Archives.

Commission on National and Community Service Board with Hillary Clinton. Photo courtesy of the author.

Corporation on National and Community Service CEO Eli Segal and Tom. Photo courtesy of the author.

To Tom Ehrlich
With Appreciation,

Bill Clinton

Signed photo of President Clinton and Tom at a meeting of the Corporation of National and Community Service. Photo courtesy of the author.

Lee Shulman, president of the Carnegie Foundation for the Advancement of Teaching with Ray Bacchetti and Tom, coeditors of the book *Reconnecting Foundations & Education*, sponsored by the Carnegie Foundation. Photo courtesy of the author.

Tom and colleagues from the Carnegie Foundation for the Advancement of Teaching—Jim Sirianni, Mary Huber, Jon Dolle, and Bill Sullivan—on a site visit to Indiana University for their book *Rethinking Undergraduate Business Education*. Photo courtesy of the author.

11

Justice for All

The White House Legal Services Program, part of the Office of Economic Opportunity, successfully supported civil legal assistance for low-income people nationwide. But it had also been controversial since it was launched. The program funded local legal-service agencies that sued landlords, businesses, and other powerful financial interests. During the presidency of Richard Nixon, Vice President Spiro Agnew launched a major effort to eliminate the program. "Why should the government pay for lawyers?" he asked over and over again, often citing one case that had gone wrong out of the many thousands that had gone right. The fact that judges were deciding in favor of lower-income people in the overwhelming share of these cases only made Agnew angrier and his abuse shriller.

The program was kept alive under a moderate Republican, Donald Rumsfeld, who was in charge of the Office of Economic Opportunity. But governors were given veto power over any grant to a local program in their states, subject to a veto override by Rumsfeld.

One of the most contentious fights was over a grant to the California Rural Legal Assistance Program, which supported migrant farmworkers in their struggles against large farm owners. Then-governor Reagan vetoed the program, only to have Rumsfeld override that veto. Federal funding for legal services expanded under President Johnson, but was

166

frozen for five years under President Nixon. The threat to abolish all funding was constant.

An Act of Congress created the Legal Services Corporation in response to that threat—to help ensure federal support for local legal services that neither governors nor the president controlled. Under the act, the corporation is directly responsible to Congress and is independent of the Executive Branch and governors. President Nixon signed the act, hoping this would help him avoid impeachment. Of course, it didn't. The act established that funding from Congress would be used to support civil legal services for about thirty million people who were living below the poverty level as established by Congress.

The act also provided that the corporation's board of directors would be divided between Democrats and Republicans. The board members President Ford initially chose were all extremely conservative, and the Senate refused to confirm them. After a long delay, a board was in place, and it turned its attention to choosing a president.

I learned that Sam Thurman was on the board. He was a friend, a former Stanford law professor, and then-dean of the University of Utah Law School. I called him and said I was interested in being considered for the position. Sam said he was not sure why I would consider it, given the turmoil that seemed to always beset legal services for people in poverty, but he would be glad to help me.

Both Democrats and Republicans on the board admired Thurman, and this was fortunate for me. It was also my good luck that Roger Crampton, dean of Cornell Law School, was chair of the board. Roger was a Republican and former head of the Office of Legal Counsel in the Nixon administration. We did not know each other, but he had heard of me and was also supportive. I later came to appreciate that Crampton was a man of great intellect and integrity.

Through a book about legal services, I recently learned that the board search committee had initially chosen three finalists for the presidency, all of whom had significant legal-services experience. Bamberger was one of the three. But the board decided it wanted someone without a legal-services background to avoid the appearance that the new corporation would simply follow the path set by the Legal

Services Program in the White House. This was certainly a factor in why I was selected. No doubt, the reputation of Stanford and its law school helped as well. During the late fall of 1975, I was interviewed several times by the search committee and was then offered the position, which I accepted commencing January 1, 1976.

Before I was chosen, I knew that the lawyers and paralegals working in two hundred and fifty-eight local programs felt beaten down and dispirited. I also knew these public officials wanted a Legal Services Corporation president who had worked in the trenches of legal services over the past five years. As an outsider, they would naturally view me with some suspicion. I realized I needed to appoint as my deputy someone this group would immediately see as one of them.

When I was being considered as president, Crampton made clear that if I were chosen, all hiring would be under my sole control, and he had cleared this stance with all board members. As soon as I received word that I had been selected, I called my friend Clint Bamberger, former head of the White House Legal Services Program, and offered him the role of executive vice president. "I want you to be my alter ego," I told him. I knew that I would necessarily be particularly focused on dealing with the board, with Congress, and with creating public support for the program. He would, I said, be primarily concerned with program operations and internal issues.

To my great relief, Bamberger immediately and enthusiastically told me that he would be pleased to accept my offer. He never mentioned that he had originally been one of the finalists to be president and the one most qualified—certainly more than I was. In retrospect, I think he did not want me to think he viewed his new position as a consolation prize.

Years later, Bamberger gave me a framed quotation from a talk in South Africa by Robert F. Kennedy: "Each time a man stands up for an ideal, or acts to improve the lot of others, or strikes out against injustice, he sends forth a tiny ripple of hope, and crossing each other from a million different centers of energy and daring those ripples build a current which can sweep down the mightiest walls of oppression and resistance."

I still have that gift on my office wall, for it reminds me of the life that Clint Bamberger always lived, "striking out against injustice."

Ellen was initially wary of moving back to Washington, which is not an easy place for spouses of government officials. While I had a wonderful experience working in the Kennedy and Johnson administrations, she had a more difficult time with primary responsibility for raising our children. A decade later, we had three children—Paul, age ten; Elizabeth, age thirteen; and David, age sixteen. And again, I would be traveling extensively. But Ellen agreed to the move, recognizing that this was an extraordinary opportunity to launch a new federal agency focused on a critically important need in our country.

For a while, Ellen and our kids stayed in Palo Alto so they could finish the school year, and I returned to Palo Alto from Washington for a weekend every other week. During that time, I stayed in Washington with my friend and former colleague, Abba Schwartz, whom I had defended before the House Un-American Activities Committee and the Senate Internal Security Committee. He had a lovely house in Georgetown, and we became closer friends.

Our son, David, understandably wanted to finish his senior high school year at Palo Alto High, and fortunately, our friend Nancy Packer agreed to let him live in her guest room for that year. We worried about leaving him behind, but he stressed he was ready to be on his own, and in retrospect, I believe he was right. Meanwhile, Ellen and I, along with Elizabeth and Paul, moved to a house in Chevy Chase, Maryland, that we rented. In retrospect, I realize that the move was particularly hard for Paul—a new location, a new house, a new school, and at the outset, no friends.

The eleven-person Corporation Board represented a range of perspectives. A majority were conservatives who nonetheless believed that people in poverty deserved representation by a lawyer when faced with critical issues involving the law. When it was part of the White House Office of Economic Opportunity, federally funded legal services grew under President Johnson, but funding had been frozen at $74 million for the previous five years under President Nixon. This funding was supposed to pay for legal services to more than thirty million people living below the federally established poverty line.

In this period, local programs supported with federal legal-services funds were concentrated largely in urban areas along the East and West Coasts, for those were the areas where bar and other local groups were most receptive. As a result, many sections of the Midwest, South, and Southwest were without any legal help for people in poverty people except through the voluntary efforts of private attorneys.

Bamberger and I soon set about planning what would be needed for the Legal Services Corporation. The board was set to vote on our appointments at its meeting in October 1976. Crampton had talked with the board members who were not on the search committee, and he told me they were all enthusiastic about my appointment and understood that I would be responsible for all hiring.

Crampton suggested that we hold a reception right after the January board meeting and invite a large group of legal-services people, Congressional members and their staff, and others who might be helpful to the corporation. I would be sworn in as the new president and Bamberger as the executive vice president. Afterward, board members, Bamberger, and I would all have a chance to mingle with the guests at the reception.

With help from those in nearby legal-services programs, Bamberger and I put together a guest list and were delighted when more than five hundred people agreed to come to the reception in a downtown Washington hotel. I had asked US Supreme Court Justice Byron White to swear us into office. He and I became good friends when our families were together at the Salzburg Seminar in Austria, where he and I were both lecturing.

In the week before the board meeting, a conservative columnist named James J. Kilpatrick wrote an angry column that was printed in hundreds of newspapers. In the column, he bemoaned that I had been chosen—a liberal Democrat who had worked in the Kennedy and Johnson administrations. But much, much worse, he wrote, was the selection of Bamberger as executive vice president, for Bamberger was "pink." He wrote that Bamberger had misdirected the legal-services program in the Office of Economic Opportunity, and he would be a disastrous leader of the new federal effort.

The board met in the hotel where the reception was scheduled. They began with a luncheon, including Bamberger, me, and ten of the eleven board members. The eleventh, Judge Revius Ortique from New Orleans, the only Black appointee, was delayed getting to Washington. At about one o'clock that afternoon, Bamberger and I were asked to leave the meeting while the board briefly discussed and then voted on our appointments. Under the act establishing the corporation, board approval was required for both of us, but Crampton had assured me this was just a formality. So Bamberger and I left the meeting room and moved to a large area next door where the reception would be held.

At about two, Crampton came out, ashen-faced, and asked me to join him in a small room adjacent to where he had been having lunch with the rest of the board. When he closed the door, he told me that at least half of the board wanted me to withdraw Bamberger's name as "too divisive." I would be approved, they said, but only if I withdrew Bamberger's nomination. In effect, Crampton reported, these board members wanted a clean start for the corporation, and this would not be possible with Bamberger in a leadership position. I later learned that the Kilpatrick column was the key to this hardline stand.

I had to decide how to respond, and in retrospect, it was one of the morally critical moments in my professional life. I did not hesitate for an instant to tell Crampton that I could not serve as president without Bamberger as my partner. I had asked Bamberger to join me, and I could not go back on my personal commitment. I had a moral obligation to keep that commitment. I also said I could only do the job at the standard I thought necessary with Bamberger as my colleague.

"If you decide you don't want me," I told him, "Then I will do everything I can to help you find the right person, and in the interim, I will do everything I can to support legal services."

To his great credit, Crampton never suggested to me that I back away from my position in the greater interest of the organization. Rather, he immediately understood and replied, "I thought you would say that, and I will support you and do everything I can to ensure you are both approved." He then went back to the luncheon room, and I returned to sit with Bamberger.

In retrospect, I realize that I answered without considering several problems that would arise if the board decided to hold firm about Bamberger. Ellen and I had already moved to Washington and rented a home. I had resigned as dean at Stanford Law School, and a search was underway for a replacement, so I could not return to that position, although I could return as a professor there. The Legal Services Corporation, having struggled for well over a year to get started, would be without leadership for much longer while a new search was organized. What had happened would no doubt be well known in legal-services circles, so finding a new leader would not be easy. And so forth. But I considered none of these critically important matters—only my moral obligation to Bamberger and my need for his partnership if I were to be successful at president.

This was not, of course, the first time I have felt the importance of following my moral compass. But it was the first time when I had to make a career-determining decision based on it.

I came back to the reception room and told Bamberger what had happened. He immediately offered to withdraw his name. But I told him that he was exactly the right person for the corporation and me and that the corporation would either be led by both of us or by neither of us.

Time passed as Bamberger and I sat in the reception room, surrounded by mountains of food. At about three o'clock, I called Justice White to tell him he should not come to swear me into office.

"Gee, Tom, I hope it works out all right," he sympathized.

Bamberger and I then made lists of close friends who were coming. We called them between three-thirty and four o'clock, explained what happened, and gave each a list of other people to call to say the reception was canceled, but not to say why. We thought the news would get out soon enough, and there was no need to cause further agitation. We also called a local food kitchen and donated the food to it.

At around six o'clock, Crampton came out to say that the board was still talking, but it was now split five to five. Revius Ortique was expected late that night. Bamberger and I went to his house for dinner and a long wait. Finally, I received a call from Crampton at eleven o'clock to say that Ortique had arrived at the meeting and voted for both of us. We would be sworn in at a board meeting the next morning.

Bamberger and I arrived together the next morning, not quite sure what to expect. The board had voted six to five to confirm us. I thought our leadership could be severely handicapped in our new roles, particularly in dealing with the minority of the board who were against Bamberger. To my pleasant surprise, this was the last serious conflict I had with the board. All the members apparently decided that they should put the issue behind them. Ironically, having gotten off to such a rocky start, the board was unanimous in supporting Bamberger and me during a series of very controversial steps we took in the next three years.

Meanwhile, we enrolled Elizabeth and Paul in schools, and Ellen found a job she enjoyed as a fundraiser for an institute at George Washington University. She always could raise money for various civic causes we supported. She could connect with potential donors and enable them to understand how their financial support would make a difference in a program they cared about. After a couple of years in that position, Ellen shifted to working as a fundraiser for the National Portrait Gallery, part of the Smithsonian Institute. She had become a terrific fundraiser, a talent that stayed with her. Unlike many people, Ellen enjoys asking people to support a cause she cares about, and she has a rare ability to encourage others to feel it is a privilege to give to that cause.

As the first employee of a brand-new government entity, I knew I had a chance to engage in real institutional architecture, which I loved. Everything had to be done at once—a place to house what would be a large staff, hundreds of regulations, and a strategy to gain increased support from Congress. We were lucky that two incredible lawyers, Louis Oberdorfer (later a federal district judge) had been serving as acting corporation president, and David Tatel (later a federal court of appeals judge) was acting general counsel. Tatel continued to serve until our new general counsel, Alice Daniel, was chosen and could start work.

A prime example of the good work of these two interim leaders was when President Ford tried to withhold a share of the Congressionally appropriated funds for the corporation on the ground that the corporation was not fully operational during much of the year. Tatel brought suit in federal court, arguing that while the president could withhold expenditures by agencies of the Executive Branch, the corporation reported only to Congress and was immune from such action. Success in that suit helped enormously in establishing the corporation as a permanent part of the governmental landscape.

Also fortunately, one employee who knew the administrative side of legal services had stayed on the government payroll. His name was Alf Corbett. He turned out to be a close friend of Steve Walters, my former student, whom I hired as my special assistant. Walters and his wife, Mabsie, had stayed with our children when Ellen and I went for six weeks to Chile, and he was later a law clerk for Chief Justice Warren Burger. Bamberger and I used a hiring consultant named Arnie Miller, later head of the White House Office of Personnel for President Carter, to help us find the key people for the new corporation. An active union of legal-services lawyers also helped us.

We wanted a diverse staff. We wanted women, African Americans, and Hispanics. We certainly wanted some Republicans. It turned out that we had the hardest time finding the right people from the last group.

Over the first few months, most of my time and Bamberger's was spent picking the key senior staff. Some were relatively easy to identify. Alan Houseman was a leading person in research on legal services for people in poverty people, and his appointment was obvious as director of research. Others had not been directly involved in legal services but had been working in programs for impoverished people in other arenas. Alice Daniel became one of the many stars as general counsel. Mary Burnett and Judy Riggs were hired to help on the Hill. We also thought it was important to hire people who were working at the regional offices of the White House Legal Services Program, and these included Clint Lyons, Bucky Askew, and Charles Jones. And we needed someone in public affairs. Fortunately, much of our success was due to networking, which resulted in hiring Harriet Ellis as public affairs director, and several others.

One of the biggest challenges was to bring on board at least one sensible Republican in a leadership position, someone who was seen as a visible, conservative Republican. One of our most able board members was Bob Kutak, who had built one of the country's largest and most successful law firms in the country in Lincoln, Nebraska. Kutak knew Bucky Hennigan, who was on the staff of Nebraska Senator Hruska, a conservative Republican. Kutak recommended Hennigan as comptroller. He was terrific, giving us legitimacy in places where I might not have been allowed in the door without him.

Conservative Republicans in Congress put a cap on all corporation salaries, and as a result, I was earning far less than I had as dean at Stanford. Most of those I hired also took pay cuts. Given my compensation cut, the board of the corporation wanted to help me in every way it could while following the statute that established the corporation and also set my salary. The board proposed that I have the free use of a modest-sized car, which would be helpful for me in driving to and from work and visiting legal-services offices but could also be used for my own purposes. One day, not long after I started, a front-page article in *The Washington Post* criticized the Board for authorizing the car and me for accepting its use. It suggested that the head of a program to help people in poverty should not have the free use of a car. On reflection, I think the article was right.

I knew that within a few weeks of taking office on January 1, 1976, I would need to fashion a budget proposal to Congress for the next fiscal year. As I mentioned earlier, funding for the federal program to support civil legal services had been frozen under the Nixon administration for five years while inflation had risen by over 30 percent. Increasing funding for legal services would be my key priority. I knew an increase was essential if the new corporation was to meet its statutory mandate to support legal services for people living below the poverty line.

We also had to grapple with the reality that there were some places in the United States where an impoverished person was totally deprived of legal-services, and some places where low-income people didn't get an even break, but at least there was a legal-services program to help them. What would be our strategy to deal with the unevenness of legal-services operations across the country? Would we say, "Let's hold up until we can fill in the gaps?" or would we strengthen existing programs that had been under the budget gun for years?

I set out to visit all members of Congress or their staff who had any role in funding legal services for people in poverty . My preliminary talks convinced me that we needed a simple message. I knew that about a third of Congress would fully support the program as long as we could show it was efficient and effective. Another third would never approve, no matter how powerful our arguments. The middle third was the key. Those members of Congress were skeptical, but my initial soundings persuaded me that we could gain their support if we developed a simple message with a potent rationale. "More funding" alone would not satisfy those who were skeptical. The skeptics included both Democrats and Republicans.

Bamberger, Corbett, and I struggled for most of a weekend to find a message until Corbett mentioned that there were eleven lawyers per ten thousand people in the United States, but far less than two lawyers per ten thousand impoverished people. I immediately realized that this potent fact could be the key to our funding request. We called it the "minimum access" plan. Over the next four years, we wanted to increase funding for civil legal services in the United States until there were at least two lawyers per ten thousand people in poverty.

Fortunately, this seemingly simple solution worked marvelously. The plan had key advantages—anyone could understand it, and it sounded reasonable. Mary Burdette was in charge of governmental relations, and she did a masterful job of steering me up and down the halls of Congress for day after day, talking with members and their staff one by one. "We are not asking for legal services at a level equivalent to what is available to the rest of our citizenry," I stressed. "We are only seeking 'minimum access'—less than a fifth of that amount, or two lawyers per ten thousand." This was the essence of the "minimum access" plan, though we had to work out complex formulas so that those sections of the country, particularly in the Northeast and on the West Coast, with more than this level would not be reduced. Indeed, they also needed increases to cover inflation, though the increases could not come as rapidly as new support for those sections of the country, particularly in the South and Southwest, with little or no federal support.

We set this goal of "minimum access" as our target over a four-year period. Congress supported the plan, and within the four years, funding increased first to $92.3 million, and then to more than $321 million. At that point, about sixty-two hundred lawyers and twenty-eight hundred paralegals were serving in 323 programs throughout the country. There were Congressional opponents, of course, but they were largely confined to proposing restrictions on the abilities of legal-services lawyers to provide help in specific areas of the law. From the outset, these lawyers were precluded from work on matters involving nontherapeutic abortions, selective service, and educational desegregation. Fortunately, there were public-interest law firms willing to bring those cases, and we did not have to raise what seemed to me and many others a substantial constitutional issue. Each year, we beat back efforts to expand that list of restrictions, though Congress did add a restraint on the representation of people known to be in the US illegally.

In that brief period, the overwhelming majority of Congress came to understand that our legal system could not operate fairly if impoverished people were denied access because they could not afford the costs of a private lawyer. We showed that these services were most often needed because individuals living below the poverty line faced an acute crisis. We produced compelling evidence of the consequences for low-income people when, for example, they were unlawfully fired from their jobs, removed as tenants from their homes, or denied Social Security or unemployment benefits. We successfully argued that our legal system depended on access to civil legal services.

Luckily, a significant share of moderate Republicans and Democrats were persuaded that funding civil legal services was a sound alternative to the blood on the streets—at least figuratively—that could result from people in poverty being disenfranchised from the legal system.

Many of those Republicans opposed other programs that resulted from President Johnson's War on Poverty. But they saw legal services as different: they were "leveling the playing field" in an arena where access to justice was involved.

Even with "minimum access" secured, however, I knew that many impoverished people would be denied civil legal services unless members of the private bar agreed to give some of their time and talents pro bono to help. A second key priority was to persuade private lawyers that this was an essential part of their responsibilities. I argued that the public had granted them a monopoly on the delivery of legal services. In return for that monopoly, the public was entitled to expect that people in poverty would be served without a fee. Bar associations throughout the country supported this view, as did the American Bar Association (ABA). I worked closely with ABA leaders to strengthen legal services. Not every lawyer agreed, of course, and some accused me of demanding "involuntary servitude." But the general response from private lawyers was extremely positive.

When private lawyers were reluctant to give their time and talents to help impoverished people with legal problems, to my surprise, they often said, "I don't know anything about housing law or Social Security benefits." When I responded that we offered short courses that helped practicing lawyers learn what they needed to know in those fields, the lawyers said, "people in poverty would not be comfortable with me." What they really meant, I finally realized, was that they would not be comfortable talking with impoverished people because they had never done that, particularly if those people were Black or Brown. I came away from this experience convinced that educational opportunities were needed for students to engage with people in poverty and this insight stayed with me when I returned to higher education administration.

A third key priority at the Legal Services Corporation was to work through these closely related issues: Why should taxpayers support civil legal services in relation to other public programs designed to help impoverished people? And since the available funding could not possibly cover all the legal needs of those people, how should the funds be allocated? I knew that the rationale for providing federal funding for civil legal services should be tied to the allocation process if it was to be persuasive as a matter of public policy. Strange as it may seem, virtually no attention was focused on the issue when the Legal Services Corporation was created. The hearings and debates in Congress on the act that was finally adopted consumed several thousand pages. The corporation's structure, how board members would be chosen, and scores of procedural issues were endlessly debated. But the underlying questions—Why legal services? How do we allocate limited resources?—were not asked in any searching way,

A particularly vexing issue was the extent to which legal-services programs should engage in efforts to reform the legal system to minimize the legal problems facing low-income people. Many within the legal-services community argued that since there would never be enough funding to adequately serve all impoverished people, primary attention should be focused on law reform. They made the case that instead of an endless stream of lawsuits to protect tenants in poverty from eviction, for example, legal services programs should concentrate on reforming housing laws to increase legal protections for these tenants. On the other side, both within and outside the legal-services community, many argued that direct service to clients was the statutory purpose of the corporation, and law reform efforts would inevitably result in reductions in funding by Congress. On this and many other issues, Bamberger and I tried to lead the corporation on a careful path between extremes.

In contrast to the closed room in which Corbett, Bamberger, and I devised the "minimum access" plan that served the corporation so well, I thought it essential to have open and extended discussions about this "why" issue and its natural corollary, "How should limited funds be allocated?" by a legal-services program. If the answer to the "why" question is that legal services are an effective means to ameliorate poverty, then law reform should be a key, if not the primary, goal of those services. On the other hand, if the answer is that the hurdles imposed by the legal system should not be insurmountable due to poverty, then priority should be given to providing legal services in those situations when a client has no choice but to use those services—when one is sued, for example. We debated openly and at length these and other responses to the fundamental issue: Why should the federal government fund civil legal services for low-income people?

Over many months, the board held extensive hearings on the issues. Councils made up of impoverished people were formed for each legal-services program to consider those issues. Ultimately, the board and I concluded, with the full approval of those working in local programs, that the client council should determine priorities for each program. As a result, housing issues might be dominant in New York, for example, while Indigenous land claims were the priority in Hawaii. When we developed this approach, only one group vehemently opposed it—the Boston Bar Association, which argued that clients could not possibly know enough to judge how scarce legal services should be allocated. But over time, even that group came to accept our position.

These were not the only major issues I dealt with as president of the Legal Services Corporation. A Congresswoman from Oregon named Edith Green caused the most important single political struggle we faced. She included a provision in the Legal Services Corporation Act that precluded backup centers. That umbrella phrase referred to a series of legal-services offices that did specialized work—one in housing law, one in family law, one in administrative benefits like Social Security, and so forth. In all, there were perhaps eight or ten backup centers, each doing vitally important work in support of local legal-services offices facing particularly difficult cases.

I asked David Tatel, who had served as interim general counsel, to write an extensive memorandum on the law—what the provision precluded and what it allowed. Under his interpretation, we could effectively do everything we were then doing as long as we did not label the doers backup centers. So, I announced that we would eliminate all backup centers.

In a separate action, I announced that we would fund a set of support centers to do essentially the same work. We were not quite that crude—we made a few changes. Training, for example, had been under the aegis of a backup center, and we brought it in-house, a move that I thought wise in all events. Edith Green was not deceived by what we were doing and screamed, but to no avail. An absolutely critical piece of legal services was saved.

Alice Daniels, our general counsel, and Steve Walters, my special assistant, needed to prepare a substantial set of regulations about allocating funds to legal-services programs across the country and the operations of the programs that received those funds. We worked with a council of legal-services lawyers, who often pushed back in response to draft regulations that seemed overly burdensome to them. We knew that opponents of federally funded legal-services programs would delight in stories of mistakes by those programs. But we also knew that the programs were operating under great pressure to serve their clients adequately. Lengthy and complex regulations made their work much more difficult. Finding the right balance between these pressures was a continuing challenge.

The act creating the corporation called for a study to determine whether it might be more efficient to fund private lawyers directly to offer the services provided by legal-services lawyers. It was no surprise that many legal-services lawyers were deeply concerned by this provision. But we also knew Congress would hammer us if we failed to carry out a completely impartial study. We hired Leona Vogt, an outstanding social science researcher from the Urban Institute, to do the study. She hired teams of lawyers throughout the country to visit legal-services offices and compare the files of cases to comparable cases by private lawyers. We were particularly helped in organizing this study by Joel Hyatt, founder of Hyatt Legal Services, which provides private legal counsel for people of moderate means on issues such as wills and divorces. All of us at the Corporation gave a sigh of relief when the Vogt report made clear that staff attorneys at legal-services offices provided as good or better legal counsel than private attorneys and at lower costs.

This and other tough matters involved time, energy, and effort for my three years as president of the Legal Services Corporation. Fortunately, this was a very successful time for the corporation, one that legal-services lawyers often refer to as "the golden years." President

Ford was in office for the first half of my tenure and President Carter for the second, but in both administrations, the corporation gained substantially in funding and maintained its independence from the White House.

During those years, I also traveled to almost every state in the union, and every place I went, I saw the most impoverished sections, urban and rural. Until then, I had never walked into a room full of hundreds and hundreds of people where everyone was Black, Latino, or living in poverty except for me. In every state, I met and worked with extraordinary lawyers dedicating their professional lives to helping impoverished people while enduring low wages, terrible working conditions, and enormous caseloads.

Once, I went to Jackson, Mississippi, and spent a long night with two African American legal-services lawyers struggling against bigotry there. The next morning, I had breakfast with the Mississippi Bar Association leaders, all white, who took turns telling jokes about how they had tricked Black people (using the N-word) in lawsuits.

I traveled to Alaska shortly after two legal-services lawyers won an Alaska Supreme Court suit declaring that not having high schools for Inuit kids violated the Alaskan Constitution. We traveled around the Aleutian Islands in snowmobiles, listening to Inuit elders debate whether high schools in Alaska—would they be *real* high schools?—would be better than high schools in Sitka or Oklahoma. Would their kids ever come back?

In the spring of 1978, my colleagues and I felt we had met our initial goals for the corporation regarding funding, structural arrangements, staffing, regulations, and other key objectives. It was time to look hard at the challenges the corporation would face over the next five years and how to best meet those challenges.

The "minimum access plan" was a success, but it left many issues unaddressed. We began with a discussion paper on the broad issues facing the corporation's future. After lengthy discussions with the board, it approved a major strategic planning process. Five further discussion papers were prepared on the major clusters of challenges. Then task forces comprised of legal-services lawyers, legal-services clients, private lawyers, board members, and others met to analyze the issues and develop recommendations.

A more than two-hundred-page volume titled *Next Steps for the Legal Services Corporation* was then published. Meetings were held across the country to discuss the recommendations and seek consensus. Out of this lengthy and complex process came a set of short-term objectives for the next two years and longer-term aims for the three following years. It was an ambitious set of plans, but I was convinced it established a realistic set of stretch goals, and I was eager to lead the corporation in the effort to achieve those goals.

I loved my time in legal services. I learned an enormous amount about life, myself, and the human condition. I learned how important legal services were and how responsive lawyers could be to helping people in poverty if we worked at it. I learned in aching detail about the human face of poverty in America. I saw and heard firsthand the challenges low-income people faced, challenges that too often were exacerbated rather than eased by the legal system.

Leading the Legal Services Corporation also gave me an essential, unique experience in institutional planning. Thorough planning of all aspects of the organization had been crucial because we were starting afresh, although building on an old base. I often drew on that experience while serving as provost at the University of Pennsylvania and president at Indiana University. The three years had been an incredibly moving and educational experience.

12

Sisyphus

Three years after moving back to Washington from California, our family was well settled. Ellen had an excellent job as a fundraiser for the National Portrait Gallery, reporting directly to the director of the gallery, Marvin Sadik. The gallery's mission is to acquire and display portraits of individuals who contributed to the development of our country's history and culture. She enjoyed meeting an interesting array of individuals, some of whom were being considered for portraits in the gallery and others who were financial contributors. She also worked from time to time with S. Dillon Ripley, who was in charge of the entire Smithsonian complex for two decades and helped transform it from what was called "America's attic" to a vibrant and popular part of the Washington cultural scene.

For a time, Ellen was also a fundraiser for the School of Advanced International Studies, part of Johns Hopkins University. In that role, she learned a good deal about foreign-policy issues and met many of those who worked in that arena.

Meanwhile, our son David, who stayed in Palo Alto to finish high school, decided to learn to fly. With our enthusiastic approval, he got a job cleaning hangers at the Palo Alto Airport in exchange for flying lessons. He soloed and then, with earnings from other part-time jobs, bought a fifth interest in a single-engine plane. When it was time to register for courses at Chico State University, where he would be a student for the next three and a half years, he flew his plane there, no doubt the only freshman ever to do so.

Our daughter, Elizabeth, attended Cathedral School, a girls' school where she actively participated in many activities. She did extremely well in her academic courses through her senior year and was admitted to Stanford University.

Ellen and I faced a moral dilemma when Elizabeth was sixteen and came home one day to tell us that one of her classmates and a good friend was pregnant. The girl desperately wanted to have an abortion but knew her parents would forbid it. Would Ellen and I arrange the abortion without telling her parents? After a lengthy discussion, Ellen and I agreed to do so. Ellen took the girl to a Planned Parenthood clinic. The girl had an abortion, and her parents never knew. Since then, Ellen and I have reflected on our dilemma from time to time, and while we continue to believe we made the right decision, we understand that many would make a different one.

Paul, our youngest son, attended Western School, a public school in our neighborhood. I am dyslexic, and unlike his siblings, Paul inherited this malady. Fortunately, there are ways to work around it, and he did that extremely well throughout his school years.

President Carter took office in 1976 and appointed five new board members for the Legal Services Corporation. While they included both Republicans and Democrats, as required by statute, all of them were far more liberal than the board appointed by Ford. They included some of my Washington friends, such as Mickey Kantor, a former legal-services lawyer active in Democratic politics, and Steve Engelberg, who was legislative counsel to then-Senator Walter Mondale. Another appointee was Hillary Clinton, then wife of the governor of Arkansas, Bill Clinton. She was soon chosen as chair of the board. She was just thirty-six years old and brilliant, both in helping shape policies and in keeping the board together so that decisions continued to be by consensus.

It was fun to have board members whose political views were similar to mine. At the same time, those board members often wanted the Legal Services Corporation to use lawsuits to reshape the legal system to help low-income people. We did this, to a degree, through cases from the backup centers I mentioned. Those centers took on complex litigation that was too difficult and time-consuming for a local legal-services program to handle.

At the same time, the politics of steering the corporation in terms of Congress became more difficult because I no longer had as many conservative Republicans on the board who could make a persuasive case to Republicans on the Hill. Roger Crampton, in particular. was especially helpful in this way. He and several other conservative board members testified before Congressional committees with me. They would look Republicans in the eye and assure them that this program was doing good things and that it was what basic constitutional rights and liberties are all about in our democracy. They repeated this message over and over again, and Republicans in the Senate and the House paid attention to them. With this new board, however, I lacked that critical means of garnering conservative support.

My job at the Legal Services Corporation was not done. We had outlined an ambitious agenda in the "Next Steps" report that was prepared with broad support from the legal-services community. Our budget had more than tripled in three years, one year ahead of schedule. The corporation was funding 335 programs across the country that operated out of about 900 offices.

After reflection, I decided that the only move that would take me away from leading the Legal Services Corporation would be another position in public service, ideally working for the president. President Carter had two years left in his first term, and I admired his achievements enormously, particularly in foreign policy. Further, he was a man of extraordinary integrity and had helped strengthen the sense around the world that the United States took the moral high ground in its foreign-policy decisions.

At that point in 1978, the possibility of President Carter being reelected was uncertain at best. If he lost in 1980, I knew I would lose the opportunity to work directly for a president for at least another four years. Further, as many of my friends in Washington reminded me, the possibility of being chosen for such a position under

President Carter or some future president was slim. As one friend said, "It's a total craps game, driven by luck." The landscape of Washington was strewn with people who wanted presidential appointments and didn't get them. Timing, networking, and good fortune were essential but were not guarantees to land such a position. The same is true today.

Other job opportunities did come my way during this period, but—fortunately, in hindsight—none worked out. Either I didn't want them or was not offered the position. Most surprisingly, being the president of the Metropolitan Museum of Art was one of those positions. I told the search firm representative I had no background for the job except that my mother worked in an art museum. But he insisted that I at least meet with C. Douglas Dillon, former secretary of the Treasury and chair of the museum board. I agreed, and over lunch at a posh New York City men's club, I quickly learned that Dillon wanted someone to run the business side of the museum while Phillipe de Montebello was in charge of art. I rejected the position before leaving the lunch table.

I was also nominated for the presidencies of the Ford Foundation, Yale University, New York University, and the University of Wisconsin system, but I or "they" decided the fit was not right. Thanks to Lloyd Cutler, a good friend and counselor to President Carter, I was one of two finalists for the Yale position.

When I was dean of Stanford Law School, I had been asked to consider being dean of Yale Law School, but Ellen and I rejected the idea. Ellen and I were dubious about a move to New Haven if I were asked to be president, but we decided it would be worth finding out more. Bill Bundy, who was on the presidential search committee and whom I had come to disrespect during my State Department days because of his stand on the Vietnam war, invited me to meet with the "corporation," the governing board at Yale.

"Ellen and I would be delighted to come visit," I said.

"Oh," he responded, "It is not necessary for your wife to accompany you. If we chose you, there will be plenty of time for her to come see the house."

"If I were to take the job," I answered, becoming increasingly annoyed, "My wife and I would be a team, and I would not think of going for the interview without her."

"A spouse coming for an interview has never been in the corporation room," Bundy replied.

"Well," I said, "that is your decision. Either she comes, or I am not interested."

Bundy called a few hours later to report that Ellen could join me but that we would both have to sneak in through the servants' entrance, which we did. The first question a corporation member asked me was, "What will you do about the difficulties at the Divinity School?" Naturally, I had read a good deal about the challenges facing Yale, but nothing suggested that the Divinity School was in trouble. The school was founded to train Christian ministers, and I later wondered if I had been asked the question because I was a Jew. In any case, Bart Giamatti was chosen and became a successful Yale president.

During my time in legal services, I was also asked to consider whether I might want to stay in public service as a federal appellate judge. In 1978, the former dean of the Harvard Law School, Erwin Griswold, called to suggest that I allow my name to be put forward for possible appointment to the US Court of Appeals for the District of Columbia Circuit. Griswold was chair of a special committee appointed to screen nominees, and he said that my background was ideal for the job. I was flattered but knew that my temperament was not suited to the role of a full-time judge. My clerkship with Judge Hand led me to understand that an appellate judge must allow issues to be formulated by lawyers for the litigants and not take a position except in response. This would have been too passive a role for me. Fortunately for the country, my Harvard Law School classmate Ruth Bader Ginsburg was ultimately nominated for the position and then for the Supreme Court, where she became one of the great justices of our time.

I had come to know and admire Cyrus Vance, then secretary of state, and Warren Christopher, deputy secretary. Christopher had been a major figure at Stanford Law School and was very supportive of my work in legal services. I regarded him as a wonderful human being and close friend. Vance was a leading figure in the New York Bar Association and was equally helpful in promoting legal services for people experiencing poverty.

Having worked with both George W. Ball and Dean Rusk, two men with different temperaments and perspectives on almost every issue, I always thought it was a mistake for President Carter to choose two people with similar outlooks and personalities to be in charge of the State Department. Both were pragmatic, cautious, case-by-case lawyers. Neither believed in a grand vision, though both were deeply committed to helping developing countries and promoting human rights.

One day in 1978, Warren Christopher called me out of the blue to say President Carter wanted to nominate me to become director of a new federal agency, the International Development Cooperation Agency (IDCA), reporting directly to the president. It seemed my dream had come true. I told Christopher I was very interested, and we met to discuss the opportunity.

Carter was deeply concerned, Christopher said, that too much foreign aid, both bilateral and multilateral, was being wasted on uncoordinated projects that were promoted by someone in the Agency for International Development (AID), the State Department, or another federal agency without any overall strategy. Foreign aid was often allocated, he continued, for what he termed "walking around money" for a foreign official whom a US official wanted to influence. Carter also believed that the extent to which a developing country respects human rights, along with a focus on long-term development, should be key factors in our foreign-aid policies. As deputy secretary of state, Christopher agreed enthusiastically with Carter's position.

Christopher told me that IDCA would be responsible for bilateral assistance through AID, the Department of Agriculture, and other US agencies and coordinating all multilateral foreign aid through US contributions to the World Bank and regional banks such as the Inter-American Development Bank. In addition, IDCA would be responsible for the Overseas Private Investment Corporation (OPIC) and a new Institute for Scientific and Technological Cooperation (ISTC). OPIC was, and still is, useful in promoting economic growth in developing

countries and emerging markets by encouraging US private investment in those countries. But the latter agency was never established
while I was IDCA director. In all events, it was clear that IDCA's main
job was overall responsibility for all aspects of US foreign aid.

I told Christopher that I would discuss the offer with Ellen and be
back in touch with him the next day. That night, Ellen and I talked
about this potential new position. We were both enthusiastic. I had
co-taught international law and economic development with Gerry
Meier, a Stanford economist, and knew a fair amount about the field.
I agreed strongly with Carter's twin priorities of long-term economic
development and human rights. The work I would be doing would
reflect, on an international level, the same values that brought me
to legal services for people in poverty in the United States. I would
be in charge of a new federal agency, just as I had been in launching
the Legal Services Corporation. And the chance to report directly to
President Carter would be a once-in-a-lifetime opportunity. The next
day, I told Christopher that I would accept the position, subject to
meeting with President Carter and hearing directly how he envisioned
my responsibilities.

A few days later, I met with the president in the Oval Office. He
knew a good deal about my background and reiterated what Christopher had told me. I was impressed by his emphasis on the need to help
impoverished people in developing countries. He briefly referred to
his early days in Plains, Georgia, surrounded by poverty.

Sometime later, Carter sent me a typed letter concerning the agenda
I had set for IDCA, and the budget needed to carry out that agenda.
Underneath his signature, he wrote by hand, "Tom, You are the boss.
Act boldly re bureaucratic coordination and efficiency. I'll back you
up. Keep me informed re problems & progress." I was—and remain—
convinced that the president was totally committed to his foreign-aid
aims.

What I had not realized was the depth of resistance to those aims
that I would find not only in Congress but also inside every agency I
worked with in the federal government. There were certainly many
strong supporters, including Vance and Christopher. But some thought

the only valid use of foreign aid was to support key US foreign-policy objectives, particularly those involving our national security.

Long-term aid, as opposed to short-term opportunistic aid alloca-tion, had periodically been a goal of past US leaders since the end of WWII, though they often failed. But furthering international human rights was a new foreign-aid objective for a president. It meant stop-ping foreign aid to countries that failed to protect the basic human rights of those within their borders.

In his 1976 campaign, Carter stressed the need to infuse morality into American foreign policy. Most important, he emphasized that support for human rights had to be a bedrock principle. In his inaugu-ral address, he underscored that human rights would be center stage in his administration. "Because we are free, we can never be indifferent to the fate of freedom elsewhere. Our moral sense dictates a clear-cut preference for those societies which share with us an abiding respect for individual human rights."

The president told me he knew I would be facing intense bureau-cratic infighting to resist a new agency trying to take over what mul-tiple different agencies had been doing. But he assured me he would support me. I did not fully realize the extent of the bureaucratic bat-tles I would face until I learned that fifteen different agencies were not only concerned with foreign aid but also felt they should be able to make decisions about the allocation of that aid. In some ways, dealing with multilateral aid was even more complicated because not only was forging agreement within the US Government—including Congress—necessary, but agreement was also required with the members of the multilateral organizations such as the World Bank and regional banks.

When I accepted the position as the first director of IDCA, I had not realized that the legislation establishing the new agency faced tough opposition from many Republicans in Congress. In essence, the op-ponents argued that a new agency was not needed to carry out goals that should be achieved by the existing agencies working together. The House and Senate approved the legislation, though by closer votes than the White House had expected. The act passed, in large part, because it was backed by Republican Senator Jacob Javits, who brought many Republicans with him.

The president had appointed Ambassador at Large Henry Owen as the White House liaison with IDCA. Owen was a brilliant foreign-policy analyst and had been director of policy planning for the State Department. We talked together before I formally accepted the position, for I knew he would see and comment on my memoranda to the president about specific issues. His primary responsibilities as ambassador at large were to organize a series of economic summits with countries around the world.

I liked Owen, and I knew his close working relationship with Carter could be helpful to me. But I was concerned that he did not seem to understand much about legislative politics, and I knew that many in Congress had strong views about the allocation of foreign aid. However, I decided I could work with him and believed, rightly as it turned out, that my experiences advocating for the Legal Services Corporation in Congress would help me. At Ellen's request, I told him that she knew my job would place burdens on her, and she wanted one perk that I needed him to arrange. That was an invitation to a state dinner in the White House. He laughed and promised to make that happen.

Soon after the passage of the legislation, Owen told me that part of the deal to gain congressional approval was that I could not be the administrator in charge of the Agency for International Development and IDCA director. I went along with that decision, which, in retrospect, was a mistake, though I probably could not have changed it. I would have been in a stronger position to gain support for the president's priorities if I had had direct authority over the AID budget and activities. In theory, I could overrule any AID decision, but in practice, I had less control than I would have wanted.

Shortly after Congress passed the legislation, I was confirmed by the Senate, as was the new head of AID, Doug Bennett, the former assistant secretary of state for Congressional Affairs. Bennett and I quickly developed a strong working relationship and became good friends.

Once again, I was the first employee of a new federal agency. Realizing that the job might last only two years (which turned out to be true), I moved as quickly as possible to hire and borrow staff. This time, the four senior people who would report to me needed Senate confirmation and FBI clearances, and the process seemed to take forever. Some I asked to work for me would say, "I'd like to do this, but I'm not going to go through that protracted ordeal." Others were reluctant to leave their jobs for what looked like a short stint in the federal government. Fortunately, over time, we put together a viable staff. Some came from the State Department, while others had worked at nonprofit organizations. Jessica Einhorn, who later became dean of the School of Advanced International Studies, was an example of the talented team I was eventually able to attract to IDCA.

Our first major cluster of tasks was to decide on the priority sectors for allocating foreign aid. We did this with a lot of jockeying and close collaboration with Owen and others in the White House staff, as well as other agencies, particularly the State and Treasury Departments. The four sectors we chose were food and agriculture, energy, health, and population. We also identified four cross-sector emphases that deserved priority attention: women in development, scientific and technological cooperation, natural resources and environmental management, and capital-saving technologies.

President Carter was unfailingly engaged with the new agency and supportive of my efforts. He often knew, in detail—actually, as it turned out, often too much detail—about particular grants and reports. He periodically called me to ask about aid to an individual country. One call I remember focused on Mali and the severity of poverty in that country.

Carter has often been accused of being a micromanager, and from my own experiences, this seemed to be true, particularly in budget meetings. All other department and agency heads and I had to develop detailed budgets for each year and present them to the Office of Management and Budget. The president often attended or sent questions to be asked on his behalf. At the same time, his attention to the difficult times individual developing countries were facing underscored the depth of his compassion and commitment to help alleviate the problems those countries were facing.

Owen always reviewed the memoranda I wrote to the president about issues, and sometimes, he asked for comments from other department and agency heads before giving them to the president. Whenever possible, of course, I first reviewed a memorandum with key agencies involved to obtain their support before sending it to the White House. Partly because Vance and Christopher had chosen me for the position, I could regularly count on their support. I regularly attended meetings of the State Department senior staff and was often able to resolve issues there. But the Treasury and Agriculture Departments regularly presented objections to my proposals, and extended negotiations were needed to resolve those objections. Sometimes, the president had to resolve them. Over time, I learned to fashion memoranda to the White House suggesting three options, with the middle option being the one I supported.

The good parts about the job were heading a Cabinet-level agency reporting directly to the president, along with the new experience of leading delegations at international meetings and representing the interests of the United States in negotiations in those meetings. I felt I was contributing to the president's goals and helping both meet the often dire economic needs of developing countries and enhance human rights in those countries. I traveled extensively in Africa, Asia, and Latin America, and with that travel came opportunities to learn a great deal about poverty in developing countries. I had little sense of the grinding reality of poverty in much of those regions until I visited, for example, Calcutta and Bombay in India and Bangladesh.

I also witnessed firsthand how much long-term good foreign aid can do for developing countries. For example, we helped promote new strains of wheat and rice in India so that that nation could achieve food self-sufficiency. There was also an enormous push for pre- and post-natal health care, and I saw the utility of simple ways to reduce mortality from diarrhea among new infants.

The powerful impact of private, voluntary organizations overseas also became clear to me. My preconceived notion that missionaries' primary task was to convert people was dispelled after spending time with Catholic and Lutheran missionaries in really tough arenas where they helped provide clean water and shelter. I was not responsible for the Peace Corps, but I spent time with Corps members at work. For example, I watched one team of Corps members in Africa who had designed a closed stove made out of mud that used one-tenth of the fuel burned by open-air stoves. What a difference that invention was making in countering deforestation.

I also learned that not all foreign aid was actually useful, however well-intentioned. An extreme example was that one of the persons responsible for the AID population sector launched a program for US planes to literally drop packages of free condoms over heavily populated areas. It soon became evident that villagers who found the condoms used them for everything except their intended purposes. On the other hand, success resulted from training nurses to travel to villages, explain the use of contraceptives to women (who would explain it to their husbands), and charge a very modest fee so that they would be understood as worth something.

I also had a number of opportunities to work with the president in person instead of just via memoranda. One occurred soon after I started the job. I was invited to a working breakfast with the president to discuss foreign-aid policy. I sat to his immediate right and so was served next. The waiter asked if I wanted grits, and I almost said, "Of course not," only to realize that grits were a Georgia staple. On another occasion, I sat with Jody Powell, the White House press secretary, and the president, watching each take bags of peanuts and pour them into glasses of Coca-Cola before swigging the whole mess down in a few gulps.

The enormous downside of the job was that, except for the president, few people in Washington—Republicans and Democrats— wanted IDCA to exist. Few senior federal officials, apart from Vance and Christopher, truly supported the two priorities of long-term development and human rights with the fierce determination of the president. Those priorities were fine, I often heard, as long as others were also recognized.

Many officials resented my stepping into their agencies' responsibilities and telling them they could not do what they wanted because

their proposed actions or inactions were inconsistent with the president's two priorities. Those in the Treasury thought that I, a young
upstart, was stealing their right to set policies for the World Bank, the
International Monetary Fund, and the regional development banks.
The same was true of the Department of Agriculture in terms of food
aid and for the US Special Trade Representative responsible for US
trade policy. I recall a particularly bitter struggle at a conference in
Rome of the World Health Programme. I stayed at the residence of
the US ambassador to Italy, which is the most elegant of all the ambas-
sadorial residences I visited. The ambassador, Richard Gardner, was
a friend from when we both taught international law, he at Columbia
University. I left his palatial home each morning to engage in fierce
battles with the Department of Agriculture, which essentially wanted
to ignore international human rights in allocating food assistance.

Even Christopher and Vance sometimes seemed to find IDCA more
of an impediment than a plus. Of course, they supported its pillars of
human rights and long-term economic development. But they sometimes saw my new agency as an obstacle because they needed foreign-
aid money to deal with policy hot spots around the world.

Those in the State Department with specific country duties thought
I was trying to steal the money they needed for their specific foreign-
policy objectives. Once, Assistant Secretary of State Richard Holbrooke, a man I respected, became furious because I was blocking
his demand that foreign aid be used to support an African leader. I
rejected it because the aid would not further long-term economic development and would be to a country with a terrible human rights
record. In Holbrooke's view, the funds were essential to persuade that
leader to do something in US interests. He stood in front of me, nose
to nose, and screamed.

Carter, on the other hand, was extremely kind to me and solicitous
of how I was doing. He realized I had few influential supporters, except for him, for the two pillars of his foreign-aid approach. They were
a tough sell, but I was firm in pressing those pillars in my foreign-aid
decision-making. Doing so won me no friends inside the federal government or overseas. Over sometimes strident objections, I vetoed

aid to a country if it had a bad human rights record or the aid was not connected to long-term economic development.

During that time, I stayed in the residences of thirty ambassadors around the world. Some yelled and screamed at me because I didn't want to do what they wanted to do with foreign aid. For example, when I left Brasilia, the US ambassador to Brazil held a large public ceremony to say goodbye. We had argued for most of the four days I stayed at his residence. He wanted foreign aid for short-term issues involving influencing current Brazilian policies. Of course, I did not agree. He knew I didn't smoke and had just a carry-on suitcase. With great fanfare, in front of dozens of senior staff, he presented me with a huge onyx ashtray weighing thirty or so pounds. The ambassador knew I'd have to lug this heavy thing around for the rest of my trip across Central and South America. Afterward, I laughed at his clever ploy. But at the time, I was furious.

I felt like Sisyphus while heading IDCA, more than I've ever felt before or since. Intense centrifugal pressures exploded in all directions, with a lot of extreme bureaucratic infighting, especially with the Treasury Department. Disputes with other agency heads became epic, spawning memo after memo after memo. Those with whom I crossed verbal swords often seemed to argue just to win rather than to further the public interest. I lost as many of those battles as I won—perhaps more.

During my time at IDCA, I was chosen to be the 1979–1980 president of the Harvard Alumni Association. One of the benefits of that role was helping choose the Commencement speaker. Early in the fall, Harvard President Derek Bok, formerly my Harvard Law School teacher, called to say that he thought inviting a public official to speak would be a good idea. If we will have a public official, I said, why not ask Carter? Bok asked if I thought he would come. I did not know, I told him, but I would ask.

A week later, I had a chance to ask the president. He responded that he had promised Tip O'Neill, then Speaker of the House, that if he spoke at any New England commencements, it would be at Boston College. So I called Bok and told him that Carter was not available. But, I asked, what about Secretary of State Cyrus Vance, whom I knew well? Bok thought that was a great idea. I said I assumed Vance would receive an honorary degree at the ceremony, and Bok assured me that would happen.

The next morning, I went to Vance's State Department office and told him that while I knew he was a loyal Yale alumnus, Harvard University would be proud to have him as its commencement speaker and that he would receive an honorary degree at the ceremony. Vance responded that he would be delighted to accept, and I then called Bok with the good news.

About forty-eight hours later, I received an angry call from Andrew Heiskell, chairman and CEO of *Time Magazine* and a member of the Harvard Corporation. "You have a problem," he told me. "Harvard's policy is not to give sitting government officials an honorary degree. You must tell Secretary Vance that he will not receive one." I said I did not have a problem, for Harvard's president had confirmed that Vance would receive the honorary degree. If Harvard had the policy he described before, the president had changed it. Heiskell was obviously not happy but said I would be hearing more later.

Sure enough, Bok called me the next day, embarrassed, and said that the Harvard policy could not be altered. He asked me to help him in a most difficult situation. I agreed to tell Vance that he would not, after all, receive an honorary degree when he spoke at the commencement that year. Bok agreed with my request that Vance receive an honorary degree at the first commencement after he resigned as secretary of state.

I went back to Vance and told him the whole story and how embarrassed I was to have to withdraw the promise of an honorary degree. Vance laughed and was gracious in telling me not to worry about it.

That spring, both Carter and Vance were grappling with a crisis— fifty-three American diplomats and citizens were held hostage by Iran. Over Vance's strong objections, in April 1980, Carter ordered military helicopters to attempt to rescue the hostages. The attempt failed disastrously. Vance resigned on principle soon thereafter.

Vance was a great secretary of state, but he was not a great speaker. Yet, at a rainy Harvard Commencement in June 1980, he gave a superb speech about America's role in world affairs. Afterward, a number of friends asked me why Vance did not receive an honorary degree. I felt I could not tell them what had happened. Fortunately, at Commencement 1981, Vance did receive an honorary degree.

As the 1980 election approached, I felt some mixed feelings. Of course, I wanted Carter to win, and I was furious when Ted Kennedy tried to beat Carter in the Democratic primary. Further, I knew that Reagan would be a total disaster in terms of support for programs that helped people in poverty—like the Legal Services Corporation. I also knew that support for long-term development and human rights would not be part of the Reagan foreign-policy agenda. IDCA would probably die unless it had four more years to be built solidly into the foreign-affairs bureaucracy.

When Reagan was elected, a small part of me was relieved that I didn't have to continue this job for four more years. I was tired from the infighting and couldn't see daylight. It was just dark all the time.

My colleagues and I dutifully prepared what I thought was a powerful briefing document for the new Reagan administration about all the important things we were doing around the globe regarding foreign aid. The incoming transition team appointed a very conservative foreign-aid team from the Heritage Foundation. The head of that team—I can still see him in my mind's eye—grabbed our fairly thick briefing document, took it off the table, and just dropped it on the floor. The only use we have for foreign aid, he said, was to promote national security in relation to the Soviet Union. Otherwise, we don't care about developing countries. The change was a tragedy for the world and our country.

Henry Owen fulfilled his promise to me, and not long after the election, Ellen and I attended an elegant State Dinner for the president of Nigeria. She sat next to the former governor of New York, Averell Harriman, a hero to both of us. After a distinguished career in public service, he agreed to join the State Department as assistant secretary of state because he thought he could still contribute to the service of his country. At the end of the dinner, Ellen asked Governor Harriman for his place card as a keepsake. "Only, Mrs. Ehrlich," he quickly replied, "if I may have yours."

One day in early January 1981, I was playing tennis and felt a piece of my back tear. I fell to the court and could not move. Two days later, I had an MRI and two days after that, I had a back operation to remove some ruptured discs. I was laid up for about six weeks, and Ellen went to the final White House lunch alone.

President Carter was a truly remarkable leader, a man of extraordinary moral stature, vision, and integrity. He was totally dedicated to doing the right thing and showed incredible tolerance for the range of the human condition. He really loved people and lived his faith. I admired him enormously and was privileged to work for him.

13

More than the Sum of Its Parts

Ellen and I planned to return to California after the 1980 election. We did not discuss it at length. Rather, we just knew we would move back. My successor as dean of Stanford Law School, Charlie Meyers, had arranged for me to be appointed to an endowed faculty chair at the school, and I would return to teaching and research.

Except that was not what I wanted to do. I had a "you can't go home again" sense and felt ready to return to a leadership position in higher education. I was particularly eager to use that position to promote my deep commitment to educating students to be engaged in public service, either as a vocation or an avocation. I had learned the satisfaction of public service, and I wanted to help prepare students to be involved actively and knowledgeably in strengthening their communities—local, state, national, or international. But no positions seemed available that interested me. Ellen was open to my trying to find another position, but she would also have been happy to return to Palo Alto.

Standford owed me a six-month sabbatical, and Ellen and I spent it in Washington so Elizabeth and Paul could finish the school year there. Elizabeth was a senior at Cathedral School and then headed for her freshman year at Stanford. David was finishing at Chico State University and looking for a job flying, which had remained his passion.

I worked for six months at the Brookings Institution, a nonprofit think tank focused on public policy issues, where I wrote a series of papers on foreign aid and legal services. One article in *Foreign Policy* magazine made the case for foreign aid in the face of the sharp shift by the Reagan administration. Most of my time was spent defending the Legal Services Corporation, as the Reagan administration went after it in a vicious and vengeful way.

Fortunately, both programs had strong supporters in Congress who defended them and ensured their budgets would not be slashed. But there was no hope that those budgets would be enhanced. Senator Ted Kennedy had been and continued to be a particularly important and influential supporter of both foreign aid and the Legal Services Corporation. As I wrote in the last chapter, I was upset that he had campaigned against President Carter in the Democratic primary. But I was enormously appreciative of all he did to help triple the Legal Services Corporation budget while I was president and then to ward off both cuts in that budget and limitations on the type of cases that could be brought by legal-services programs the corporation supported.

The failure of the new administration to appoint my successor effectively eliminated IDCA. My staff found other positions, mostly in nongovernmental organizations. The death of my agency did not cause me grief, but I viewed the turn away from President Carter's focus on long-term economic development and human rights as a tragedy. Unlike the Legal Services Corporation, IDCA needed four more years of a Democratic administration to survive its infancy.

In March of 1981, just as our family was starting to plan the details of our return to California, a search firm called to ask if I would consider being a candidate for provost of the University of Pennsylvania. At the time, I knew little about Penn except that my mother had gone there, that Benjamin Franklin founded it, that it was a great university, and, of course, that it was in Philadelphia.

Significantly, though I do not know how I had learned this, I also remembered that Penn's first provost, William Smith, came to Franklin's attention through an essay Smith wrote describing a mythical utopian community called Mirania. It contained a college to train citizens in their civic responsibilities. At colonial colleges at that time, the classics were taught almost to the exclusion of other disciplines. With brilliant foresight, Smith devised a curriculum for Penn that addressed the practical problems of living, working, and governing in Pennsylvania. Civic service was an expected obligation of the first graduates of Penn—a sensibility that I had come to understand and admire.

Ellen and I talked about this possibility at length and agreed that I should certainly consider the position. I interviewed with the search committee and was one of two people recommended to the new president, Sheldon Hackney, a widely respected historian of the post-Civil War South. Not long thereafter, Hackney invited Ellen and me to visit him and his wife, Lucy. We spent several relaxed hours talking around their kitchen table. Ellen and I took an instant liking to both Sheldon and Lucy, and we knew almost immediately that this was the right job.

After our dinner together, Hackney soon offered me the job. I accepted on condition that I could be home every weekday night to help our son, Paul. His dyslexia continued to be a challenge, and I wanted to aid him in handling a new school in every way I could.

I became Penn's twenty-fourth provost in 1981 and the first one appointed from outside the faculty since 1868. I did not realize then that the provost at Penn had considerably more authority—over student and academic affairs and over much of the budget—than at other universities. This authority existed in large measure because Penn had no president, only a provost, until Harold Stassen in the 1950s, though Benjamin Franklin founded Penn in the eighteenth century. My mother was thrilled that I would be helping to lead her alma mater, particularly because she left Penn without a degree and with some irritation.

Before I turn to my new role as provost, I'll mention other happenings in our family. Not long after I started at Penn, I finally persuaded my father and mother that she should drop the psychiatrist who had been treating her for thirty years and turn to a new one. The new doctor immediately took her off most of the medications that had been prescribed for years. She soon became much more cheerful and active. At Penn, we became close friends with Lee Copeland, dean of the Graduate School of Fine Arts, where my mother had been a student.

At some point, I told Copeland the story of my mother's inability to gain a Penn degree.

In 1983, Copeland organized a special symposium on designing the environment. Ellen and I were there, as were my parents. To my complete surprise, during the symposium, Copeland announced that my mother would be awarded an honorary master's degree in architecture, dated June 19, 1924, the date my mother should have graduated from Penn. Tears streamed down my face as she walked down the aisle to receive the degree before the whole fine arts faculty. It was a moving and exhilarating moment for her, my father, and me. The recognition for her professional work meant a great deal to us. Receiving the degree she had earlier been denied was a special delight.

During the time of the ceremony, my parents had been staying with my Philadelphia aunt and uncle, Frances and Elias Wolf. Two days after the ceremony, my mother fell down a flight of stairs in their house and died of a massive stroke. I am forever thankful she had been rightfully honored. These are words from what I said at my mother's memorial service:

> As I look back, I see more clearly than before that she helped me to realize how much one person can do to make powerful and profound differences in all dimensions, personal and professional. She did that, full of love, with pride and determination.

My father had focused his life on nursing my mother and protecting her as much as possible from whatever might aggravate her illness and depression. At first, he felt lost. Several widows in Cambridge were eager to snap him up, but he had no interest in them. He started to drink heavily. I took him on a trip to Edinburgh for the four-hundredth anniversary of Edinburgh University. The Duke of Edinburgh was there, and we chatted with him for about fifteen minutes. My father and I then traveled together across Scotland.

Within a year of my mother's death, my father had reconnected with Frances Borg, the fun-loving widow of a Harvard classmate, John Borg. She was a delightful person, and they immediately clicked. I don't know if my father stayed overnight with her the first time he visited her, but it was not long before they were a regular couple and were soon engaged.

Frances literally threw out all my father's clothes and restarted his wardrobe—Gucci socks, Calvin Klein underwear, and haircuts at the Pierre Hotel. She owned a wonderful home in White Plains designed by the great architect Edward Durrell Stone and a swish apartment on Park Avenue. They were married on her back lawn, and she gave Dad a white Jaguar with red leather interior, his dream car. For the next five years, they had a wonderful life together. Dad absolutely adored Frances, and she him. They traveled and had fun—the kinds of fun that Dad had never experienced. Frances had lots of money, and while they kept some accounts separate, money was never a problem. It was to be spent. And they did.

Meanwhile, Ellen's mother, Topsy, was living a full and active life in Glencoe, Illinois, after her husband died. While she had several opportunities to remarry, she enjoyed her life on her terms, full of friends and activities.

Topsy frequently visited us, and we took many trips together. She was a delightful person, filled with joy. She came with us for a month to Salzburg, Austria, for example, in the late 1960s, when I was teaching in a legal studies program at the Salzburg Seminar. Ellen, our kids, and I lived in Schloss Leopoldskron, an eighteenth-century palace overlooking a lovely lake, while Topsy stayed in a nearby hotel. My students were mid-level European government officials. I taught a class on international law in the morning and hiked with our son David every afternoon. Supreme Court Justice Byron White was also teaching there, and he and his son, Barney, often hiked with us. Some evenings, we went to the wonderful Saltzburg Festival.

In her nineties, Topsy lost her short-term memory and then almost her entire memory by the time she was ninety-five. Her housekeeper, Christine, had been with her since her marriage. Still, the last couple of years were extremely difficult, particularly for Ellen, who had to manage her mother's household, including full-time daycare, from two thousand miles away. The end finally came in November 1999.

Even though we still owned our house in Palo Alto, which we had rented, we decided to buy a home in Philadelphia. Our friends Joan and Frank Goodman both taught at Penn, and Joan told us about what she thought would be a great house for us. We agreed, and with the help of a loan from my parents, we made an offer, which was accepted. Our new home was a Tudor house in Bala Cynwyd, a suburb of Philadelphia. A railroad station was nearby, and I could take the train to Philadelphia and then walk to Penn.

Ellen quickly found a fundraising job at Planned Parenthood in Philadelphia. We both were and still are strong supporters of that organization, and her new position gave her a chance to help a cause she cared about deeply. Her colleagues soon saw her as a star in her work. A high point for her was picking up Mrs. Anwar Sadat at the Philadelphia airport and bringing her and her two bodyguards to a Planned Parenthood fundraiser that Ellen had organized. Ellen had a delightful time talking to her at length.

Our son and daughter, David and Elizabeth, were both happy I would be in a new job with new challenges that I would enjoy. Paul, however, had only reluctantly agreed to go to Philadelphia if we promised that our new house would have a yard, a fence, and a dog. We bought our new house with that promise in mind. It wasn't long before we brought home Becky, a beautiful golden retriever. Our house was in a lovely neighborhood, and it was the first time we had a place to live we could really call our own in the East.

Meanwhile, after graduating from Chico State University at age twenty-one, David was licensed to fly commercially but was too young to fly for a major airline. For the next two years, he flew first for a regional airline and then for a private business in Houston. At twenty-three, he was finally eligible, and Northwest Airlines hired him. He had disliked flying for the business and said it was a joy "to see Houston for the last time in the rearview mirror."

Elizabeth was just starting college at Stanford. From the start, she had a full and successful time in her undergraduate years, both socially and academically. She and her future husband, Peter Dumanian, met at Stanford and fell in love, to Ellen's and my great pleasure.

Paul attended the Shipley School in Philadelphia, following a year at a school that especially prepared him to handle his dyslexia. Fortunately, Radio Shack had just started selling home computers, and we bought one for Paul to use for his homework. It enabled him to write papers that we could review together and correct spelling mistakes without Paul having to copy the papers again. Like my own dyslexia, it never stopped him from doing what he wanted to do.

I loved the provost's job at Penn and was able to shape the position to fit my academic and planning interests. Hackney, who had been president at Tulane and provost at Princeton before that, had no interest in handling the academic affairs of the university as long as I kept in close touch with him, which I did. Focusing on academic matters at Penn was what I wanted to do, always checking with Hackney regarding any significant decision before I made it. I consistently learned from him and was a much better provost because of his wisdom. We liked and respected each other, worked well together, and became close friends.

Hackney's first year as president was a rocky one. Many faculty members distrusted him because they wanted the extremely popular former Penn provost Vartan Gregorian to be chosen. When the trustees selected Hackney, Gregorian promptly resigned and soon became president of the New York Public Library.

Soon after being appointed, I went to New York City to meet Gregorian. While he was plainly furious at the Penn trustees for not choosing him, he was always kind and generous to me. We became good friends and worked together in future years, both in Campus Compact—more about that organization later—and through his support for my work when he was president of the Carnegie Corporation and I was a senior scholar at the Carnegie Foundation for the Advancement of Teaching.

As I began my new role, I thought about the leadership lessons I had learned as dean of Stanford Law School, president of the Legal Services Corporation, and director of IDCA. I wrote them in a notebook I kept of useful ideas and insights.

First, spend at least a third of your time on mid- to long-range planning after the first six months or so on the job. If you do not lead institutional planning, what I call "institutional architecture," no one else will. Second—and this can be especially a challenge at research universities and large government agencies—work very hard to make the whole of your institution more than the sum of the parts. This means making as sure as you can that everyone who works at your organization feels part of a community with a responsibility to support it. Finally, along with managing your institution, focus primary attention as a leader on a few key clusters of issues where you want to make permanent changes. Make absolutely certain that faculty and staff understand those issues and that they know you are there to support them, but also be sure they realize your support is conditional on their full-throttle backing of your position on those issues. Too often I have observed leaders set dozens of items on their institutional agendas and end up without succeeding in any of them.

As a Stanford Law School dean, the key issues were new buildings and recruiting a more diverse faculty and student body. At the Legal Services Corporation, the issues were tripling the budget through the "minimum access" plan, hiring a strong and diverse staff, and enabling legal-services lawyers in programs funded by the corporation to feel they were members of one team with strong support from the corporation. At IDCA, as President Carter made clear to me, those key issues were to focus foreign aid, both bilateral and multilateral, on long-term foreign aid and human rights.

During my first six months as Penn provost, I visited each of the university's twelve schools; talked with their deans and department chairs; and met with leaders of various faculty, staff, and student groups. I also spent a day separately with several other provosts whose leadership I admired. I sought a short tutorial from each. They were flattered to comply, and I learned a great deal in the process.

Against the background of what I learned, Hackney and I decided that the most significant issue I needed to tackle was designing and implementing a campus-wide academic planning process for the next five years. That effort would involve setting university-wide academic goals and ensuring that each of the twelve schools developed its own academic aims, consistent with the university's goals. A key part of that plan was to enable Penn to be and be seen as one university, not a collection of separate fiefdoms.

I already knew some of the university's challenges that needed to be addressed within the planning process. For example, we needed to diversify the faculty by attracting more minority faculty members, and we needed to diversify the student body by increasing the numbers of minority students and attracting students from across the country rather than mainly from the East Coast.

Our first step was to create a new Academic Planning and Budget Committee comprising several deans, faculty, and students, each chosen by their elected representative bodies. I chaired the committee. The group and the Council of Deans became the focal point of Penn's academic planning for my years at Penn, and it is still in operation. For help, I reached out to Bob Zemsky, a professor from the School of Education with wide experience in academic planning. Bob helped me again when I was at Indiana University and became a close friend.

The initial efforts of the Academic Planning and Budget Committee made clear that the whole of the University of Pennsylvania was less than the sum of its parts, and we needed to engage in a major, university-wide academic planning exercise. Without getting into the weeds of the planning, six areas emerged as university priorities for the next five years—minority faculty and students, undergraduate education, graduate PhD education, educational outreach, research capacity, and ties with Philadelphia. A separate task force was created to analyze each area and propose ways to meet its challenges. At the same time, every school was charged with developing its own five-year plan. Each area's planning effort was charged with establishing baseline data based on honest assessments of the current situation and how success in meeting the challenges would be measured. Reports to the university community were issued regularly, requesting comments and suggestions. Nothing like this had ever been done before.

The planning process did not work perfectly—no such process does. But it worked extremely well. Over eighteen months, we came up with plans to identify, build on, and connect Penn's strengths in teaching, research, and service. Penn's twelve schools prepared their own five-year plans against the guidelines and objectives we had established for the university. This exercise helped strengthen Penn, bringing the schools together on the same page, at least in terms of the outcomes we sought. Most deans responded with enthusiasm to the planning process and sought to make the Penn slogan, "One University," an academic reality. A couple of deans resisted but nonetheless complied with the planning mandate.

Early on, we were faced with deciding whether to close one of the schools—Public and Urban Policy. The grounds were that the program was not academically strong and attracted relatively few students. Only a small number of faculty members taught there. After assessing and debating the issue for a year, the Academic Planning and Budget Committee decided the school should be closed. This was the right decision in terms of academic standards, but the closure raised howls among some of the faculty. We found places for the school's tenured faculty in other departments and met with the school's alumni to explain our decision. Most accepted it, though they understandably were not pleased.

The first five-year academic planning exercise led to a significant strengthening in the entire Penn academic enterprise. Midway through the process, we took stock and made several midcourse corrections. These covered goals that were either too ambitious or not ambitious enough. In the last year of the five years, we started a new five-year planning process. By then, the university community was used to setting goals—often stretch goals—and explaining, with evidence, why the goals were met, exceeded, or too ambitious.

Being provost gave me the opportunity to look out across all the university schools and departments and begin to understand their particular strengths and challenges. Penn is not only the largest of the Ivies but also the most diversified. I decided to try to visit every department in the university—more than 120 of them—over three years, spending an hour or two at each. This meant an average of almost one per week, apart from summer months, over three years, though in some weeks, more were scheduled, and in some, less. I wanted to learn the comparative strengths of each department. And I would always ask how I could help build on those strengths.

The faculty was interested in my offer of help, of course, and I was interested in learning about them and their disciplines. These tutorials taught me a lot. Department faculties generally greeted me enthusiastically and gave me an overview of themselves and their academic fields. The one exception was the Psychology Department, known as one of the best in the country. In essence, its faculty announced that I could not possibly understand what they were doing. When I responded that those in math, economics, and many fields in medicine and engineering had found ways to educate me even though I was a layman, they softened a little, but I don't think they ever believed I could understand their academic world.

My university-wide perspective as provost importantly helped me capitalize on opportunities to make the whole of Penn more than the sum of its parts. One small example was that two of the strongest schools, the Wharton School and the Medical School, each had their own stationery, which did not mention the university. I insisted they use the standard university stationery, like the other schools. I allowed them to keep the school's name at the bottom of the stationary, but up top, where people look first, the stationary had to read "The University of Pennsylvania." Both schools eventually capitulated, but not without a struggle. Their resistance pointed to a larger issue. Although every school was strengthened by being part of the university, deans often had a limited grasp of the university perspective. Ludwig Wittgenstein wrote, "The fly in the bottle doesn't know the shape of the bottle." Deans, I realized, needed to get outside the university bottle to understand its shape. In retrospect, I realized that I had not done a good job of that when I was Stanford Law School dean.

Schools of social work have a unique lens through which to see and work with the communities around them. The lens can be of enormous value to a university. The University of Pennsylvania takes its responsibilities as a citizen of West Philadelphia seriously. When I came to Penn, however, I soon concluded that the Penn School of Social Work and its dean lacked concern about how, or even whether, the university met those responsibilities. The school had strong ties to social-service agencies in Philadelphia, but the school had made little effort to help forge those ties to the university as well. Fortunately, a new dean I hired, Mike Aiken, completely changed this dynamic. He developed a number of strong interschool ties in teaching, research, and service that helped link his school, other schools, and the whole university with the Philadelphia community.

The medical school was sprawling and complex. Fortunately, it was led by a strong dean. He and I agreed that he should be in charge of the multihospital complex under the university umbrella. In our view, the primary reason the university owned hospitals was that our medical school needed patients for research and teaching. But many, both in and out of university medical affairs, believed the vice president for medical affairs should lead the hospital complex. The dean and I were glad that the hospital complex served its patients but felt strongly that the university's primary obligation was education and research. Shortly after I left Penn, responsibility for the hospitals was shifted away from the dean, just as I feared.

Penn had a centralized approval system for faculty appointments, promotions, and tenure cases. As a result, I reviewed every dossier for appointment, promotion, and tenure, aided by an advisory committee of deans and faculty. With the committee's advice, I rejected a number of proposals by school faculties to grant tenure. My decisions were grounded in my view that if individuals I had serious doubts about were as strong as supporters claimed, they would find positions elsewhere. If I were right, the university would save millions of dollars in compensation.

Only twice did I overrule a department and grant tenure when it was opposed. This is a much harder decision to make, and in my view, it should happen rarely, if ever. One case involved the Department of American Civilization, which had grown out of the History Department. A remarkable assistant professor was considered for tenure. Her expertise was in studying who was reading Harlequin romances, why they read them, and what impact their reading had on their lives. The American Civilization Department claimed her work wasn't American civilization, characterized the work as unimportant, and rejected her. In my view, as well as that of the advisory committee and many scholars in the field across the country, her book and articles on how Harlequin romances impacted American life were stunningly impressive. The department was shocked that I overruled them and awarded her tenure. The conflict left scars, as these things always do. She left Penn in a year or two to be chair of a literature department at another university.

I also hired many administrators. Deans were most important. I thought the Wharton School needed the leadership of a person who was, at that time, head of a major accounting firm. He had also served as board chair of a university, had a PhD, and had been involved in a wide range of university activities. But he was not a traditional academic. I succeeded in making the appointment, but it was a tough sell to persuade the Wharton faculty that the individual had exactly the qualities that the school needed as a dean to fill the position.

One of my surprises as provost was the number of situations involving graduate students allegedly being sexually harassed by faculty members, often their faculty advisors. In response, Hackney and I issued a statement in 1982 with a number of guidelines for behavior. The most controversial was the following.

> No nonacademic personal ties should be allowed to interfere with the academic integrity of the teacher-student relation. That integrity is at risk when sexual relations occur between them. What might appear to be consensual, even to the parties involved, may in fact not be so. On this basis, we believe that any sexual relations between a teacher and a student are inappropriate.
>
> In order to discourage such relations, in acting on complaints that come to our attention . . . we will presume that any complaint of sexual harassment by a student against an individual is valid if sexual relations have actually occurred between them. The presumptions might be overcome, but the difficulties in doing so would be substantial. In short, any teacher enters at peril into sexual relations with a student.

In a *Daily Pennsylvanian* opinion article, I wrote, "This is strong stuff and is meant to be." Reactions were generally positive, but we also heard complaints that we had created "a presumption of guilt" and that "blanket rules cannot cover all situations in this area." Even today, most colleges and universities preclude only sexual relations between faculty members and students when the faculty members have some authority over the students. Hackney and I went much further, and I think correctly.

A major project I worked on was expanding and diversifying our undergraduate base from one narrowly focused on New York, New England, and New Jersey to one truly national in scope. Lee Stetson, the dean of admission, became a good friend, and we worked together to expand Penn's presence in those parts of the country where we expected to find large numbers of prospective students eager to attend an Ivy League school. Bob Zemsky once again lent his planning expertise in undertaking a mapping project that enabled us to pinpoint our efforts. California, Arizona, New Mexico, and Texas were identified as potentially fertile ground, and we soon set up a separate office in Los Angeles. We developed a strategic marketing plan to reach out to top-tier schools like New Trier High in Winnetka, Illinois, and aggressively recruit students to come to Penn, making it a national school in a way that it was in name but not in fact. Our efforts steadily changed the character and makeup of the student body over time.

I also taught a law or undergraduate course in each of my six years at Penn, just as I had regularly taught at Stanford Law School. At Penn Law School, I taught professional responsibility. For undergraduates, I began a series of courses that linked community service to academic study. My conversations with John Gardner at Stanford and my time leading the Legal Services Corporation underscored the need for colleges and universities to educate students to be knowledgably engaged in meeting their obligations as citizens. Consequently, at Penn and later at Indiana University, my undergraduate courses included Altruism, Philanthropy, and Public Service; Ethics and Professions; and Law and Society.

Teaching continued to be a joy for me—both stimulating and fun. I felt then, and still feel, a special adrenalin charge when helping students learn. Whether their lightbulbs came on slowly or in a flash, I found it deeply satisfying to engage in learning with students. No less important, teaching enabled me to meet students in a classroom setting where we were all learners rather than in my office dealing with a grievance they had brought to me.

I also led a seminar called "What Is Evidence" that drew on faculty from different disciplines, including a historian, lawyer, sociologist, and physicist, among others. We looked at social problems through the lenses of our academic disciplines and gained new insights as a result.

Hackney and I worked hard to communicate regularly with students, faculty, and staff. I gave a talk to incoming freshmen each year and followed up with columns in the student newspaper, *The Daily Pennsylvanian*. I reached out to faculty and staff through frequent articles in *The Almanac*, which carried news of the university. Hackney and I also wrote numerous special reports on the academic planning process and other important issues at the university.

I had to handle a steady stream of controversies. That is part of the lifeblood of any college or university. Whatever the problem at hand, it inevitably became more serious if we were not open about what was going on and why.

Yes, there were plenty of student grievances, and many of the most volatile ended up in my office. I had at least one student sit-in at my office every year while I was provost. Many of them were related to issues of race. This was when student protests aimed at US investments in South Africa were increasing all over the country, and there was an active Penn student movement to press for divestment by the Penn trustees. Hackney and I met frequently with the trustees to discuss divestment in South Africa, particularly in the summer of 1986. Since the trustees were rarely available in the summer, my office was a convenient target for the protests.

Student groups also objected to what they perceived as inadequate support for the Black studies curriculum and for attracting more Black and Hispanic students. At the time, traditionally white, all-male fraternities dominated the central part of the campus, creating an environment that was often seen as unwelcoming to women and minority communities.

When dealing with sit-ins, I learned it was important to find out who the students were as individuals and to treat them with respect for their views, however irritating it might be to have them sitting in my office when I was trying to get my work done. Humanizing the situation was key, and feeding them doughnuts and cookies often helped. My aim was to help the protesters understand that they were part of the university rather than just declaring, "I care deeply about this. Now you go do something, Mr. Provost," It was their university as well.

It was also important to try to work with protestors to articulate a reasonable sense of their demands. Usually, at the start of a sit-in, all their demands were declared nonnegotiable. I often thought the demands were right on the merits. I agreed, for example, that Penn should have more minority faculty, staff, and students. In those conversations, I attempted to educate the protestors, without being pedantic, about the real financial situation of the university.

A persistent difficulty when dealing with sit-ins was the lack of anyone in charge with whom to negotiate. Some students said they didn't believe in leadership, so they didn't want anybody to be their leader. I might work out a settlement with a student or students who purported to lead a demonstration, only to be told that others in the group did not like the settlement, and the sit-in would continue.

Over time, however, I did become better at handling criticisms and protests. The student newspaper, *The Daily Pennsylvanian*, was invariably on the administration's case for one alleged misdeed or another. Sometimes, the paper was right, but it often possessed such a tone of moral righteousness that it was difficult not to be irritated even then.

I naturally kept looking for a humorous way to poke back at the student paper. I finally found it when the paper printed a picture of a truck belonging to a pest-exterminator company named "Ehrlich Exterminator" in big letters on the side of the truck. The caption of the picture read, "There goes the provost, getting rid of things again." I immediately called the editor in chief, Jeff Goldberg, and explained, "My grandfather owns that company. You can criticize me—it's part of my job to take criticism—but it's not fair to make fun of him. He is an old man." Shocked and ashamed, Goldberg promised never to show such a picture again. The paper then remained silent about me for several months. Decades later, Goldberg was the accomplished editor of *The Atlantic*, and I had a chance to tell him that I had made up the story and had no living grandfather. We laughed together.

Ellen and I made many good friends at Penn, and even though I was provost, we were able to keep my role separate from those relationships. Lee and Rolaine Copeland were friends from our first year, and we spent vacation time together in Rockport, Maine, and years later in New Zealand. Frank and Joan Goodman were already friends when we came to Penn, and we became even closer. The dean of the School of Social Work, Mike Austin, and his wife, Susan, were two others. And we felt a special friendship with Lucy and Sheldon Hackney and traveled with them. Somewhat to our surprise, we also became good friends with a number of the Penn trustees, including the head of the board, Al Shoemaker, along with Saul Steinberg, and particularly Leonard Lauder, all influential business leaders. I came to have great respect for their judgments and grateful for their support of Penn and the aims that Hackney and I shared.

In many ways, my job at the University of Pennsylvania was ideal—fascinating issues to work on, the chance to develop and put into operation institutional architecture, engagement with both academic and student affairs, a supportive president, and lots of friends. Before becoming provost, my knowledge of an entire university system had been episodic. My six years at Penn gave me insights into the workings of an entire university in ways that being the dean of Stanford Law School could not. The scope of administrative responsibilities was more wide-ranging, involving issues related to a broad array of academic disciplines and administrative issues. My time as provost prepared me for a new leadership opportunity and the next significant step into an even larger world of public service.

14

Hoosier Heartland

In 1986, during my fifth year at Penn, as much as Ellen and I enjoyed our experiences in Philadelphia, it seemed time to start looking for a university presidency. At age fifty-three, I felt ready to take on that challenge. I was eager to lead a public university, ideally one that covered a whole state.

Ellen and I did not feel limited by geography because our children were no longer at home with us. David and Elizabeth were married, working, and living in California, while Paul was a student at the University of Oregon, intending to attend law school after graduation.

Presidents of public universities are generally chosen from those who had worked in those institutions, so I realized finding a position might be difficult. I had been a student and administrator at private universities. But I came to believe that public universities were the main street of American higher education, and I wanted to work on that street. Those institutions educate more than three-quarters of all undergraduate students and about half of all graduate students. A significant majority of disadvantaged students attend public colleges and universities. Public institutions have responsibilities to serve the citizenry of their states and communities that private campuses do not have. A public university would bring to the foreground issues of access, like my time at the Legal Services Corporation and IDCA, in addition to the issues of academic excellence that I engaged with at Stanford and Penn.

At just this time, John Ryan announced he was retiring as president of Indiana University (IU), and a search was underway for his successor. He had served sixteen years, from January 1971 to July 1987. I knew little about IU except that a leading figure in higher education, Herman B Wells, had been its president and it was one of the Big Ten. A call from a search firm suggested that I meet with the board of trustees president, Richard Stoner, and vice president, Harry Gonso, and I agreed.

Before the meeting, I read as much as I could about IU and its history. I was struck that the first president of Stanford, David Starr Jordan, had been president of IU, which seemed a signal that this might be the right match. (It was only years after I had left IU that I learned of Jordan's role in promoting the eugenics movement, a severe stain on his reputation as a higher-education leader.) The university was founded in 1820. It had grown steadily from a small seminary in Bloomington to a major university with eight campuses. Bloomington and Indianapolis were the two main research campuses. The other six were spread across the state so that no citizen, apart from those in the southwest region, would be more than fifty miles from an IU campus.

Stoner, Gonso, and I met in a private room at the Philadelphia airport for about three hours. Before the meeting, I wondered whether I might be rejected not only because I was educated at—and helped lead—only private universities but also because I had worked in the federal government in Democratic administrations. I was a politically active liberal who wore bow ties and was a Jew. I could imagine that any of these parts of my past might be enough for Stoner and Gonso to look elsewhere.

Both men immediately put me at ease, and I quickly realized they were interested in whether I could successfully lead IU, not the matters I had wondered about. Stoner was vice chairman of the board of Cummins Inc, one of only a few Fortune 500 companies in Indiana. Gonso was a partner in one of the leading law firms in Indianapolis. He was a hero in Indiana because he had been the quarterback on the

1967 Indiana University team that went to the Rose Bowl. None had since.

Over the course of our meeting, I came to know and admire both men. I felt sure they would support me if I were chosen. This would be important, I knew, because the board of trustees had only nine members: six appointed by the governor, including one student, and three elected by alumni. This was in striking contrast to Stanford, with more than thirty trustees, and Penn, with more than forty. I probed whether partisan politics would affect the choice of president. They assured me that it would not, even though Indiana was a dominantly Republican state at the time. Stoner told me he was an active Democrat but had been appointed and reappointed for many years by both Democratic and Republican governors. Robert Orr, a Republican, was governor at the time, but Democratic governors had been elected previously.

I told Stoner and Gonso that my strengths were in academic planning and the implementation of academic plans, what I called institutional architecture. It turned out that this was exactly what they were looking for. They both felt the university was adrift academically and wanted the next president to address that directly. I outlined at some length the academic planning process that I had led at Penn and described the main challenges I had faced and how they were handled. Stoner and Gonso told me their perceptions of the university's strengths and limitations.

Shortly thereafter, Dick Stoner called to say that former Indiana University president Herman B Wells would be visiting Philadelphia on his way from Indiana to Florida and would enjoy meeting me. It does not take much knowledge of geography to realize that Philadelphia is somewhat of a detour between Indiana and Florida, so I realized that suggesting Wells was stopping in Philadelphia in the natural course of things was an exaggeration. I was thrilled. For decades, I had read about this great man of higher education, one of the three most important American educators in the second half of the twentieth century, along with James Conant of Harvard and Clark Kerr of the University of California, Berkeley.

Wells and I visited together for most of the afternoon in my office. He began by telling me that he had not been on the Penn campus since the celebration of Penn's bicentennial. We were then in the process of organizing the university's 250th celebration, and I began to gain some sense of his reach back through time. Wells was eighty-four years old when I first met him in my office. He had been president of Indiana University from 1937 to 1962 and had profoundly shaped the university that was increasingly of interest to me. It was a small regional university when he started and an internationally renowned institution when he retired.

I asked Wells what he thought was most needed to strengthen Indiana University. He encouraged me to lead aggressively in the academic realm. His support was extremely helpful during my years at IU in developing and implementing an ambitious academic agenda. During those years, when I had a problem with a group of faculty members, I could tell them that I had discussed the matter with "Herman," which almost always helped.

Stoner then invited Ellen and me to visit the Bloomington campus. We readily agreed, but on the condition that my consideration for the IU presidency would be confidential. I did not want to weaken my role as Penn provost by the news I might be leaving.

A Cummins Engine plane took us from Philadelphia to Bloomington and did so for subsequent trips until I became president. We stayed in a special set of rooms, the Metz Suite, at the top of the Indiana Memorial Union, one of the largest facilities of its kind in the world. The suite was filled with hunting trophies—heads of lions, tigers, and more—brought back from Africa by Dr. Metz. A little spooky!

Ellen and I felt totally relaxed during our stays at IU. If the visits worked out well, that would be wonderful, but if not, at least we would enjoy ourselves. I quietly met with the full search committee, which seemed to go well. I sensed that most of the committee members wanted someone from the outside as president—someone who would focus on enhancing IU's academic strengths.

I learned that the trustees chose Ryan, who was retiring as president, seventeen years earlier over a single weekend when they concluded his predecessor could not continue. Ryan had been the university vice president overseeing the regional campuses. At that time, many faculty members were furious that there had been no full-scale search and did not view Ryan as having strong academic credentials. As I came to understand how much Ryan had done to strengthen IU, I realized he was a fine leader. As a prime example of his leadership, he helped engineer a collaboration with Purdue University, where IU was in charge of the joint Indianapolis campus (called IUPUI), and Purdue was in charge of the joint Fort Wayne campus. As a result, the threat of starting a new public university in Indianapolis was averted. This was the only such partnership in the country and worked well, in my view. (After I left IU, both partnerships were dissolved.)

At Stoner's request, Terry Clapacs, the IU vice president in charge of facilities, gave Ellen and me a full tour of the Bloomington and Indianapolis campuses. We struck an instant friendship, and over time, he became my best friend at the university, along with the dean of the School of Music, Charles Webb.

At a concert on campus during our visit, I was struck that the evening program listed it as Number 1203. I asked how many years back the numbering had started. It turned out that this was the 1,203rd concert that year! The Music School was the greatest of any university, with more than fifteen hundred music majors, six full orchestras, nine operas a year—each double-cast—and much more.

We also attended a basketball game in Assembly Hall, which was a sea of cream and crimson. At Penn, I often went to basketball games in the Palestra, so I thought I knew how loud a cheering crowd could be. But the IU fans brought the decibel level to a whole new pitch. That was the 1987 season when IU went on to win the NCAA championship. Little did I know what awaited me with the coach of that winning team.

I made two more visits to the campus to meet with various groups, and although I talked to hundreds of people during the months of the selection process, word never became public. I told Hackney of our interest, and he was very supportive. He said, "If that's what you want to do, I'll do my best to support you."

During our visits, Ellen and I became convinced that Indiana University would be the right place for us. One couldn't walk down a street in Indiana without seeing people who had attended the university themselves or their children or relatives had. They viewed IU with pride as "their university." As president, I would be responsible for strengthening that pride through bolstering the academic enterprise.

Meanwhile, Stoner arranged for the board of trustees to visit Ellen and me in our Bala Cynwyd home. The aim, of course, was to enable the trustees to see us entertaining and judge whether we could successfully handle that important dimension of our prospective jobs. Ellen would not be paid if I were chosen as president, but it was clear to us, as it was to the trustees, that the presidency was a two-person job. To the surprise of our neighbors, two stretch limousines pulled up in front of our home, and the trustees came in for dinner. For the next three hours, we chatted as the trustees came to know us, and we came to know them. Apart from Stoner and Gonso, we had not met any of them. Fortunately, we all seemed to like each other. I knew Stoner and Gonso would be close friends for Ellen and me, and I suspected this would also be true for several other trustees. And I believed I could work with all of them.

About a week later, Stoner called to offer me the presidency of Indiana University. I said I was extremely flattered and would be back in touch. Ellen and I were clear we would accept, but I wanted advice on what should be included in the contract. Luckily, Gary Posner, a good friend from my days at Penn, led a higher-education search firm and helped me prepare a list of provisions to include. A few days later, Stoner and I talked again, and we worked out the details of the contract. I knew I would be head of IU's separate fundraising organization, the Indiana University Foundation. We arranged that part of my compensation would come from the foundation, and the university would pay the remainder.

I also visited the governor at the time, Robert Orr. I told him what I was sure he already knew: that I was a longtime, active Democrat, but I would put aside partisan politics as long as I was IU president. I did not want to take the job if my past political activities would hurt the university. As Stoner had assured me, Orr stressed that his support for IU was nonpartisan and would ensure it stayed that way as long as he was the governor.

March 4, 1987, was my birthday, and it was also the first time Ellen and I were introduced to the university community in Bloomington. I also spent time with the chancellors of the Bloomington campus, Ken Gros Louis, and the Indianapolis campus, Jerry Bepko. Over the years we worked together, both became good friends.

Along with a whirlwind of speeches, handshaking, and multiple meals, Ellen and I began to gain a sense of the warmth and friendliness of the IU community of which we would be a part. Over the next weeks, Ellen and I visited all of the IU regional campuses, talked at length to each chancellor in charge of those campuses, and also met students and staff. By the end of the whirlwind visits, my mind was a blur.

The IU campuses are spread across the state, so it would be difficult for me to visit each campus regularly except by air. Fortunately, IU owned two small airplanes, which enabled me to travel easily to two or three campuses in a day. I was also blessed with a wonderful driver who would drive me to Indianapolis and elsewhere in Indiana so I could work during the drive.

On August 1. 1987, I became IU's fifteenth president. My first task was to come to know the then-current senior staff whom I had not met. These included three vice presidents, the general counsel, and the head of the IU Foundation.

I concluded that IU was fortunate to have as my new partners not only Clapacs, Bepko, and Gros Louis but also Judy Palmer as vice president for planning, and Jerry Tardy as executive director of the Alumni Association. I quickly clicked with both Palmer and Tardy. In subsequent years, Tardy and I traveled together to visit IU alumni clubs in the US and abroad.

I regretted that the university's senior leadership included no persons of color and only two women, Palmer and Peggy Elliott, the chancellor of the IU Northwest campus in Gary. Elliot had been on the search committee that chose me. Fortunately, I could approve the nomination of Charlie Nelms, an outstanding African American administrator, as chancellor of IU East in Richmond, and sometime later of Emita Hill as chancellor of IU Kokomo. After I left IU, Nelms went on to become president of North Carolina Central University.

The vice president for administration and finance had retired, and I needed to start the search for a new one immediately. I wanted someone who would not be afraid to change established practices. A series of warning signals had been raised after I had been chosen and before I became president, and those convinced me that administrative changes would be needed.

One example came from an IU senior staff member's visit to my office at Penn. He told me I would be pleased to know that the president's office kept two sets of books. One was made public, while the other, which included a large amount of discretionary funds, was known only by the president and two senior officers. He said the idea was that the president could allocate those discretionary funds however he wanted without criticism. The idea of two separate sets of books appalled me, and I knew a prompt change was needed to ensure that the university's full financial picture was available publicly.

Stoner suggested John Hackett, the Cummins Engine chief financial officer, could be a good fit. I considered others and then chose Hackett. To put the matter gently, he ruffled many feathers in the IU administration, a tendency that was exacerbated because he had no prior experience in higher education. But from my perspective, he did his job well. When Hackett left, I appointed Palmer as vice president for finance and Clapacs as vice president for administration, believing it was time to separate those two critically important roles.

I soon realized that the vice president of public affairs would not be able to publicize IU in the ways I thought necessary. To replace him, I was able to attract Doug Wilson, who held the same position at Miami of Ohio University.

In my view, the head of the IU Foundation was also not the right person for the job. When I visited his office, the furniture was shabby and the office a jumble. He made it clear that he thought if his surroundings looked poor, this would attract contributions to IU. When

I was dean of Stanford Law School, I learned that the opposite was true. Both an individual and an institution need to look successful to attract donor support.

Thanks to both Clapacs and Tardy, I heard about an ideal new head of the IU Foundation, Curt Simic. An IU graduate, he was then heading the University of California at Berkeley Foundation and was frustrated by a lack of support from the administration. He was eager to return to IU and quickly turned the foundation into an effective fundraising machine. As head of the foundation board, I could be sure that the foundation's efforts were focused on the top university priorities.

I also concluded that the current general counsel needed to be replaced. He was used to being consulted only when a troublesome legal issue about a university policy had arisen. I wanted a general counsel who would be involved in university policymaking from the start and give advice not just when the university got into trouble but also, more importantly, beforehand to avoid trouble. I became convinced that the associate general counsel, Dottie Frapwell, was the right person for the job if she would spend a year as my special assistant before taking over the general counsel position. She agreed and soon became the best general counsel with whom I have worked, as well as a dear friend.

Finding the right vice president of research at the University Graduate School took several years, but when George Walker took that position, he did an outstanding job, enhancing graduate education at IU and significantly helping increase research funding.

The senior staff and I grew to respect and care for each other. We became close colleagues and close friends. They often had different views on particular issues, and I encouraged them to present their opinions as strongly as possible. I particularly urged them to make clear when they thought I was going to make a mistake. As I told them, "I don't ever want you to think, let alone say, 'I could have told you the path you are on would be a problem.' Tell me now so I and your other colleagues can weigh the concerns you might otherwise keep to yourself." Once a decision was made, however, I made clear everyone had to support it clearly and publicly.

We met weekly and regularly spent time considering not only the problems we were facing in the immediate future but also tough issues that might arise and how to deal with them—the suicide of a student, the embezzlement of university funds, and so forth.

Each summer, the senior staff and I, along with our spouses, went on a retreat with two aims in mind. The first was to plan how to handle the challenges we knew would arise—from the legislature, faculty, alumni, and students or staff. The second was to bond more closely as friends who worked together. One year, we went to Camp Brosius, run by the Alumni Association. Another time, we were at a resort in Kohler, Wisconsin. Perhaps the best was a retreat at historic New Harmony in southern Indiana, which had been two different utopian communities in the early nineteenth. A wealthy Texas couple named Owen had helped rebuild the whole town as it had been more than a century earlier, with financial support from the Lilly Endowment. New Harmony was Ellen's and my favorite getaway place. We went as often as we could and became close friends with Jane Owen, who led the restoration of the town her husband's ancestor had created.

Finally, in terms of staffing, I had to decide what to do about a resolution from the University Faculty Council. The council was made up of representatives from the faculty councils of all eight campuses, and I was chair. The resolution, adopted before I became president, proposed that a new university position be created—provost and vice president for Academic Affairs. The trustees had chosen me to strengthen IU's academic standing and I did not want to turn over that responsibility to someone else. On the contrary, doing that job was a key reason I wanted to become IU president. As a result, I did nothing about the resolution. I suspected that when I left IU, a new president would have a different view. Shortly after my successor was selected, the position of provost and executive vice president was created.

Ellen and I did not understand until I was chosen as president that we would have not one but two houses to live in—both of them extremely attractive. Bryan House, on the Bloomington campus, was named for William Lowe Bryan, a great IU president from 1902–1937, after serving earlier as vice president from 1893–1902. In 1970, Bryan

House was renamed the William and Charlotte Lowe Bryan House in recognition of Charlotte's many contributions. But I will continue to refer to it as Bryan House, as it was popularly called.

Bryan House is a center-entrance Georgian home situated at the highest point in the middle of the Bloomington campus. During our time at IU, it had entertaining rooms, a kitchen, and a pantry on the first floor, two bedrooms and a study on the second floor, and three guest rooms on the third floor. We loved the house as soon as we walked through it for the first time with former president Ryan and his wife, Pat.

The decor of the house, however, was not to our taste. Heavy drapes hung around the living room windows, for example, making the house seem dark even on the brightest day. Clapacs ensured the house and beautiful grounds were fashioned to our liking. He hired Kendra Webb and Celicia Upper, who had a two-person interior decorating firm in Bloomington. They did a wonderful job. A special bonus was that Ellen and I became fast friends not only with our decorators but also with their husbands, Charles Webb, dean of the School of Music, and Henry Upper, the associate dean. Over our years at IU, our friendship with the Webbs and their sons deepened into a lifelong bond, just as was true of Terry Clapacs and his wife, Phyllis.

Ellen and I realized that we could use Bryan House as what we called "a high-class bed and breakfast place." Over the years, we invited scores of distinguished visitors to IU to stay with us. Within the first few months of our arrival, for example, Isaac Stern, Yo-Yo Ma, and Emanuel Ax stayed together at Bryan House with us while they were teaching master classes at the School of Music. On the last day of their stay, they played a morning mini-concert for us, our household staff, and Ellen's mother, who was visiting.

We also entertained many friends and our family at Bryan House. I paid the university a monthly amount to cover all the expenses for private entertaining. Every Thanksgiving, for example, we hosted our children, my parents, and a number of aunts and uncles. Our most exciting private gathering was when our daughter, Elizabeth, and Peter Dumanian (whom we call our "son-in-love") were married. I can still see Elizabeth walking down the beautiful staircase in Bryan House, her long white dress flowing behind her.

Lilly House in Indianapolis was a gift to IU from Eli Lilly, the founder of Eli Lilly and Company, the great pharmaceutical firm. The house is on Sunset Lane, one of the most beautiful streets in Indianapolis. Mr. Lilly gave IU his home and all its furniture, books, and other furnishings, including a Gilbert Stuart painting of George Washington and an extensive set of Murano glass tableware. The house had a beautiful ballroom on the top floor with a stunning mural covering the wall. We had a delightful disc jockey Valentine's dance there for Elizabeth and Peter, along with many of our colleagues and friends.

We lived in Lilly House much of the time the legislature was in session and regularly entertained key House and Senate leaders there, as well as distinguished visitors to IU, such as the writer Umberto Eco and prospective faculty we were trying to recruit to IU. We also had a variety of private gatherings there, such as hosting a book club with a mix of members, including the mayor of Indianapolis, Bill Hudnut, who became a close friend.

Many of Ellen's efforts on behalf of IU did not involve me. She quickly became known as an effective IU ambassador to the surrounding communities. She focused on strengthening the ties between IU and Bloomington, Monroe County, and Indiana. One of her strengths was as an experienced fundraiser, and she joined the Monroe County United Way board. She soon suggested that the board add a new level of individual support that would be given special recognition, and she solicited individuals she knew could contribute at that level. The move significantly increased support for Monroe County United Way. After a year, she was asked to join the Indiana statewide United Way board, and a few years later, she joined the United Way national board. As a result, she had an important impact in enhancing support throughout Indiana and beyond for nonprofit agencies that help the disadvantaged.

A special pleasure for me was benefiting from the mentorship and example of former president Herman B Wells, whom I already mentioned. He taught me, in his own words, to "dream great dreams" and to work with confidence to make them a reality.

When we arrived at IU, I learned much more about this extraordinary man. He had a remarkable sense of the past, but his vision of the future was the hallmark of his genius. All through the early years of his presidency, he kept plans in his desk of how the university could and should develop physically and academically. He presided over the realization of those plans as the years went on, steering a small Midwestern college toward greatness.

Wells reached out around the world to establish international programs that made IU better known in some parts of Asia and Europe than in the United States. He worked closely with private and public institutions of higher education for the benefit of the entire state. Most visibly, he understood that a beautiful physical environment can enhance the learning of students and faculty. He ensured that as the Bloomington campus grew, it would retain its natural beauty, its architectural cohesion, and the atmosphere of a small campus that belied its large size.

When we arrived, the noise from the battles Wells fought throughout his presidency had faded with the passage of time, and only the results of his victories remained in view—great academic programs that he developed, beautiful buildings to house them, and strong leaders to guide them. Wells also frequently told me of struggles he lost, though the pain of those defeats had faded.

However, one of Wells's innovations proved unsuccessful in the long-run, and it became my problem to deal with. The 18/20 retirement program essentially provided that faculty members or senior staff who worked long enough at Indiana University could retire at age sixty-five, receive full pay, and not draw on retirement savings until age seventy.

Wells put the program into effect because he thought it would encourage faculty and senior staff turnover and enable IU to attract more of the best scholars and administrators. Whether or not it was a mistake at its inception, by the time I arrived, it was clear that the program would bankrupt the university, and it couldn't continue. When I took a close look at the program and its cost to the university, I was irritated that it hadn't been dealt with sooner. It was not on my agenda at the start, but we had to deal with it. We set up a commission to study the question. Sensible faculty were involved, and they agreed the program could not continue. Then the question became how to eliminate the program going forward while continuing it for existing faculty and senior staff since we couldn't change their contracts. For several months, the problem and proposed solution were in the foreground of my administration as the contentious issue moved through the faculty senate and then to the trustees. If the transition failed, it could derail my academic agenda, so I paid close attention as it progressed.

Even before we arrived in the Hoosier State, I was told the president should prepare an annual State of the University address, generally delivered in August. I responded that I knew little about the state of the University, but I would prepare a paper on the university in the state, a play on words since one of my aims was to enhance the role of Indiana University in promoting the state's economic growth.

My paper, "Our University in the State," spoke directly about my educational perspectives and the university's missions of academic distinction in undergraduate education, graduate education, and research, along with enhancing access to an IU education and Indiana's economic growth. It was also my first take at underscoring that while each campus was distinctive, IU was One University. The message was similar to the one I developed at Penn regarding the twelve schools there.

I sent a first draft and many succeeding drafts to wider and wider groups of faculty and other advisors, seeking to gain their counsel on the issues involved and to garner their support. In addition to those inside the university, I included the governor and other political leaders. The process worked well, and as a result, I wrote a paper each year of my presidency on a different key cluster of issues important to the university community. For example, one was on the arts, and another on the sciences.

Some deans gave me detailed feedback about how their schools were contributing then—and would in the future—to the goals I had suggested. Other deans seemed defensive, concerned that their schools might be overlooked or left behind. From those early interactions, I realized that a few deans could not engage in the academic planning process because they feared any change might weaken their schools or their leadership. I worried their schools would suffer as a result.

On October 11, 1987, my inauguration took place with ceremonies in both Bloomington and Indianapolis. Local clergy—a rabbi and a priest—opened and closed those ceremonies. My good friend, Mary McPherson, president of Bryn Mawr College, spoke at one ceremony, and one of my favorite former Penn colleagues, Henry Glassie, spoke at the other. Glassie was among the most significant folklorists in the world, and one of my early actions was to persuade him to join the outstanding IU Department of Folklore.

My inaugural address was titled "Education and Values." It did not focus on the tasks ahead for the IU community, as did my "Our University in the State," but instead discussed the moral frame within which those tasks should be addressed. "We are in a time when the roots of individual morality are strained, in a climate of moral uncertainty. It is worth inquiring what roles a university can have in reinforcing the roots, in clearing the climate." I spoke about how a university can educate about values and also epitomize those values. The value of freedom or liberty was first on my list, and I quoted my mentor, Judge Learned Hand: "The spirit of liberty is the spirit which is not too sure it is right." I then considered the values of reason and respect. "History suggests," I said, "that no community can maintain an environment of liberty without an environment of mutual respect and that both are needed to allow the exercise of reason to flourish." Then I turned to what I called "the morality of learning—a morality that recognizes the importance of learning for its own sake and for the sake of the learner."

There was more, but these snippets should provide a sense of the tone I was trying to set for the concerted efforts I had in mind to strengthen the academic enterprise at IU. I closed by saying, "More than a quarter century ago, my wife, Ellen, and I returned to live in the Midwest, where she was born. Since then, we have moved to the East, to the West, and back again to the East. Now, and finally, we are home in Indiana." Everyone who heard or read my speech knew that an unofficial Indiana state song was "Back Home (Again) in Indiana."

Those two addresses, one on substance and one on tone, were the initial steps in the academic planning process that I began with a small group of faculty and administrative leaders months after becoming president. My former Penn colleague, Bob Zemsky, was a helpful advisor throughout the process. Ultimately, more than four hundred individuals from all campuses, working in task forces, were involved in a year-long collaborative effort.

There is no single right approach to university planning, but it is always necessary to establish design principles to guide the process. One of ours was that we wanted a comprehensive academic agenda for the entire university on all eight campuses, including more than eight hundred degree programs, the academic work of more than four thousand faculty members, and a student body that then numbered over eighty thousand. (Enrollment rose to a high of ninety-six thousand in the next five years). We needed to be general to be comprehensive. At the same time, we wanted to avoid producing yet another vague document full of puffed-up aspirations that could be readily ignored. Our answer was an agenda that covered three broad areas: undergraduate education, graduate education and research, and economic growth for the State of Indiana. Those were the three areas I had identified in the initial paper, "Our University in the State."

Within each of the three areas, a number of task forces drawn from faculty and students spelled out specific initiatives, fifty-three in all. For many of these initiatives, progress was measurable in quantitative terms. The results were published in draft form for faculty and others to comment on in a paper titled "IU: One University—Indiana at Its Best." It set out an ambitious agenda for strengthening the University in every academic aspect. As examples, the initiatives included these three:

> Require a strong and sustained commitment on the part of each campus to increase substantially both the numbers of African Americans and Hispanics and the numbers of women on our faculty—a commitment that recognizes that faculty can serve as role models and mentors only if their diversity matches the inherent diversity of the student body.

Develop common academic experiences for all undergraduates
on all eight campuses; a prime vehicle could be the many ar-
tistic and creative treasures in Indiana.
Develop new standards for assessing educational performance—
by both students and faculty.

At regular intervals, my administrative colleagues and I published
progress reports for the university community on how well each campus was doing to achieve the goals of each initiative. Competition
naturally arose among the campuses, and if one had stalled regarding
a particular initiative, the progress of others often acted as a spur. More
important, each campus learned from the others and borrowed each
other's good ideas.

This process of interaction among campuses furthered a key
purpose of the academic agenda—to draw its eight campuses together as "One University with Eight Front Doors." That became our
mantra. Treat everyone equally and not view the university system
as having two research campuses and six less important regional
campuses.

The natural pressures, both academic and political, within any institution of higher education are centrifugal, particularly when multiple
campuses and local politics are involved. Adding to the problem was
the impulse to overly centralized system-wide functions in the main
research campuses. For example, if IU Northwest, the campus in Gary,
Indiana, wanted to replace one of its cars, someone in Gary had to
drive 197 miles to Bloomington, get the car registered, and then drive
back to Gary. Doing so, of course, annoyed everybody at the Gary
campus, who rightly thought they were being treated as second-class
citizens. So, as academic planning continued, we undertook initiatives
to emphasize that every campus was important, and to find ways to
link them together. That was possible especially through art and music
festivals that traveled from one campus to another.

The most important "One University" initiative was FACET—the
Faculty Academy on Excellence in Teaching. The program was started
and administered by a faculty member named Eileen Bender at IU

South Bend. Each year, the faculty of every campus chose outstanding teachers who received a stipend and met to share teaching tips and to mentor other faculty members to become better teachers. Several books of these tips were published by the IU Press and widely distributed to faculty on all IU campuses. FACET is still going strong, more than three decades after it was launched.

Four overarching academic goals of my administration over the initial years emerged as a result of the planning process. One goal was improving the education of what I came to call our "new majority" students—older than traditional college age, going to school part-time, holding down a job, and often also raising a family.

In the regional campuses, a majority of the students were first-generation, older, and part-time with families. I gave an award for the most outstanding student to a brilliant woman on the Fort Wayne campus. A couple of weeks later, I received a call from the head of the English Department, where the woman was studying, saying, "Would you mind calling the student because she's dropped out of school?"

I called the student and asked, "What's going on? You're the brightest student on the whole campus. You can do anything!"

"You see, I'm married," she replied, "and I am married to a guy who didn't go to college. I feel myself separating from him, and my marriage is much more important than my education. I am sorry to leave, but that's what I am going to do." That experience gave me a new perspective of the challenges facing those in the student new majority. Fortunately, we were able to help her husband enroll in college with a scholarship, and things worked out for them both.

In my years at IU, I taught both traditional-age and new-majority undergraduates—the former in Bloomington and the latter in Indianapolis. In my third year, I taught a course on ethics in the professions via interactive television, linking a class of traditional-age students in Bloomington and a class of primarily new-majority students in Indianapolis. For the first time, I understood directly what faculty colleagues have told me—many insights can be gained by each group of students learning from the other. I watched while what could be described as "two-way mentoring" intensified.

As an example, I was teaching "The Letter from a Birmingham Jail" by Martin Luther King, Jr., which I had done many times before. At the start of the class, I asked the students whether they cared enough about a social cause to go to jail for that cause. After a pause, I turned to a student and repeated the question. She was quiet for more than a minute. Then she said, "No. You see, my brother is in jail for the rest of his life. I am at Indiana University so that I do not have to go to jail." Suddenly, I gained a whole new insight into the iconic document I had taught so often.

In earlier eras, university presidents taught classes in moral philosophy to seniors. The university president was expected to articulate moral values for the institution. In the fall of my last year at Indiana University, I taught a group of seniors in a seminar, "Philanthropy, Altruism, and Public Service." In the wake of the relativism that scarred the 1960s, it had taken some time for moral inquiry to regain its standing, and too often, the radical right or left claimed a monopoly in this realm. But the presidency of Herman B Wells underscored to me that a university president should seek to teach about important moral issues.

A second key goal was increasing the numbers of African American and Hispanic students and faculty. We developed the Hoosier Plan for Minority Enhancement, a university-wide strategy to raise the overall percentage of African American and Hispanic students at IU to 10 percent, equal to the percentage of minorities in Indiana's population. The Hoosier Plan stated specific enrollment goals for each campus and the population the campus served.

In an important effort related to the Hoosier Plan, we reached out to six leading, historically Black universities and colleges with the help of an IU alumna, Gloria Randle Scott, president of Bennett College. (At her request, I became a trustee of Bennett College after I left IU.) I arranged with Bloomington campus science departments to host faculty from those institutions to work during summers in the labs of the IU departments—labs with much better facilities and IU faculty who could mentor faculty from those institutions.

A third overarching goal was enhancing undergraduate retention and graduation rates. We initiated detailed faculty discussions of the goals of the baccalaureate degree and the means to assess the extent to which those goals were realized. We decided on the core competencies one should gain as an IU graduate and then analyzed whether and how those competencies were achieved. This aim was realized, in part, by the creation of the Wells Scholars Program.

When I came to Indiana University, I was troubled that many of Indiana's best high school students were leaving the state for college—to go to Harvard, Berkeley, Michigan, Stanford, and other leading institutions. IU had worked to raise its admissions standards over the past decade and had modest success. But the very best students, with few exceptions, still went elsewhere. The Wells Scholars Program was designed to help change that. High schools throughout the state were invited to nominate one or two of their best students for full-tuition scholarships. Those nominees had to be not only academically outstanding students but also well-rounded leaders.

The program faced a tough challenge in the Faculty Council because many thought a public university should only give scholarships based on financial need. I sympathized with that view but thought this program was needed if the university were to enhance undergraduate education. Fortunately, a majority of faculty agreed that athletes should not be the sole recipients of financial aid without regard to need. Success with the faculty was assured when Wells agreed to lend his name to the program, the first time he had done so.

Fifty of the best nominees were invited to the Bloomington campus for a weekend, much as outstanding football and basketball recruits came to be interviewed. Twenty-one were offered a full scholarship and the opportunity to work closely with faculty members in their areas of particular interest.

I was worried about how well the program would fare, for I knew that the young men and women offered the first Wells Scholarships were also offered scholarships at major private and public universities throughout the country. I was sure the program would succeed, however, when twenty of the twenty-one accepted. Even more important, our admissions director told me that some two hundred applicants for the program, many of whom would not otherwise have come to

Indiana University, selected IU even though they did not receive a Wells Scholarship. They chose the university because they wanted to attend an institution with high expectations. During my tenure, I saw five classes of Wells Scholars and was persuaded that the program raised expectations for undergraduate education at IU by a considerable margin.

The final overarching goal was to augment substantially the funding of externally sponsored research. IU was behind other universities in the American Association of Universities, the national organization of research universities. We were able to do this to a degree with enhanced funding from the federal government, the state legislature, and private philanthropy, but never to the extent that I had hoped, apart from the medical school, which increased external support by a significant amount.

These were our four major goals over my first years as president, together with one administrative objective: to build a transparent budgeting system that would enable academic priorities to lead, not follow, in the budget process.

I quickly learned that IU's budget lacked transparency and consistency. There was no principled, unified, and widely understood rationale for why schools and other academic units were budgeted the way they were. For a public university, in my view, this state of affairs was outrageous.

In response, I decided to switch the IU budget system to responsibility-centered management (RCM), the budgetary approach used at the University of Pennsylvania. Some faculty and administrators objected, fearing the switch would hurt the units where they worked. Discussions about the switch eased many of the concerns, but some still lingered. Most new presidents take office with an initial bank of goodwill capital to use for innovative changes. I used a substantial amount of that capital to gain agreement for RCM. It was well worthwhile in terms of revenues earned and expenses reduced.

The IU switch to RCM provided a consistent and transparent tool for promoting academic strengths, identifying academic priorities, and ensuring that funding allocations would follow. In my view, the advantages were obvious, and the system is still in effect at IU.

As the academic planning progressed, I also reviewed every faculty appointment, promotion, and tenure decision, as I had done at Penn. I did this with the advice of an academic council that I created and whose members I appointed. Those members included the chancellors of the Bloomington, Indianapolis, and rotating regional campuses, along with several school deans.

I made some mistakes in taking on this responsibility. To be appointed or promoted to a tenured position, faculty had to be outstanding in one of three areas and at least satisfactory in the other two. Those areas were teaching, research, and service. Early on, I turned down for promotion to a tenured position a faculty member at IU Northwest. He had written a math textbook, which he argued was outstanding scholarship. I rejected his promotion on the ground that writing a textbook was not scholarship; it was part of teaching. The faculty member sued and might well have won. Luckily, at about the same time, Ernest Boyer, president of the Carnegie Foundation for the Advancement of Teaching (where I later worked), published a seminal book, *Scholarship Reconsidered*, that argued faculty could contribute to academic disciplines in multiple scholarly ways, including textbooks. In retrospect, I concluded that I was wrong and the faculty member was making an important contribution to scholarship and reversed my decision.

Working closely with the legislature was a key part of my responsibilities. With the help of Don Weaver, a staff member focused on governmental affairs, I met regularly with the governor and members of the House and Senate and testified before the relevant committees. Indiana had a Commission on Higher Education, which had to approve each new campus degree, and I also spent a good deal of time with the commission members.

My colleagues and I took two key major steps that strengthened IU's support from the legislature and standing with its representatives. The first was to persuade the Purdue president, Steve Beering, that our two universities should present our budget requests together and for the same percentage increases. Beering had been dean of the IU School of Medicine, and we quickly became friends. Beering and I then persuaded the other five public universities in Indiana to join us in what we called the "Commitment to Quality Consortium." Instead of competing for special advantages from the governor and legislature, I concluded that the whole state would benefit if its public universities worked together. I believed IU would be better off as well.

The second step was triggered by a visit I made early in my tenure to Representative Pat Bauer, then chair of the House Ways and Means Committee and later Speaker of the House. I made my basic pitch to him about the importance of IU to the economic success of the state. In response, he essentially said, "You are a nice fellow, Tom, and when I hear what you said from my constituents, I will be supportive." With the trustees' approval, I used private donations to hire a firm that knew how to do grassroots organizing. Two trustees and I interviewed several firms and chose one in Washington that I knew from my time working there.

The firm designed what we called "Hoosiers for Higher Education." We chose IU alumni for the positions of captain and lieutenants for each House and Senate district in the State. Those alumni agreed to read the materials we sent them and to stay in close touch with the legislators representing their districts, speaking about IU to those legislators as often as they could. Twice a year, we also invited every legislator to Bloomington, accompanied by their constituents who were captains or lieutenants, for a full day. Many of the legislators who came were IU graduates, and many of those who were not IU graduates also came. We had a program that highlighted talks by outstanding faculty, as well as discussions of IU's financial needs. Each "IU Day" also included a football game in the fall and a basketball game in the spring. Hoosiers for Higher Education had an important effect on the state support IU received. I also traveled around the state, sometimes with Beering, talking with our alumni about what was going on in their universities and what they could do to help.

Unsurprisingly, my interactions with the legislature sometimes met with resistance I could not overcome. One example was the efforts that the medical school dean, Walter Daly, and I made to concentrate all undergraduate medical education in Indianapolis. At that time, several of the regional campuses, including South Bend, provided the first two years of medical training. Daly made a compelling case, I thought, that dividing medical education in this fashion was unwise academically and more expensive as well. I went to see Representative Bauer, whose comments led me to Hoosiers for Higher Education. He told me bluntly that if IU tried to make the move I supported, it would lose its funding for medical education. Naturally, I dropped the plan.

The Black Monday 1987 stock market crash spawned a number of legislative battles during my first years. I tried a variety of steps to connect with legislators. In order to demonstrate the importance of funding for public universities, for example, Ellen and I held weekly dinners at Lilly House in Indianapolis when the state legislature was in session.

Working with Congress and federal agencies was also part of my responsibilities. Fortunately, Indiana was represented then by a number of outstanding legislators. Two of my favorites were Senator Richard Lugar, a Republican, and Congressman Lee Hamilton, a Democrat. When I first came to see Senator Lugar, he invited his whole staff to what turned out to be a seminar on IU's needs and how the senator could best help to meet those needs. Similarly, Congressman Hamilton, whom I had known from my days at the Legal Services Corporation and IDCA, was helpful in gaining approvals for IU projects that needed federal support. Over time, Hamilton became a close friend, and our friendship continued after I left IU.

The university-wide academic planning process unfolded well on many fronts during my first years. By 1993, the initial five-year planning effort resulted in significant academic gains across all eight IU campuses. We then started a new planning effort to build on the momentum and to further strengthen parts of IU that needed to be enhanced and areas of academic excellence where further gains were most possible.

In my first year at IU, however, I learned an important lesson: intercollegiate athletics can be an all-consuming diversion from the academic goals and planning of a university president. Coach Bob Knight led the IU basketball team to the NCAA championship in 1987. Knight was justly lauded for the championship. But nothing prepared me for the State of Indiana's love affair with basketball. Harvard, Stanford, and Penn paled against the Big Ten (now eighteen universities) for intercollegiate athletics being at the heart of student life.

Knight had become a legend on campus and throughout the state long before I arrived. How would an Ivy League type from the East Coast react to basketball as the Hoosier lifeblood? Many asked that question. In fact, I always liked the game and learned to love it in Indiana. But there were some bumps along the way—big bumps.

Knight was a great teaching coach, but he was also a bully with a strong temper and a foul tongue. He could be like a little boy who tests his parents by stepping as far over the line as he can and seeing when he's going to get slapped down. Knight was also brilliant in many fields, history particularly, and very generous to the university library. And he took care of the student players who could survive his brutal coaching style.

Our initial exchanges were pleasant enough, but in December of 1987, he was infuriated by a referee's ruling and ordered his team to leave the court partway through an exhibition game with a Soviet squad in Bloomington. The media blasted Knight and sought my reactions. When I checked with the coach, he admitted he had made a serious mistake. I issued a public statement criticizing him. He was apparently furious at this, since he had never been chastised or sanctioned by my predecessor, even though he threw a chair across the basketball floor in anger in a game against Purdue in 1985 and regularly screamed obscenities at his players.

All was relatively quiet until April 25, 1988. Television newscaster Connie Chung was interviewing Knight at courtside and asked him how he handled stress. He replied, "I think if rape is inevitable, relax and enjoy it." A video clip of the comment was included in the nightly TV news across the country. It was repeated in newspapers and other media throughout the next day.

I again rebuked Knight publicly, this time more sharply, after trying unsuccessfully to contact him. "Coach Knight was not speaking for the university during the interview with NBC correspondent Connie

Chung," I said, in part. "I deplore his reference to rape, and his coarse language was in very poor taste." Knight was in a rage—mad at Connie Chung for, in his view, baiting him into making the offensive remark after several hours of her own street talk that was not aired, and mad at me for criticizing him publicly, particularly since I had not heard his version. He had been snookered by a woman, and the fact that I had tried to reach him before speaking made no difference.

For the next seven days, the matter was on the front page of every paper in the state. At the time, the University of New Mexico was looking for a new head coach, and Knight was courted. UNM's president brought his plane to Bloomington and flew Knight back to New Mexico where Knight already had a ranch. The aim was to persuade Knight to leave IU and come to coach at the University of New Mexico.

It was the week of IU commencements, and I presided over nine ceremonies in those seven days—Indianapolis had two—traveling on one of IU's small planes to each campus. Every time I arrived, I was surrounded by the press. What would I do if Knight left? I received more than ten thousand letters from irate fans. The one I liked most went something like this: "I am seventy-eight years old, in a wheelchair, and the only thing I care about is IU basketball. You can take your goddamn bow ties and go back where you came from." I framed that letter and kept it on display for times when I might get too full of myself.

A group of angry students marched on Bryan House, our campus home. Even the governor, Robert Orr, called to ensure I really understood just how important Knight was to five and a half million Hoosiers. The Bloomington Faculty Council passed a resolution supporting me, and many from outside Indiana wrote, backing my action. But the majority of comments from inside the state was critical.

I didn't know what would happen. *Should I do nothing more?* In that case, I believed Knight would leave. He was a great coach. None could deny that. But he was a terrible role model and a misogynist. His comments were deeply objectionable to every decent-thinking person, and particularly offensive to women. *Shouldn't he leave?*

On the other hand, I believed there were many bigger and more important things going on at IU than basketball—things that needed attention. We were in the middle of system-wide implementation of our academic plans, involving all the schools and all the campuses, and that needed to be the priority.

I recalled what happened to a friend of mine, Hunter Rawlings, who was president of the University of Iowa. In his first year, he announced the elimination of freshman eligibility for football and basketball, which I thought was a good idea. The alumni became so outraged that the crisis basically derailed his academic agenda for a whole year until he withdrew his proposal.

In the end, with reservations and with assistance from Dick Stoner, I reached out to Knight and asked him to stay. If Knight's comments were made by a coach today, I have no doubt I would fire him. At the time, some in Indiana, and many more outside the state, thought that is what I should have done. Years later, I was visiting Indianapolis and took a taxi from the Lilly Endowment to Shapiro's Delicatessen. As I got out of the taxi and paid the fare, the cab driver, who had been silent during the entire trip but clearly recognized me, said, "Well, Mr. President, I still think you should have fired his ass when you had a chance."

Given all that needed to be done for the sake of the university and state, I still believe I made the correct decision. The crisis passed. In subsequent years, Knight and I had good relations. He regularly invited me to watch practices. His running commentary while he sat next to me at courtside taught me a lot about basketball. At his request, I visited the locker room after every home game to talk with the team. And Knight and I chatted at length about historical events that interested us both. We even coauthored an op-ed piece for *USA Today*, making the case that when there is a sports misdeed of a significant kind, the coach should get punished and not the players.

That turbulent time during my first year taught me firsthand how totally diverting issues of intercollegiate athletics could be from the job of a university president. My very able successor, Myles Brand, publicly rebuked Knight for choking an Indiana player during practice. Brand said he would fire Knight if he misbehaved again. Knight did so again, and Brand fired him, as he should have. Unfortunately, Brand's own agenda for the university effectively came to a halt then, and he was unable to carry out many of the important initiatives that he had developed. Knight died on November 1, 2023, as I was finishing this memoir.

A few other matters also threatened to divert attention and energy from strengthening academics. Perhaps the most serious was a sit-in at my office. As opposed to the near routine of sit-ins at Penn, only one occurred during my entire presidency at IU. The IU Foundation, which I chaired and was separate from the university, had been given a farm in Mississippi before my time. It was valued at $1 million, and we spent around $100,000 a year to keep it going. We had no interest in keeping this farm and were trying to sell it. We could only find a single buyer, a waste disposal company. We did a careful review to ensure that the company wouldn't dump toxic waste at that site. We also talked to the NAACP about the sale because the farm was located in a predominantly African American community.

We concluded that it was fine to sell; the local community leaders and the NAACP supported our decision because it would bring jobs. But a group of environmentalists claimed the sale was environmental racism because toxic waste would be dumped and destroy the lives and livelihoods of poor Black people in the area. They connected with a student group on campus, who were outraged, marched in, and sat in my office.

Fortunately, I had a plan. I told the students that I proposed to hire an independent person, an alumnus who had taught at IU and was well-known and widely respected on campus. I would ask him to conduct an independent evaluation of the sale. If he concluded the sale was a mistake, I pledged we would not sell the farm. We would sell it only if our alumnus approved. The students agreed to my proposal in what was, I believe, a teachable moment for them. The alumnus concluded that the plant would not harm the community and we should definitely sell the farm.

After the first year at IU, Ellen and I became convinced that someone was watching out for us because Indiana University turned out to be exactly the right place for both of us. To those who had welcomed us so warmly, it might have seemed an unlikely combination—an East

Coast Jewish liberal coming to the heart of the Midwest, where the Ku Klux Klan dominated not so long before—in a conservative state, with only twenty-five thousand Jews out of 5.5 million residents. During our time at IU, however, we did not hear a single antisemitic remark, and the university had a superb Jewish Studies program.

Because there were so few Jews in the state, I had made it clear to the trustees and others before I became president that Ellen and I were Jewish. After my appointment, I reviewed my fall appointment calendar with my assistant and noticed that homecoming had been scheduled on Yom Kippur. I called Dick Stoner and said, "I want you to know I can't possibly come to homecoming, and I think it's important to have the president at homecoming, particularly for his first time." He agreed, and immediately, the date of homecoming was changed, even though events had already been scheduled for that weekend. Although nobody publicly announced why homecoming had been changed, the Jewish community in Bloomington somehow knew I was behind it. I became their hero for a while.

Later, I brought together clergy from the thirty-four different faith groups in Monroe County, where Bloomington was located, to discuss ways they might help engage students through small-group experiences. I knew that many of our students came from small towns, and they needed small-group experiences to avoid falling through the cracks. The clergy all came, except for the rabbi of Hillel on the Bloomington campus. I tried unsuccessfully on numerous occasions to find this rabbi. Furthermore, the Hillel building looked terrible.

I called the president of the national Hillel office in Washington DC, Richard Joel, whom I didn't know, and said, "I've got a real problem. I'm the first Jewish president of Indiana, and I can't find the Hillel rabbi. "

After listening to my story, he said, "I'll be out there next week with my assistant. If what you say is confirmed by what I find, the rabbi will be gone, and we'll find a new one." He came to Bloomington, and following three days of intense interviewing, he agreed with me.

"I only ask two things," he said. "One, you help us find a new rabbi. Two, you help build a new Hillel because this one's a mess." I said yes to both.

Ellen became chair of the fundraising efforts for the new Hillel. The Simon family from Indianapolis, owners of many shopping centers, were looking for a way to honor their mother and agreed to fund it. I wasn't on the search committee, but I assisted in finding a new rabbi. In the process, I talked to many potential Jewish donors who were thrilled that somebody was paying attention to Hillel and Jewish students at IU. We built a splendid new Hillel and brought to IU a young woman rabbi named Sue Shifron, a native of Indianapolis, who sparked a dramatic reawakening of spirit and interest among our Jewish students.

More generally, religion was central to the lives of most Hoosiers, and we tried to ensure ample opportunities for local clergy to engage with students. We held sessions for freshmen in their residences where a couple of students from different faiths told their peers about their religion and why it was important to them. Most of the Indiana students had never met a Catholic, a Muslim, a Mormon, or a Jew. In addition, we also had strong religious studies programs on the Bloomington and Indianapolis campuses.

In the spring of my second year at IU, I decided, if the weather was good, to hold the Bloomington campus commencement in a single ceremony at the IU football stadium, which held fifty-two thousand people, rather than hold multiple commencements in Assembly Hall, which held only seventeen thousand. I asked a nun at the Newman Center, which served the IU Catholic community, to give the invocation, knowing she was beloved there for many years. The only limitations, I insisted, were that she did not refer to Jesus Christ, as IU was a public university, and that she spoke no more than two minutes. We wanted to keep the ceremony to under an hour. There would be forty thousand or more sitting in the hot sun in the stadium if the weather was fair. The nun agreed. Commencement day was beautiful, and the nun walked to the front of the stage as the ceremony began. She spread her hands wide and prayed, and prayed, and prayed.

When she finally sat down, she had been praying for close to ten minutes. After the ceremony, I came up to her and said, "Sister, your prayer was beautiful, but you agreed to pray for only two minutes, and you prayed for ten."

"Yes, Mr. President," she replied. "But I have served at the Newman Center for decades, and those guys [she was referring to the priests] never allowed me to say the public prayers. This was my chance. Did you really think I would limit it to two minutes?" I laughed and said I understood.

As I have written, one of the pleasures of our lives at IU for both Ellen and me was the opportunity to do so many things together, and we traveled all over the state as a team, where we were treated with warmth almost everywhere we went. I spoke at many Rotary Clubs, Lions Clubs, and other organizations. In the process, I learned a great deal about what Hoosiers were doing in the state, how they lived, and what their concerns were. An added bonus was that our son Paul was a law student at the University of Notre Dame and visited us often.

We also traveled together outside Indiana. Our most memorable trip was during our last year at IU, when I received a grant from the Rockefeller Foundation to spend five weeks at the Foundation's elegant Bellagio Center in Italy. We had a large bedroom looking out over the entire length of Lake Como. There I wrote my final essay on "new majority" students in the annual series, "Our University in the State." I worked in a sixteenth-century guard house for four or five hours in the mornings, and Ellen and I had time to explore the area throughout the rest of each day.

Ellen and I loved working as a team. We grew closer, realizing how much fun we had in our new collaboration. We delighted in being partners in fundraising, dealing with the state legislature, and working with the multiple constituencies of Indiana University. Our move brought us together in new ways.

I took a number of steps to reach out to the citizenry of the state and beyond through a series of what I called "IU windows to the world." IU is not exactly at the crossroads from or to any place, and I thought it important that we find ways to highlight the university's strengths.

These included launching and hosting a series on IU's public broadcasting station, WTIU. The program was called *Pro & Con*. It included

IU faculty members discussing with me issues of interest and concern to the public, ranging from the death penalty and animal research to contemporary music and teaching. My assistant, Juliet Fry, and I avoided hot-button political topics but chose controversial ones and selected faculty with different perspectives. One show, for example, asked whether the personal conduct of an artist should affect how we view the artist's art. Should we care in viewing Picasso's paintings of women that he was a misogynist? The show was taped at the WTIU facilities in Bloomington and broadcast during the spring and summer months by nearly all of the PBS stations in Indiana and many across the country.

Through an IU alumnus, I could also write a regular column for Scripps-Howard newspapers. The column was distributed to all the newspapers in the chain, and they could choose whether or not to print a particular column. Many hundreds did, and it proved an excellent means to publicize IU. The articles were mainly about education, but I also wrote on a wide range of other matters just because they interested me. One of my columns, for example, was titled "Why Read Middlemarch?" which I wrote because it is one of my favorite novels. Most of the publicity was favorable. But in one column I wrote on capital punishment, I suggested that I would rather have my hand cut off than spend a year in jail. Many readers were outraged that I seemed to believe in cutting off the hands of criminals, which was certainly not my intent.

Another IU alumnus in Indianapolis, Buert SerVass, bought the rights to the then-defunct *Saturday Evening Post* and offered me the chance to write articles for publication in that magazine. I decided to write a series called "Bible Stories." Each story told my views on the contemporary meaning of well-known stories in the Bible, such as the tales of Abraham and Isaac, Job, and Jonah and the whale. To my pleasant surprise, the stories seemed to resonate with many deeply religious Christians in Indiana.

The most important "IU window to the world" was Indiana University Press. It was and remains one of the most distinguished university presses in the country. It published about 140 books a year, balanced carefully between scholarly academic books, popular books for Indiana citizens such as accounts of IU basketball, coffee-table volumes on works by major Hoosier Impressionist artists such as William Forsyth, and books of more general interest. A strength of the IU Press was that it specialized in a dozen or more fields, such as women's and gender studies, Jewish and Holocaust studies, and film studies.

I regularly gave IU Press books as gifts to visitors to the Bloomington campus from the US and around the world. I occasionally had to defend the IU Press when it published a particularly controversial volume. A biography of Yasser Arafat was one example. I received a plea from a group of Jewish faculty who urged me to stop the publication on the ground that it would give Arafat undeserved publicity. I responded that the IU Press chose the books it would publish, it had an outstanding reputation, and I had no intention of interfering.

I also helped the Big Ten arrange with a PR firm to make compelling short TV ads about our universities to be shown during breaks at televised basketball and football games. In the past, these ads had all looked exactly alike—they often included a student bending over a test tube—and it was not possible to tell which university was involved. The new IU one I liked best showed a young man sitting in chair in a darkened room with his back to the camera. He started speaking in what is clearly an Asian language. After a minute, the young man swiveled around, the lights come on, and he said in perfect English, "Indiana University teaches fifty-seven languages. Japanese is one of them."

Mine was a public, always visible position. The day after Ellen and I moved into Bryan House, we went in shorts and T-shirts to Kroger's grocery store in Bloomington. We hadn't been back to our house an hour before a new IU friend called to welcome us, adding that he heard we went to Kroger's in our shorts. As it happened, John Ryan, my predecessor, rarely went anyplace without wearing a three-piece suit. It struck me that day that Indiana University was a warmer and friendlier environment than what we were used to, and one in which there were no secrets, at least in terms our personal lives.

Ellen and I went to lots of meet-and-greet lunches, dinners, and other official functions. Ellen shone at these, particularly because she almost always could find something interesting about the person she was talking with. We both had a good time at these events, and we learned what those we met enjoyed about IU and what they thought could be improved. I spoke regularly at these gatherings and became increasingly relaxed in doing so. One reason was that I had asked a faculty member in the Theater Department to come to my talks from time to time and coach me on how to improve my public speaking.

Thinking back, Ellen and I agree that among these events, our time with Audrey Hepburn was a special highlight. The IU School of Nursing (the largest in the country) is home to the Sigma Tau International Honorary Society. That organization invited Hepburn to receive its first Distinguished Award and asked me to be master of ceremonies and to introduce her. Hepburn and I chatted for a while, waiting for the ceremony to begin, and I noticed she seemed very nervous. "How can you be nervous?" I asked. "I love you, as do millions of others around the world." She said she had not spoken at such an event before. As something to say, I told her Ellen and I were soon going to Switzerland to hike near Murren and see Ellen's relatives in Zurich.

"You must stop and have lunch with me when you are there," she responded. We regularly heard people we met suggest—just to be polite—that we stop by to see them, knowing they have no interest in our doing so. It did not occur to me that Hepburn was serious. But the next morning, I received a handwritten note from her with a beautiful drawing she did on the cover: "Dear Tom, Just to say that I had the best time talking with you last night. You helped me forget my 'nerves' . . . almost! Thank you for honoring us with your distinguished presence and for your easy, charming M.C.ing. I enclose our address and telephone number. Please come."

Could we refuse such an invitation? Of course not. So, we spent a magical day with Hepburn and the man she was living with in her home, a lovely farmhouse several centuries old near Lucerne. We talked and laughed and walked for an hour and then had a delicious lunch outdoors. Throughout the day, she was absolutely charming as well as gorgeous, dressed in blue jeans and a sports shirt. It was the treat of a lifetime

Years passed. Ellen and I thought we would stay at Indiana University perhaps as long as a decade. Then Dick Stoner, the wonderful board president and my good friend, retired. Ellen and I reflected on the matter and decided that the following year would be a good time for us to return to California. We had been away from our children and grandchildren for twenty-one years. We missed them and wanted to be near them and especially to come to know our grandchildren as they grew up. Ellen had had open-heart surgery two years earlier, and I worried about her health. Our youngest son, Paul, also had open-heart surgery, and we worried about his health as well. I had received awards and honorary degrees, but these were no substitute for being close to our family. After long and careful reflection, Ellen and I decided at the end of our sixth year, 1993, that the next academic year would be our last.

I believed my colleagues and I had accomplished much of what I had thought the most important to do—strengthen the academic enterprise. The university-wide academic planning exercise had succeeded. We had built up the faculty in many important areas and strengthened, diversified, and expanded the student body. The university was in sound financial shape despite difficulties the state had faced in earlier years.

Ellen and I were given a wonderful send-off when we left IU. A gala was held in the Musical Art Center, and there were many parties. The legislature passed a resolution in our honor, and we received scores of letters of appreciation for our efforts to strengthen IU. As I joked to Ellen, my head had swollen so much that I needed new hats. We loved IU, and we felt loved.

As I concluded seven years as president of Indiana University in 1994, I reflected on what had made the journey of that job so invigorating and fulfilling. I was reminded of advice I heard years ago from the president of Stanford University, Wallace Sterling. I tried regularly to pass the advice on to students: "A university education should equip one to entertain three things: a friend, an idea, and oneself." My IU education during these seven years equipped me well to entertain all three.

Ties to friends were the most obvious benefits. I could comment at length on faculty and staff members who became close personal friends as well as colleagues. Their friendship relates to my joy in entertaining ideas, for they took the time to teach me about an extraordinary range of fields and to give me a dazzling array of insights. As for entertaining myself, in the process of learning how to be president of Indiana University and trying to be the best president I was able to be, I also learned a good deal about my own limitations and strengths.

A most important lesson was how carefully I needed to listen—to students, to faculty, to staff, and to alumni and friends of the university. I often felt comfortable with my position on an issue, only to find myself challenged—frequently by students—and impelled to reanalyze and revise my view.

My time in Indiana helped me grow in countless ways and appreciate, far more clearly than could have been possible before, what an extraordinary opportunity I had to lead an excellent university in a great Midwestern state.

PART IV

SERVING

15

Back to Our Family and to California

By 1994, our three children had all moved to the West Coast. They reminded us on more than one occasion that anybody who didn't live there was crazy. With that advice in hand and our grandchildren waiting for us in California, we knew it was time to return to Palo Alto and reclaim our house. When we left Palo Alto, Ellen had made clear to me that "Since you cannot seem to keep a job, we must keep our house." And we did, renting it for the prior twenty-one years. I knew I wanted to continue working. *What would I do?*

At first, I assumed I would rejoin the Stanford faculty in the Law School. Paul Brest was then-dean of the law school and a good friend.

"Paul, I'm coming back," I told him. "I think I would like to resume teaching at the law school."

"I'll talk to the faculty," he promised, "and I'll be back in touch."

After two months, Paul finally called me. "Tom," he said carefully, "we'd love to have you come back, and we'll give you an office. We're glad to have you teach what you want to teach, but it will be as an adjunct faculty member."

My feelings were hurt. The Stanford Law School faculty didn't want me as one of their own, despite the fact that, as dean, I had led the school and helped hire many of the faculty and raised the funds for the school's new buildings. Since leaving Stanford, I had also published a book of essays, coauthored a volume of teaching materials, and taught both law students and undergraduates at Penn and IU. I didn't think I lacked credentials, but the faculty did not share that view.

It took some time to ease my wounded pride. Fortunately, I had already accepted an offer from a good friend at Duke University, Joel Fleishman, to visit Duke for four months, beginning in the fall of 1994, while Ellen and I unwound from the pressures of leading IU. During that time, I realized this rejection might prove to be an opportunity. I had changed since being a professor and then dean of Stanford Law School; my life, interests, and priorities were no longer the same. Returning to Stanford, sliding back into the familiar, would have been a mistake. I began considering what I *really* wanted to do. What did I *really* care about? The answer soon became evident: educating undergraduates to become engaged citizens.

My interest in civic education was not new and had grown stronger during my career. When I was president of the Legal Services Corporation, the reluctance of most private lawyers to offer pro-bono services to people in poverty, especially those who were people of color, had been an epiphany for me. Those private lawyers, I realized, were unwilling to work in impoverished communities because they rarely, if ever, interacted with people of economic, racial, and ethnic backgrounds other than their own. They were afraid to do so. Their education had not given them structured opportunities to work with people different from themselves.

Among the many books I read over the years that had an impact on my thinking, John Dewey's *Democracy and Education*, published in 1916, was one of the most influential, despite his difficult prose style. Dewey proposed two then-radical insights about American society. One was that most citizens, not just the elite, can have a life of the mind. The other was that a life of the mind is inadequate to the challenges of American democracy. Our society requires civic engagement to realize the potential of its citizens and its communities. And, he argued, education was the key to that engagement. As has become a cliché, democracy is not a spectator sport.

Over time, I realized that colleges and universities must prepare undergraduates with the civic knowledge, skills, and attributes they need to become responsible and engaged citizens. Most college and university mission statements announce that their campuses were educating students to meet that need, but too few did so. This meant, I realized, that civic learning that lasted for a lifetime should be an integral part of the curricula and cocurricular lives of students as they grew from adolescence to adulthood. It also meant that civic education that was solely *about* how the civic wheels of governments turn was not enough. Students need to engage in that work as well. They would then not be afraid to work with—and as importantly, learn from—those with far fewer resources and from varied backgrounds and walks of life.

My experiences with Campus Compact fueled my commitment to preparing students to become involved in the civic life of their communities—local, state, national, and international. My daughter, Elizabeth—one of its first employees—introduced me to the organization when I was provost at Penn. Campus Compact was cofounded in 1985 by Howard Swearer, Timothy S. Healy, and Donald Kennedy, the presidents of Brown, Georgetown, and Stanford Universities, along with Frank Newman, the former president of Rhode Island University and then head of the Education Commission of the States.

The original focus of Campus Compact was on promoting student community service as a way to counteract the self-centered image of undergraduates as the "me generation." Tutoring kids, cleaning up parks, and working in community kitchens would help students understand the importance and satisfaction of community service. When I became IU president, I joined the Campus Compact board and soon became chair of the board. The organization had multiple state affiliates, and I also helped launch the Indiana Campus Compact.

By the early 1990s, Campus Compact membership had included some five hundred presidents of universities and colleges, a number that doubled over the next decade. During that time, my colleagues and I slowly learned that Campus Compact campuses needed to go beyond creating service opportunities for students and find ways to link community service with academic learning in order to be taken seriously by students and faculty. I heard these comments all the time: "Community service is a nice thing to do in the afternoon if you have some free time, but it's not really important. It certainly doesn't significantly impact the learning processes in an academic sense, and that's really what's important." To overcome that mindset, I and others at Campus Compact became convinced that community service needed to be infused into the curriculum.

As a result, Campus Compact launched a major initiative focused on integrating community service with academic study through structured reflection. We came to understand that civic engagement is not a dimension of learning that can be pasted on a student's character while she or he learns calculus. Rather, it is a complex combination of cognitive and emotional learning. Service connects thought and feeling in a deliberate way, creating a context in which students can explore how they feel about what they think and what they think about how they feel. The interaction of academic study and community service, linked by structured reflection, offers students opportunities to consider what is important to them—and why—in ways they too rarely experienced otherwise.

The initiative was initially met with resistance from faculty in many disciplines. They claimed that time spent doing community service would detract from academic learning. We had to show with empirical evidence that the reverse was true. The integration we were championing would enhance academic learning, just as academic learning enhances community service.

Fortunately, faculty in various fields began writing articles to support this position. Some faculty, for example, taught two sections of the same course and could show that students in a section with a service-learning requirement performed better on the same tests than students who did not have that requirement.

We gained additional support from another national organization, the American Association for Higher Education (AAHE). Its ten thousand members were faculty and staff interested in undergraduate teaching and learning. AAHE was headed by a dynamic leader, Russ Edgerton, who became a close friend. I was elected by the members to chair the AAHE board and worked closely with Edgerton. Over time, AAHE published a series of twenty-three monographs on how service learning could be integrated into different disciplines.

Edgerton also helped me understand that service learning is one of a number of modes of active learning that he termed "pedagogies of engagement." Service learning engages students in reaching outside the walls of the school and into the surrounding community, as opposed to closed classroom learning. It is not, of course, the only form of civic education, but I think it is the most powerful, particularly when linked with problem-based learning and collaborative learning. Problem-based learning can be built around a community problem, like homelessness, which is the starting point in designing a course. As students advance, they tackle increasingly difficult aspects of the problem using increasingly sophisticated techniques and increasingly complex knowledge bases. The problem approach is key in preparing students for active participation in the ongoing renewal of democracy because it calls for citizens to identify community problems and work communally to resolve those problems. Collaborative learning is a pedagogy particularly targeted toward enhancing the skills and abilities required to be a productive team member. It is also integral to a democratic society in which citizens interact with each other, learn from each other, grow with each other, and together make their communities more than the sum of their parts.

By the time Ellen and I left IU for Durham, North Carolina, and our time at Duke, I was clear that educating undergraduates to be engaged citizens would be my professional focus when we returned to Palo Alto. With that in mind, I accepted the position of distinguished university scholar in the California State University (CSU) system, which is the largest university system in the country. Santa Clara University and CSU had both expressed interest in hiring me; I chose the latter because it was a public university and offered the opportunity to not only teach service-learning courses but also engage deeply in the creation of the institutional architecture of community-service learning. Barry Munitz, the SCU chancellor, asked me to develop a network of community-service centers across all twenty-three campuses within the California State University system. A few of those campuses had community-service centers but most didn't, and all lacked system-wide coherency.

But first, Ellen and I were ready to unwind in Durham, North Carolina. We had great fun there for the next four months. We felt as though we were playing house. We traveled in North Carolina from its coast to Ashville, visiting local artists in their studios and appreciating the beautiful scenery.

I also enjoyed teaching an undergraduate course, "Altruism, Philanthropy, and Public Service," and finishing a book, *The Courage to Inquire*, about lessons learned at IU. No less importantly, I learned to write on a computer. At IU, I worked with secretaries and dictating machines. Marilyn Saunders, head of the president's office, understood my every need and ensured it would be met. But now I knew I would have no secretarial or other support except on a limited basis. Microsoft's Windows had not yet come onto the scene, and I used DOS. But I did learn, and by the end of our time at Duke, I could write on the computer as fast or faster than I could dictate. My parents had insisted I take typing lessons one summer as a boy, and I renewed my gratitude to them for enabling me to acquire that skill.

We left Durham for South Africa, Zimbabwe, Australia, and New Zealand over the course of six weeks. It was the trip of a lifetime. In South Africa and Zimbabwe, we stayed with friends Ellen had known since her days in England on the Experiment in International Living as a high school student. South Africa was fascinating because independence had just come. I could still remember meeting with Bishop Tutu when I was working for President Carter. Tutu told me there was no chance of a shift away from white rule without terrible bloodshed. Miraculously, we saw that did not happen.

Zimbabwe was a thrill since we stayed on our friends' sixty-thousand-acre ranch and had a chance to visit wonderful game preserves and Victoria Falls. New Zealand was special because we met our friends Rolaine and Lee Copeland there. Lee had been dean of Fine Arts at the University of Pennsylvania when I was provost there. We hiked the Milford Track and traveled throughout the South Island. Then onto Australia, Sydney, and the Great Barrier Reef. It was a glorious trip.

On January 1, 1995, Ellen and I returned to Palo Alto, refreshed and eager to be with our family and old friends. Our son David was a captain for Northwest Airlines and lived in Chico, California, with his wife, Maureen, and their four daughters. Our daughter, Elizabeth, now a family therapist, lived with her husband, Peter, in the Bay Area with their three children. And our youngest son, Paul, was in Portland, Oregon, with his wife, Hillary, and had just started working as a lawyer with a private law firm. It was a joy to know we could see our children regularly and enjoy our grandchildren as they grew up.

Elizabeth and Peter met us at the San Francisco airport and took us to our temporary apartment on the Stanford campus. We stayed in that apartment for six months while our Palo Alto house was completely gutted and redone. Thanks to Copeland's brilliant design, our home was transformed from a small tract house that served us, three children, and a dog into an elegant, "grown-up" home for two. Paul's bedroom became Ellen's study, Elizabeth's bedroom became my study. David's bedroom became the guest room. Our bedroom was entirely reshaped to give us a huge closet, and so forth. We spent far more than the $33,500 we originally paid, but housing prices had shot up all over the Bay Area since the birth of Silicon Valley tech companies. In the years since we returned, those prices exploded. How fortunate we were that Ellen insisted we keep that house while we were away for twenty-one years. It was the best investment we ever made.

I began at California State University by working with faculty and staff leaders across the campuses on a new strategic planning exercise, "The Cornerstone Initiative." One key aim was to make service learning and civic learning fundamental parts of the educational experiences of CSU students. Our efforts had two key objectives: (1) engage students at each CSU campus in at least one community-service learning experience prior to graduation and (2) offer a continuum of community-service opportunities at each CSU campus, including a wide variety of community-service learning opportunities, as well as extracurricular and cocurricular community-service experiences. To implement that part of the strategic plan, the system-wide Office of Community Service Learning was established in the chancellor's office. The first of its kind in the country, this office oversaw and coordinated implementation of service learning on the twenty-three CSU campuses.

By the time I left California State University in 2000, the community-service learning program had grown so rapidly and with such enthusiasm that the CSU board of trustees passed a resolution calling on the chancellor and each CSU campus president to "ensure that all students have the opportunity to participate in community service, service learning, or both." Also in 2000, California governor Gray Davis authorized $2.2 million to support the development of new service-learning courses and support infrastructure across the CSU. In the 1999–2000 academic year alone, twenty-nine thousand California State University students were enrolled in some one thousand service-learning courses. My passion for community-service learning had taken root in helping an institutional transformation.

During my first few years back in California, I also assisted in building the service-learning institutional architecture at San Francisco State University (SFSU). Robert Corrigan, the president of SFSU, was interested in expanding community-service learning at the university. The offices of California Campus Compact were relocated to the campus. Corrigan also founded the San Francisco Urban Institute, a nonprofit research and action center that served to link the university and its strengths with the city, its opportunities, and its needs. Under the leadership of Professor Brian Murphy, who became my close friend, the institute sponsored a series of projects that promoted student and faculty learning and research on the one hand and the resolution or amelioration of city concerns on the other. The institute was both an academic and an administrative unit, reporting directly to the university president.

Corrigan also invited me to host a yearlong seminar on community engagement with faculty representatives from each of the eight colleges of the university. The report from that seminar led to the establishment of the SFSU Office of Community Service Learning. In addition, I had the opportunity to teach a series of service-learning courses and learn from that experience as I worked to promote civic education at SFSU and beyond.

While I was engaged in the national efforts of Campus Compact and the American Association of Higher Education to strengthen civic education and service learning across the country, I hoped to help find ways for the federal government to promote opportunities for all citizens to engage in community service. I knew from my time at the Legal Services Corporation what a difference federal support could make.

In his 1989 inaugural address, President George H. W. Bush spoke about his vision of Americans volunteering to help their less fortunate fellow citizens and urged "a thousand points of light" to further that vision. A year later, the Thousand Points of Light Foundation was created to honor those who did outstanding volunteer service.

There was bipartisan support for the federal government to support public service, particularly by young people. The president wanted federal funding for his new foundation, and Democrats in Congress wanted funding for other programs that provided public service opportunities on a large scale. A deal was made, and the National Community Service Act of 1990 became law. It included an appropriation for the foundation and a White House role in setting up and appointing a new federal commission to study and fund experimental public service programs.

As soon as I learned this, I sought and received help from Indiana senator Lugar to become one of the twenty-one directors to be nominated by the president and confirmed by the Senate as members of the Commission on National and Community Service. Potentially, I suddenly had a much larger palate to help support my passion for public service. Programs to promote public service among college students were part of the commission's mandate, and so were K–12 schooling, youth corps, and national programs. The commission was called on to submit its report in 1993,

At the first commission meeting, I suggested Catherine Milton as having the perfect background to be the commission's executive director. Though I did not know her personally, I did know that President Donald Kennedy of Stanford University had chosen her to lead a new Stanford center for public service, the Haas Center. She had a wealth of experience in organizing and implementing programs involving volunteers and had received rave reviews from people whose judgment

I trusted. Milton was quickly hired and became a superb executive director, as well as a close friend.

The commission first worked hard analyzing the potential for supporting community-service programs in the areas of school-age young people, higher education, youth corps, and national-service models. Programs that focused on youth would have primary attention. The next steps were to develop guidelines for competitive grants in each area, allocate funds to the strongest applicants, and then evaluate the results so that the Commission could propose a plan for permanent federal support of national and community service.

I was an active director throughout these steps and was board chair during the Commission's last year. In the process I learned a great deal about the potential and the challenges of programs to provide community-service opportunities to their participants. I worked closely with national service programs such as Teach for America, City Year, and Public Allies—as well as state and local programs— and continued to learn about the ways community service could help shape the lives of program participants.

In his 1993 inaugural address, President Clinton spoke of the need for public service by citizens throughout the country. "In serving, we recognize a simple but powerful truth: we need each other. And we must care for one another." Later that year, Clinton signed legislation that merged several public-service agencies, including the commission, to form a single federal agency, the Corporation on National and Community Service. Clinton announced that a new national service program would be called AmeriCorps. I wanted to continue engaging and learning in the work of the corporation, as I had for the commission. I reached out to Hillary Clinton, former chair of the Legal Services Corporation, and she and California senator Feinstein helped ensured that I was chosen.

President Clinton made clear that national and community service was one of his signature programs, and AmeriCorps grew rapidly. Unfortunately, its leadership lost some of the bipartisan support that had made the commission successful. It was only when former Senator Harris Wofford became CEO of the corporation that it attracted strong Republican as well as Democratic support in Congress.

AmeriCorps steadily grew, and I continued to learn about the potential of community service on a national scale.

I was particularly pleased that a separate program, called Learn and Serve, was created specifically to fund service learning and related civic-education programs in higher education and in K–12 schools. This gave an enormous boost to service learning, which became the fastest-growing pedagogy in higher education until online learning exploded. I felt great satisfaction to have been part of that transformation. By the year 2000, there were few four-year colleges or universities in the country that did not have a center to support civic-engagement programs. And a new peer-reviewed journal was created to publish research in the field.

Since my time in the Army Reserves, I had been a strong advocate of requiring youth aged eighteen to twenty-four to spend at least a year in civilian or military public service. I knew how my own experiences had helped shape my character through working closely alongside men with very different backgrounds and perspectives than my own. I was convinced that programs like the Peace Corps, but on a much larger scale, could similarly have a lifelong impact on the young women and men who participated. After a decade on the board of the commission and then the corporation, I was even more convinced of the value of public service. AmeriCorps is still voluntary today, but it now places more than two hundred thousand individuals annually with nonprofit, faith-based, and community organizations. I cherish my opportunities to have helped make this happen. I increasingly thought it was time for me to start writing about what I had learned about in my years promoting service learning and community service.

The first five years after returning to California had its challenges. Ellen and our son Paul previously had heart surgery, experiences that made us all more aware of our human frailties and our abiding love for each other. We were finally back home in the same house we had bought so many decades ago, though it was completely remodeled. It didn't feel like coming full circle for us, however, but rather completing a spiral. We returned to California at a different level, a different age, and a different time.

Ellen quickly became an active volunteer and fundraiser for an organization in Palo Alto that served disabled children and their families. She reconnected with old friends and made scores of new ones.

Looking back, those same five years at the end of that long spiral were creative and invigorating to me professionally. My passion for community-service learning had broadened, deepened, and took root in significant structural ways in the Cal State System, impacting tens of thousands of students. With the knowledge I had gained as part of the commission and then the Corporation for National and Community Service, I was practicing what I preached, taking the time to research and think through the development and implementation of civic responsibilities courses, sometimes bringing the community to the students and not just the other way around.

I think the health scares my family and I had made me increasingly sensitive to the entwined synergies between spirituality and civic engagement for students. By spirituality, I mean the will and capacity to be part of something larger than oneself, which I believe is built into our human DNA. Many of the experiences students have while in college reinforce this desire to build a good life, one in which their work, along with their personal and civic lives, is part of a larger community. Whether or not spirituality is expressed in terms of organized religion is less important than holding a deep sense of community, one in which students realize that focusing only on oneself in a narrow, materialistic sense is not enough—it is not a life well lived. Engaging in civic work and bettering one's community allows students to learn and grow through experiences that are part of being truly human and also deeply spiritual.

Research shows that development occurs at an accelerated rate during times of transition, and college is one such time when traditional-aged undergraduates are growing into young adulthood. For this reason, the college years are also a time of significant identity formation. Many students have important learning experiences in college when they are part of a larger community and can learn from others who are different than themselves.

Structured opportunities for learning and reflection within our institutions of higher education, especially service-learning courses, help create the desire within students to become lifelong learners as they develop a deeper sense of self, identity, and spirituality. These involvement opportunities can show students there are many paths to spirituality while developing as civically minded citizens who are willing and able to participate in our democracy during college and after graduation. Through this process, the trajectories of their lives often shift so that civic service to others and to their communities becomes an integral part of who they are and how they choose to live their lives.

When students become involved in civic service, it is rarely with the thought that this will be a pathway in a search for meaning and purpose. But that is precisely what I have often witnessed happens to students. They realize their good fortune only after they are well along that path.

Not long after we returned to Palo Alto, I met Lee Shulman, then a distinguished Stanford professor of education. He was interested in my work on service learning specifically and civic education more generally, and we talked at length over coffee in a series of sessions. In the process, we became fast friends. I came to realize that Shulman was among the best teachers I had ever known, always raising questions for me and others to consider. I did not imagine then that he would also have a profound impact on my own work in the years ahead.

That impact occurred because the president of the Carnegie Foundation for the Advancement of Teaching, Ernest Boyer, had died, and its board was seeking a new president. I had known and admired Boyer and his work. He had stayed with us at Bryan House when we were at IU. And I had spoken in his place at the inauguration of the new Stanford home of the Haas Center for Public Service when Boyer was too ill to be there.

Russ Edgerton, the remarkable leader of the American Association for Higher Education, was on the Carnegie board and asked me whether I thought Shulman would be an able president. My immediate response was that this was a great idea. I also knew the chair of Carnegie, Stan Ikenberry, who had been president of the University of Illinois when I was at IU. Russ and I arranged for Ikenberry and Shulman to meet at my house. Ikenberry became a fan of Shulman, just as

Edgerton and I were, and Shulman was chosen as the new president. Shulman made it a condition of his agreement that Carnegie move from its home in Princeton, New Jersey, to the Stanford University campus, and both the board and Stanford agreed.

Soon thereafter, Shulman asked me to work with him part-time to help shape a new administration for Carnegie, which I did. Not long afterward, he invited me to join him as a senior scholar, working full-time on issues of civic responsibility in higher education as well as other matters that might interest me.

I remembered I had been warned by some colleagues that if I became a university administrator, I would never be able to return to teaching and research. I had proven to myself that this was not true regarding teaching and wanted to prove it was untrue regarding research, for there was much I wanted to write about. With a position at Carnegie, I could do just that.

An added stroke of good fortune occurred when I learned that Anne Colby, a distinguished psychologist and author, would be coming to Palo Alto to accompany her husband, Bill Damon, who had become a Stanford professor. I had never met Colby, but in one of my courses, I had used a book that she and Damon wrote, *Some Do Care*. I learned from this powerful book that moral values are inevitably woven through civic responsibility—they are two sides of the same coin—a truth that has run through my work ever since. Colby and I met and decided we wanted to work together, and Shulman readily agreed that Colby would also be a senior scholar at Carnegie.

During the next eleven years, Shulman shaped Carnegie into a magical place for me and other senior scholars. We worked together in small groups, but we were all eager to help any of the other senior scholars who could benefit from our assistance. The groups usually included one or two Stanford graduate students who worked with us; we were both their teachers and their colleagues, and many of them became important faculty scholars in their fields.

In total, I coauthored, edited, or coedited seven books during that period. Three of them related directly to civic responsibility in higher education, which was the title of the first of the volumes. Two of my

other coedited books focused on philanthropy and higher education;
one was on how and why young people should engage in public service,
and one was on infusing liberal learning into undergraduate business
education.

The book encouraging young people to engage in public service is a
special favorite of mine because I wrote it with a remarkable Stanford
undergraduate, Ernestine Fu. An editor told me I needed a youth voice
if I were to make the volume appeal to young people, and Fu provided
that and an extraordinary range of contacts with youth organizations
engaged in community service. In the process of research and writing
the book, we became and still are fast friends. Her life and work continue to exemplify youth civic engagement at its best.

Over time, Shulman and Colby became two of my closest friends
along with two other Carnegie colleagues with whom Colby and I
worked closely. Bill Sullivan brought his background in philosophy
to that work, as did Mary Huber, an anthropologist by training. We
each had complementary talents. Colby had worked as a psychologist for years and was a superb writer who knew the field of survey
research, about which I was ignorant. I was also involved with a score
of other projects at the Carnegie Foundation such as creating a new
campus classification system to highlight institutions that succeeded
in strengthening the community engagement of their students.

While at Carnegie, George Mehaffy, a vice president at American
Association of State Colleges and Universities, asked me to help him
launch a new organization, the American Democracy Project (ADP).
This was a nonpartisan, multicampus network educating future generations in democratic practices. It now includes about three hundred
broad-access public campuses across the country, educating some
three million students.

At the launch, we used one of the books I cowrote at Carnegie,
*Educating Citizens: Preparing Students for Moral and Civic Responsibil-
ity,* as the core text. It was a study of the ways entire campuses could
promote education for citizen responsibility, viewed as both a civic
and moral imperative. ADP quickly expanded. But we soon found
that most of the programs on its campuses concentrated solely on

community service without attention to educating students to be engaged in public-policy issues and politics. Students who served tutoring kids, for example, usually did not explore the public-policy issues involved in why volunteer tutors were needed. My Carnegie colleagues and I then did what academics often do, we researched and wrote another book, *Educating for Democracy: Preparing Undergraduates for Responsible Political Engagement*.

We made three major findings in that book. First, the twenty exemplary programs and courses we studied—ranging from a two-year program to individual courses—all had significant and positive effects on students in terms of their political engagement. Second, contrary to what many public commentators were saying, the courses and programs did not alter the ideological positions of these students from conservative to liberal or vice versa. And finally, a faculty or staff mentor was central to students' political engagement.

I then worked with a group of nine campuses over three years to determine whether they could educate their student bodies as a whole with the knowledge, skills, and attributes needed for responsible political engagement. The results were stunningly successful. Eight out of the nine campuses prepared most of their students for lives of involvement in public-policy issues and politics.

Ellen and I were able to travel abroad frequently during these years, and we took special delight in hiking trips to France and Italy. Over the sixty-seven years of our marriage, we visited forty-nine countries in South and Central America, Europe, Africa, Asia, and the Middle East, along with Canada. On work assignments, I visited fourteen more nations. In addition, one other trip stands out in my mind. It was to China, occasioned by an invitation from Fei Jiang, a professor at Northeast Normal University in Changchun. She and the university's president visited me at Stanford to say they wanted fourteen of my books translated into Chinese, and a leading publishing company in Shanghai would publish them. I agreed with enthusiasm, and they invited Ellen and me to come to Changchun to sign the agreement. Ellen did not feel up to the trip, but I took my daughter Elizabeth with me, and we had a wonderful time. Then, for my ninetieth birthday present, Fei Jiang and the university president came back to California and presented me with two elegant boxes of the translated books.

Lee Shulman decided to retire as president of Carnegie in 2008. I had assumed I might stay at Carnegie and continue to write. But the new leader of Carnegie wanted to shift the organization's focus, and all of the senior scholars left. I then asked the dean of the Stanford Graduate School of Education, Deborah Stipek, if I might come there and teach. She and the school faculty agreed, and I became Stanford faculty member as I did in 1965, this time as an adjunct professor.

The timing was right, and since then, I have been teaching a course called "Leadership and Administration in Higher Education," using a series of case studies about tough problems faced by campus leaders. Preparing for the course gave me a chance to bring together leadership lessons I learned at Stanford, Penn, and IU. I was also able to use those lessons in a program sponsored by the Aspen Institute and designed to prepare aspiring community college presidents to be effective leaders in those roles.

In addition, I have been teaching an undergraduate course called "Democracy in Crises: Learning from the Past." This course focuses on US democracy and uses a series of case studies of important events in our national history to explore what happened to American democracy at key pressure points and why. I use this historical exploration to shed light on how the current political challenges might best be handled.

I created the course because I frequently heard comments, especially in the wake of the 2016 election and particularly from students, that our democracy had never before been in such a devastating crisis. I would respond that we did have a Civil War and that throughout our history, our democracy has been severely tested frequently—in wartime and in peace. I remind them of the Andrew Jackson administration and the parallels to our current quandaries. Some students said yes, but there was a spirit of compromise in earlier eras that had been lost. I responded that this was only partially true.

I told the students that I worked in the federal government during six administrations, and in all those times, there were moderates on both sides of the aisle to support the programs that I led—legal services for the impoverished people, foreign aid, and national service. That has changed. But I also refer them to a passage from the course book we use, *Democracy: A Case Study,* by David A. Moss: "Democracy in America has always been a contact sport in our country. Words like 'cooperation' and 'consensus' may sound appealing and even comforting, but American democracy has survived and thrived from one generation to the next on the basis not principally of harmony but of conflict—sometimes intense conflict—mediated, generally, by shared ideals. The critical question is what makes a conflict either constructive or destructive."

Shared faith in our democracy is the glue that holds America together, making partisan conflict constructive rather than destructive, and that glue is losing its grip. But I am still doing what I can to help new generations shift back to the era when the tensions were constructive.

One of my college professors, Samuel Huntington, concluded his book, *American Politics: The Promise of Disharmonies* with these words: "Critics say that America is a lie because its reality falls so far short of its ideal. They are wrong. America is not a lie; it is a disappointment. But it can be a disappointment only because it is also a hope."

I have hope.

Epilogue

E llen and have been blessed with good fortune. After owning our small house in Palo Alto for fifty-five years, we sold it and moved to a wonderful independent living facility called Vi at Palo Alto. When this book is published, I will almost be ninety-one and Ellen ninety. It was time.

Health challenges have made this clear. I had prostate cancer, which, fortunately, was successfully treated, and a blocked colon that might have ended my life. I wake up each morning suffused in gratitude for our lives and the sixty-seven years we have been together. At our age, it is often hard to make new friends. Ellen and I have made scores of them where we now live.

Our three children and their children and our nine grandchildren are doing well. David and his wife, Maureen, live part of the time in Chico, California, and the rest at Lake Tahoe. He is still flying, now for Delta Airlines, where he is a senior pilot. Their four daughters, Brigid, Hannah, Reilly, and Casey, have all graduated from college and are working in California. Brigid is now married to Tyler.

Elizabeth, and her husband, Peter, moved two years ago to San Francisco, where they live in Noe Valley with a stunning view of the entire city. Elizabeth works as a family therapist, as she has for many years. Grant, their youngest son, is living in San Francisco. Their eldest son,

Jay, and his wife, Rachel, are living in Seattle, as is their daughter Kate and her husband, Conor.

Paul and his wife, Hillary, live in Portland, Oregon, with their two boys, Henry and Benjamin. Paul is now general counsel for Adidas America, the sportswear company.

Ellen has been reading up a storm ever since we moved. I now take long walks each morning and often talk by phone to our grandchildren. If I had said more than, "Yes, sir," to my grandfather, it would have been a big deal. Now I can talk with grandchildren as well as children and friends for an hour or more. That is a joy.

When COVID hit, I no longer could do research, so I decided to try to write a novel, which I did with the help of a Stanford writing course. It's titled *The Search: An Insider's Novel about a University President*. It chronicles a public university president struggling to maintain the primacy of academics over athletics. (It is published by Indiana University Press.) I had such fun writing it that I wrote a second novel, again aided by a writing course. This novel is a murder story taking place in an independent living facility like the one we live in.

As I write these last words, Ellen and I just returned from visiting with our adorable new great-grandson, Simon, for the first time. We were on Bainbridge Island, near Seattle, where our granddaughter Kate was married to Conor. And I officiated, as I had at the wedding of her brother, Jay, to Rachel. Next week we will be at the wedding of another granddaughter, Brigid, and her fiancé, Tyler.

It doesn't get better than that!

INDEX

For Indiana University Press

Gary Dunham, Acquisitions Editor and Director

Brenna Hosman, Production Coordinator

Katie Huggins, Production Manager

David Miller, Lead Project Manager/Editor

Dan Pyle, Online Publishing Manager

Stephen Williams, Assistant Director of Marketing

Jennifer Witzke, Senior Artist and Book Designer